Acknowledgments

D0896208

The authors and publisher would like to thank the following reviewers and consultants:

Karin Abell
Durham Technical Community College, Durham, NC

Sandra Anderson
El Monte-Rosemead Adult School, El Monte, CA

Sandra Andreessen
Merced Adult School, Merced, CA

Julie Barrett
Madison Area Technical College, Madison, WI

Bea Berretini
Fresno Adult School, Fresno, CA

Mark Brik
College of Mount Saint Vincent, The Institute for Immigrant Concerns, New York, NY

Debra Brooks
BEGIN Managed Programs, Brooklyn, NY

Rocio Castiblanco
Seminole Community College / Orange County Public Schools, Sanford, FL

Sandy Cropper
Fresno Adult School, Fresno, CA

Carol Culver
Central New Mexico Community College, Albuquerque, NM

Luciana Diniz
Portland Community College, Portland, OR

Gail Ellsworth
Milwaukee Area Technical College, Oak Creek, WI

Sally Gearhart
Santa Rosa Junior College, Santa Rosa, CA

Jeane Hetland
Merced Adult School, Merced, CA

Laura Horani
Portland Community College, Portland, OR

Bill Hrycyna
Franklin Community Adult School, Los Angeles, CA

Callie Hutchinson
Sunrise Tech Center, Citrus Heights, CA

Mary Jenison
Merced Adult School, Merced, CA

Mark Labinski
Fox Valley Technical College, Appleton, WI

Rhonda Labor
Northside Learning Center, San Antonio, TX

Lisa Lor
Merced Adult School, Merced, CA

Eileen McKee
Westchester Community College, Valhalla, NY

Jennifer Newman-Cornell
College of Southern Nevada, Las Vegas, NV

Sonja Pantry
Robert Morgan Educational Center, Miami, FL

Eric Rosenbaum
BEGIN Managed Programs, Brooklyn, NY

Jodi Ruback
College of Southern Nevada, Las Vegas, NV

Linda Salem
Northside Learning Center, San Antonio, TX

Evelyn Trottier
Seattle Central Community College, Lynnwood, WA

Maliheh Vafai
Overfelt Adult Center, San Jose, CA

Nancy Williams
Bakersfield Adult School, Bakersfield, CA

Contents

Contents

English in Action 2nd edition is a four-level core language series for English language learners. It is a comprehensive revision and expansion of *English in Action 1st edition*. The revision has allowed us, the authors, an opportunity to refine the text. We are writers, but we are also teachers. When writing a unit, we can immediately try it out in the classroom. Activities, tasks, and exercises are added, deleted, and changed in an on-going process. Students provide daily and honest feedback.

This first book is designed for students who have had little exposure to English, including new arrivals or adults who have lived in the United States for many years, but have never formally studied English. The text assumes that students are literate in their native language.

The units in Book 1 branch from self to school, family, home, jobs, and community. The contexts are everyday places and situations. The units build gradually, giving students the vocabulary, the grammar, and the expressions to talk about the situations and themselves. Students see, hear, and practice the language of everyday life in a great variety of exercises and activities. Because this is the first book and students are unsure of themselves, there is ever-present support in the form of grammar notes, examples, vocabulary boxes, and so on. By the end of Book 1, students should feel comfortable talking, reading, and writing about their lives using basic English phrases and sentences.

Each unit will take between five and seven hours of classroom time. If you have less time, you may need to choose the exercises you feel are the most appropriate for your students. You can assign some of the activities for homework. For example, after previewing **Writing Our Stories**, students can write their own stories at home, instead of in class. The short descriptions that follow give you an idea of the sections in each unit.

Finally, the book comes with an audio component. The listening activities in the units are motivating and interesting. They provide other voices than that of the teacher. We have encouraged our adult students to buy the book/audio package. They tell us that they listen to the audio at home and in the car.

Changes to this Edition

There are three new or adapted units in the second edition. Unit 9: Transportation is a brand new unit. The students discuss different modes of transporta-

tion, and how they get to and from class, home, and work. The grammar focus is on present continuous questions. In Unit 11, students talk about their daily schedules and study routines. Students talk about when, where, and how to study. The grammar focus is simple present tense. Several teachers requested that the future tense be included in Book 1, and Unit 15 is a new unit that fulfills this need. In Unit 15, students talk about their weekend plans and activities in their communities. The grammar focus is the future tense with *be going to*.

The new features in the second edition include the following:

- **Word Builder** is an opportunity for students to practice the Dictionary vocabulary.
- **Word Partnerships** are word collocations related to the Dictionary vocabulary.
- **Working Together** activities are partner and group activities that are now spread throughout the units. Look for the partner icons.
- **Sharing Our Stories** allows students to read and talk about each other's writing.
- **English in Action** is a two-page spread that gives students practice in life skills related to the topic of the unit. For example, in Clothing and Weather, students practice returning items to a clothing store. In A Visit to the Doctor, they make a doctor's appointment and fill out a patient information form.

Dictionary

Each unit opens with a one- or two-page illustrated **Dictionary**. Students are asked to listen and repeat each item. Teachers realize that one repetition of vocabulary words does not produce mastery. Ask students to sit in groups and study the words together. Stage spelling bees. Play word bingo. Look for the same items in the classroom or school environment. Students must also study the words at home.

Word Partnerships

This is a new feature, which usually appears at the end of the **Dictionary** section. It provides students with common high-frequency collocations using vocabulary from the **Dictionary**. Have students practice using these collocations in sentences of their own creation.

Word Builder

This is another new feature that provides additional practice with the vocabulary from the **Dictionary**.

Have students refer to the **Dictionary** if they need help completing these activities. Many of the activities in this section include structures from the unit and recycle the grammar from previous units.

Active Grammar

Three to six pages of structured exercises and activities present and practice the grammar of the unit. This first book integrates the new vocabulary and the grammar throughout all the activities in the unit. At this level, grammar mastery is not the goal, but rather an introduction to the basic structures of English and a feeling of comfort and security in the new language. As students progress through this section, they will find a variety of supportive features. Artwork and photos illustrate the context clearly. Word boxes show the verbs or nouns to use in the answers. Those who have used the first edition will see that there is enhanced grammar support within the units with full, colored grammar charts and sample sentences. In addition, students can look at the grammar charts in the appendix for a summary of all the grammatical points covered in the book.

For many of the exercises, the entire class will be working together with your direction and explanations. Other exercises have a partner icon—students can try these with another student.

Working Together

Working Together activities are more cooperative, encouraging students to work in groups, role-play, or exchange information in a more active way. You can walk around the classroom, listening to students and answering their questions. Encourage this free flow of the language, replete with mistakes and hesitancies, as it is an important step in gaining comfort and fluency in English. If your students represent several different languages, group students with classmates who speak a language other than their own.

Pronunciation

Within the **Active Grammar** section is an exercise that focuses on pronunciation. These exercises are specific pronunciation points that complement the grammar or vocabulary of the lesson, such as the sound of plural *s*, contractions, numbers, syllables, and so on.

The Big Picture

This is our favorite section. It integrates listening, vocabulary, and structure. A large, engaging picture shows a particular setting, such as a restaurant, a doctor's office, or an office supply store. Students listen to a short story or conversation, and then answer questions about the story, fill in exercises, review structures, or write conversations.

Reading

A short reading expands the context of the lesson. We did not manipulate a selection so that every sentence fits into the structure presented in the unit! There are new vocabulary words and structures. Teachers can help readers learn that understanding the main idea is primary. They can then go back over the material to find the details that are interesting or relevant. If students can find the information they need, it is not necessary to master or look up every word.

Writing Our Stories

In this writing section, students first read a paragraph written by an English language learner or teacher. By using checklists or fill-in sentences, students are directed to brainstorm about their own schools, families, jobs, and so on. Students then have an opportunity to write about themselves. Several teachers have told us about the creative ways they share student writing, including publishing student magazines, designing a class Web page, and displaying stories and photos taken by their students. **Sharing Our Stories** directs students to read and understand one another's stories.

English in Action

The unit concludes with a two-page **English in Action** section. It provides practice in the everyday skills students need to interact as citizens, family members, students, and workers. The activities that follow include role plays, forms, and problem-solving exercises to help students become more comfortable in these real-life situations.

The complete *English in Action* package includes everything necessary for students and teachers to facilitate learning. Visit **elt.heinle.com** to learn more about available resources.

Fun, engaging, and action-packed!

A **"Dictionary"** section begins each chapter with a picture dictionary–style presentation of key vocabulary words to illuminate word meaning.

NEW TO THIS EDITION!

"Word Partnerships" provide students with frequent collocations to promote fluency.

NEW TO THIS EDITION!

"Word Builder" activities provide additional vocabulary practice and encourage students to get a deeper understanding of the target words.

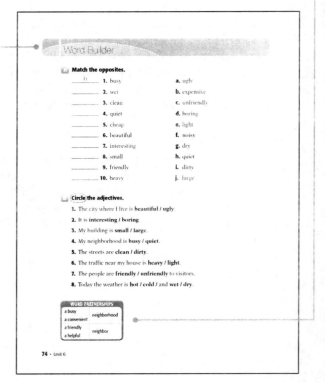

Fun, engaging, and action-packed!

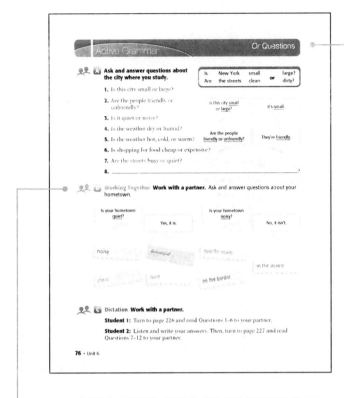

"**Active Grammar**" sections present clear, contextualized grammar explanations along with a rich variety of practice activities.

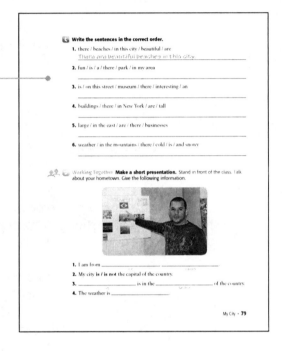

UPDATED FOR THIS EDITION!

"**Working Together**" activities build learner persistence through cooperative tasks, enhancing the classroom community.

"**Working Together**" activities build workplace skills with teamwork tasks like labeling, presenting, etc.

"**The Big Picture**" sections include integrated skills practice around a story or conversation, motivating students to listen and use new grammar and vocabulary.

Fun, engaging, and action-packed!

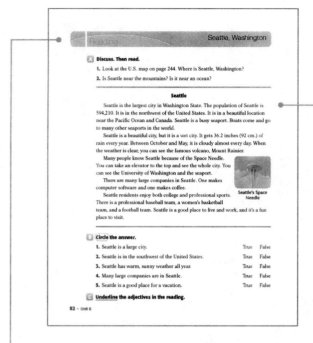

Interesting readings based on the unit theme recycle the vocabulary and grammar presented earlier in the unit.

"Reading" sections provide before-you-read discussion questions, encouraging students to think about the reading topic.

"Writing Our Stories" sections expand students' literacy by giving a closer look at real people in real communities and guided, practice activities to help students write about themselves.

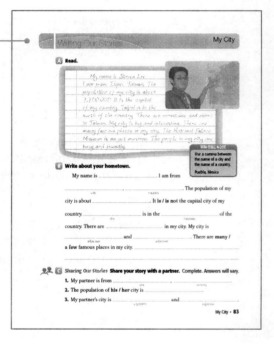

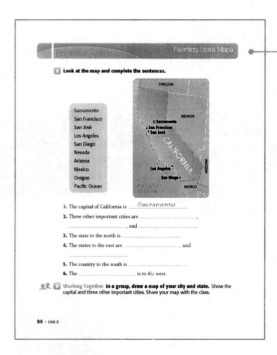

NEW TO THIS EDITION!

"English in Action" sections practice the everyday skills students need to interact and solve problems in the real world.

Liz and I work at Union County College in Elizabeth, New Jersey. We teach at the Institute for Intensive English, a large English as a Second Language program. Students from over 80 different countries study in our classes. Between us, Liz and I have been teaching at the college for over 40 years! When Liz isn't writing, she spends her time traveling, taking pictures, and worrying about her favorite baseball team, the New York Mets. I love the outdoors. I can't start my day without a 15- or 20-mile bicycle ride. My idea of a good time always involves being active: hiking, swimming, or simply working in my garden. I also enjoy watching my favorite baseball team, the New York Yankees.

Barbara H. Foley
Elizabeth R. Neblett

Hello

Dictionary: One to Ten

  Listen and repeat.

(CD1 • TR1)

• Have students listen to the audio, following along in their books as they listen to each phrase: *one student, two students,* and so forth.

• Play the recording again, prompting students to repeat each word along with the audio. Repeat this step until students feel comfortable saying each phrase.

• Have students say *one student, two students,* and so on, as you point to each photo one at a time.

• Check comprehension by pointing to photos at random and calling on individual students to say the appropriate phrase.

Unit 1 Hello

One to Ten

 Listen and repeat.

one student   two students   three students

four students   five students   six students

seven students   eight students   nine students

ten students

2 • Unit 1

More Action!

Have students arrange themselves in groups in response to your prompts: *one student, two students,* and so on. Check comprehension by having groups stand up out of numeric sequence. For example, say *five students,* gesturing for the group with five students to stand up or raise their hands. Repeat with other vocabulary. If necessary, point to the appropriate picture in the book to help support comprehension.

More Action!

Bring to class batches of ten objects such as paperclips, books, pencils, pennies, etc. Have partners arrange objects in numbered groups up to ten (one pencil, two pencils, and so on). Have partners share their groupings with the class. One student can point to each grouping while his or her partner describes them in the pattern *one book, two pencils,* and so on.

  Listen.
CD1·TR2

  Working Together **Introduce yourself to two classmates.**

A: Hello. My name is Miguel.

B: Hi. I'm Elena.

A: Nice to meet you, Elena.

B: Nice to meet you, too.

I am = I'm

Complete. *(Answers will vary.)*

1. My first name is _____.

2. My last name is _____.

WORD PARTNERSHIPS	
first	
middle	name
last	

Elena Blanco
First Name: Elena
Last Name: Blanco

Hello · **3**

Nice to Meet You

   Listen. (CD1 • TR2)

Have students listen to the audio while looking at the people in the photo. Have students listen again, repeating each line. Ask while pointing to each person in the photo: *What's his name? What's her name?*

Working Together Introduce yourself to two classmates.

Point out the note box with the contraction *(I am = I'm)*. Call on pairs of students to read the dialogue aloud. Then invite students to take turns introducing themselves to at least two other classmates.

Complete.

• Point to the two sentences and complete them using your own first and last names.
• Point to the photo on the right and ask: *What's her first name/last name?*
• Ask students to complete sentences using their own names.

Teaching Tip

You will probably not have time to use every suggestion in this *Teacher's Guide.* Feel free to use the suggestions that are appropriate for your class and work best for you and your students.

Teaching Tip

In some cultures, a person's middle name is the last name of his or her mother before marriage. In some cultures, people don't use middle names. Ask students what the custom is in their cultures.

Word Builder

🔊 **A Listen. Then, listen again and repeat.**
(CD1 • TR3)

• With books open, have students listen to the alphabet. Then have them listen again and repeat each of the letters.

• Point out the note box and the terms *capital letter* and *lowercase letter*. Point out the difference in the way that lower-case and upper case letters are written.

🔊 **B Listen and write the letter you hear.**
(CD1 • TR4)

Have students listen to the audio with books closed and write the letters in the air with their fingers. Then with books open, play the recording again, inviting students to write the letters they hear on the blank lines in their books.

👥 **C Working Together Practice your spelling.**

After following the directions in the student book, have students repeat the activity using their own names.

🔊 **A Listen.** Then, listen again and repeat.
CD1•TR3

Aa	Bb	Cc	Dd	Ee	Ff	Gg
Hh	Ii	Jj	Kk	Ll	Mm	Nn
Oo	Pp	Qq	Rr	Ss	Tt	Uu
Vv	Ww	Xx	Yy	Zz		

A = capital letter
a = lowercase letter

🔊 **B Listen and write the letter you hear.**
CD1•TR4

1. _C_
2. _F_
3. _H_
4. _W_
5. _L_
6. _Z_
7. _S_
8. _G_
9. _J_

👥 **C Working Together Practice your spelling.**

Student 1 Close your book. Listen to your partner spell names 1–7. Write the names on a sheet of paper. Then spell names 8–15 slowly for your partner.

Student 2 Spell names 1–7 slowly. Now close your book. Listen to your partner spell names 8–15.

1. Paula	**6.** Daniel	**11.** Garcia
2. Carlos	**7.** Joanne	**12.** Walker
3. Victoria	**8.** Anthony	**13.** Mitchell
4. Jeffrey	**9.** Elizabeth	**14.** Brooks
5. Debbie	**10.** William	**15.** Johnson

4 • Unit 1

More Action!

Divide the class into two teams. Assign one team letters from the first half of the alphabet. Assign the second half to the other team. Ask each team to think of words starting with their assigned letters and to write them on the board. Students won't have much vocabulary but should be able to come up with simple words such as *apple, book, cat,* etc. The team with the most correct words wins.

A Listen and read.

CD1·TR5

A: What's your first name?

B: Ana.

A: What's your last name?

B: Santos.

A: Please spell that.

B: S-A-N-T-O-S.

B Working Together Ask five students their names.
Listen and write their first and last names.

> What's **your** first name?
> What's **your** last name?
> Please spell that.

1. __(Answers will vary.)__ _____

2. _____ _____

3. _____ _____

4. _____ _____

5. _____ _____

C Read.

My name is Sandra. **His** name is Tuan. **Her** name is Erica. **Their** names are Serena and James.

D Say your classmates' names.

His name is Tuan. Her name is Erica. Their names are Serena and James.

Hello · 5

Active Grammar: My/Your/His/Her/Their

A Listen and read.
(CD1 • TR5)

Have students listen to the audio with books closed. Then they listen again with books open. Pairs of students read the dialogue to the class.

B Working Together Ask five students their names. Listen and write their first and last names.

Have students move around the classroom and ask each other their names, using questions from the Helpful Expressions box. Students can check each other's work to make sure the spelling of their names is correct.

C Read.

• Say *My name is _____* while pointing to yourself. Point to several different students as you model the sentence patterns: *His name is _____. Her name is _____.*
• Read aloud the illustrated sentences in the book. Then, form pairs of students, and have partners take turns reading the sentences to each other.

D Say your classmates' names.

Ask a volunteer to stand up. Ask the class: *What's his* (or *her*) *name?* If necessary, model how to respond using a complete sentence. Repeat with other volunteers.

More Action!

Guide students in searching the Internet for the meaning of or any other information they can find about their names. Model how you would report on your name. For example: *My name is Lana. It means beautiful place. It is from Ireland.*

Teaching Tip

Students don't like to hear their names mispronounced. Ask the class to take the time to learn how to say each other's names correctly. This may mean that some students will need to say their names several times and help others with pronunciation.

Hello · **5**

Active Grammar:
To Be

W **Read the chart and look at the pictures.**

• Model the sentences in the chart substituting countries represented in the classroom. For example: *She is from Vietnam. He is from Mexico.*

• Pronounce the names of countries in the box. Ask if students come from any of these countries. Have them point out these countries on a classroom map or on the map on page 243.

• Tell students to look at the three rows of drawings. Go around the class indicating individual pictures and asking where each person is from. For example: *(#6) She is from Peru. (#5) He is from Russia.*

A **Read the chart and look at the pictures.**

I	am	from the United States.
You	are	from China.
She	is	from Mexico.
They	are	from Haiti.

Use *the* with these countries:

the Dominican Republic
the Philippines
the Republic of Congo
the United States
the United Arab Emirates

More Action!

Have students bring items to class from their respective countries, such as articles of clothing, candy, books, newspapers, or souvenirs. Display them in front of the class. Have each student explain: *It is a wooden doll inside another doll. It is from Russia.*

B Complete with *am / is / are*.

1. They ___are___ from New York.
2. Denise ___is___ from Greece.
3. Pedro ___is___ from the Dominican Republic.
4. They ___are___ from the United States.
5. I ___am___ from Bogotá, Colombia.
6. My sister and I ___are___ from Lisbon, Portugal.
7. Mr. Martinez ___is___ from Boston, Massachusetts.
8. Mr. and Mrs. Martinez ___are___ from Boston.
9. Miss Lee ___is___ from Korea.

Mr. Frank Martinez   **Mrs.** Ana Martinez   **Miss** Lily Lee / **Ms.** Lily Lee

C Working Together **Work in a large group.** Look at the world map on page 243. Ask and answer questions about your countries. Point to your country on the map.

Where are you from?

I'm from the United States.

Where is he from?

He is from Brazil.

D Write about the students in Exercise C. (Additional answers will vary.)

1. ___Carlos___ is from ___Colombia___.
2. _____ is from _____.
3. _____ is from _____.
4. _____ is from _____.
5. _____.

Hello · **7**

Complete with *am/ is/are*.

Ask students to complete the exercise on their own. Then ask them to share their answers with the class. Provide feedback and have students make corrections to their work if necessary.

Working Together Work in a large group. Look at the world map on page 243. Ask and answer questions about your countries. Point to your country on the map.

Circulate as students work and verify that they are forming sentences with a variety of subjects and pronouns, including *I, you, he, she, we,* and *they*.

Write about the students in Exercise C.

More Action!

Take a census. Ask students to tell what countries they are from. Have one student write all the countries in a column on the board as the other students call out the names. Next to each name, the student at the board shades in a square for each student from that country. Which country has the most shaded squares? Which has the fewest?

Active Grammar: Contractions

  A Listen and repeat.
(CD1 • TR6)

Have students listen to the audio while looking at the full and contracted forms. Have them listen again, repeating both forms. With books closed, ask them to listen and repeat again.

B Pronunciation: Contractions Listen and repeat.
(CD1 • TR7)

Have students look at their books while listening to the audio. Repeat the full and contracted forms of each sentence. Practice the pronunciation of country names that students are seeing for the first time.

C Dictation Listen and complete. (CD1 • TR8)

Explain that students will hear eight sentences. Each sentence will either be in the long form (not contracted) or the short form (contracted). Students should complete each sentence in their books so that it matches the way that the sentence is pronounced on the audio. When they are finished, write answers on the board so students can check their work.

A Listen and repeat.
CD1·TR6

I am	→	I'm
you are	→	you're
he is	→	he's
she is	→	she's
it is	→	it's
we are	→	we're
they are	→	they're

B Pronunciation: Contractions Listen and repeat.
CD1·TR7

1. He is from Mexico. → He's from Mexico.
2. She is from Vietnam. → She's from Vietnam.
3. I am from Russia. → I'm from Russia.
4. He is from China. → He's from China.
5. I am from Haiti. → I'm from Haiti.
6. She is from Peru. → She's from Peru.
7. He is from Cuba. → He's from Cuba.
8. She is from Egypt. → She's from Egypt.

C Dictation Listen and complete.
CD1·TR8

1. __I am__ from Mexico.
2. __She's__ from Alaska.
3. __They're__ from Chile.
4. __We're__ from Cameroon.
5. __He is__ from Ukraine.
6. __I'm__ from Italy.
7. __It is__ from Vietnam.
8. __You're__ from Colombia.

8 · Unit 1

More Action!

Have students play a memory game. Choose five or six students to stand in front of the class. The first says his or her name and where he or she is from. For example: *My name is Jean-Paul and I'm from Haiti.* The next student says: *His name is Jean-Paul and he's from Haiti.* Then he or she introduces himself or herself. Each student must introduce all those who have already spoken before introducing himself or herself.

A Ask and answer the questions with a partner.

Min (China)

Her name is Min.

She's from China.

1. What's her name?
Where is she from?

Adolfo and
Alfredo
(El Salvador)

Their names
are Adolfo
and Alfredo.
They are/
They're from
El Salvador.

2. What are their names?
Where are they from?

Hong (Vietnam)

His name is
Hong.
He is/ He's
from Vietnam.

3. What's his name?
Where is he from?

Aruna (India)

Her name is
Aruna.
She is/ She's
from India.

4. What's her name?
Where is she from?

John (Canada)

His name is
John.
He is/ He's
from
Canada.

5. What's his name?
Where is he from?

Rosa and
Consuelo
(Guatemala)

Their names
are Rosa and
Consuelo.
They are/
They're from
Guatemala.

6. What are their names?
Where are they from?

My name
is...
I am / I'm
from...

7. What's your name?
Where are you from?

Active Grammar: Questions

A Ask and answer the questions with a partner.

• Group the students in pairs. Student A asks the question and Student B gives the answer. Walk around the room as students work through the activity, giving help with pronunciation.
• When most of the pairs have completed the activity, tell them to switch roles and do it again.
• Put pairs together to form groups of four. Student A of one pair asks Student A of the other pair about his or her partner. *What's his/ her name? Where is he/ she from?* Student A answers. Then the other pair of students asks the same questions. Repeat until all four students have introduced their partners.

More Action!

Have one student silently choose a classmate as the subject of a guessing game. Other students must ask yes/no questions until they guess the correct person. If necessary, model how to ask questions such as: *Is his name Stelios? Is he from Greece?*

Looking at: Driver's Licenses and ID Cards

Write.

- Ask students to look at the Edison School ID and the Florida driver's license. Explain (or elicit) the meaning of *ID number, driver's license,* and other new words.
- Go through the activity first orally, calling on students to read each sentence and say whether it belongs on the driver's license or the school ID. Then ask them to complete the exercise.

Match.

Have students complete the matching activity on their own. Review the answers orally by asking one student to read the question and another to give the answer.

Looking at

A. Write.

a. His first name is Hong.

b. ~~Her first name is Luisa.~~

c. Her last name is Reyes.

d. His last name is Lin.

e. His street address is 12 Bay Street.

f. Her ID number is 44387.

g. She is a student at Edison School.

h. He lives in Tampa, Florida.

i. His zip code is 33615.

STUDENT ID **Edison School**
Name: Luisa P. Reyes
ID Number: **44387**
Luisa P. Reyes
Signature
2-LAN 44387

1. Her first name is Luisa.
2. Her last name is Reyes.
3. Her ID number is 44387.
4. She is a student at Edison School.

Florida Sunshine State
DRIVER'S LICENSE
F65942-953950-947392
HONG LIN
12 BAY STREET
TAMPA,
FLORIDA 33615
Hong Lin
ORGAN DONOR

1. His first name is Hong.
2. His last name is Lin.
3. His street address is 12 Bay Street.
4. He lives in Tampa, Florida.
5. His zip code is 33615.

B. Match.

c	**1.** What's his name?	**a.** Her name is Imelda.
b	**2.** Where is he from?	**b.** He is from Mexico.
a	**3.** What's her name?	**c.** His name is Hector.
e	**4.** Where is she from?	**d.** I'm from Poland.
f	**5.** What's your name?	**e.** She is from the Philippines.
d	**6.** Where are you from?	**f.** My name is Dorota.

10 · Unit 1

More Action!

Ask students to bring similar forms of identification from home, including driver's licenses, green cards, passports, or other IDs. Display them on a table in front of the room. Have pairs of students ask and answer questions about the forms. For example: *What's his/her first name?* *What's his/her ID number?*

Teaching Tip

Some students may be uncomfortable displaying items that contain personal information. If so, they need only ask and answer questions about identification the other students have brought.

Listen.

Tomás   Jenny   Erica   Hiro   Marie

 Listen again and write each person's name.

Tomás   Hiro   Erica   Marie   Jenny

 Listen and write the answers.

1. _____ Tomás _____   3. _____ Erica _____   5. _____ Hong Kong _____
2. _____ Hiro _____   4. _____ Haiti _____   6. _____ Answers will vary. _____

 Listen. Write the number next to the correct answer.

_____4_____ **a.** He is from Japan.

_____2_____ **b.** I'm from Peru.

_____3_____ **c.** His name is Hiro.

_____5_____ **d.** Her name is Marie.

_____1_____ **e.** My name is Tomás.

_____6_____ **f.** She's from Haiti.

The Big Picture: My Classmates

 Listen. (CD1 • TR9)

Have students listen to the audio while they point to each of the five people. Then ask them what they remember about the people.

 Listen again and write each person's name. (CD1 • TR9)

Have students listen again while they write the names of the people on the lines.

 Listen and write the answers. (CD1 • TR10)

Have students listen to the questions first without writing anything. Then listen again, giving students time to write the answer. Help students check their answers by playing the audio once again.

 Listen. Write the number next to the correct answer. (CD1 • TR11)

Have students listen first. Then play the audio again, as students fill in the correct answers.

More Action!

Have pairs of students take turns. In each pair, Student A gives an answer to an unasked question by making a simple statement or by naming a person. Student B must think of a question that goes with the answer. For example, if Student A says *Marie and Hiro,* Student B may ask, *What are their names?*

Teaching Tip

Most students will not understand everything on the audio. Assure them that the best way to understand rapid spoken English is to focus on the key information they need and let the rest go. Suggest that here they listen only for the students' names and their countries of origin.

Reading:
The English Language

A. Circle the countries where English is spoken.

• As a pre-reading activity, ask students to look at the list of countries. Read the list aloud and ask students to repeat after you.
• Ask students to circle the names of countries where English is spoken.

B. Read.

• Have students close their books. Read the passage aloud. Ask a few general questions such as: *How many languages do people speak in India?*
• Read the passage again with books open. Ask some of the same questions again.
• Ask students if there are words they don't know. Work with them to make guesses at the meaning of unknown words such as *official*, *politics*, and *business*.

C. Complete the sentences.

Ask students to find the sentences in the reading which have the missing information needed to complete the sentences.

A. Circle the countries where English is spoken. (Answers may vary.)

(the United States)	Japan	China	Mexico
Colombia	(Britain)	(Ireland)	India
(Australia)	Russia	(Canada)	South Africa

B. Read.

English Around the World

Many people around the world speak English as their first language. People in the United States, Great Britain, Ireland, and Australia speak English.

In India, there are 21 official languages, but English is the language of politics and business. In South Africa, there are many languages, too, but many people speak English.

For you, English is a new language, but you can speak some English, too. You know words like *car*, *man*, *woman*, and *money*. You know sentences such as *I'm a student* and *I'm from Mexico.*

English is a language with different words and new grammar. It will take time to learn. Many people around the world speak English. Soon you will speak English, too.

C. Complete the sentences.

English	grammar	languages	People	world

1. ___People___ in the United States and Australia speak English.
2. In India, there are 21 official ___languages___.
3. Many people around the ___world___ speak English.
4. English has new ___grammar___.
5. Soon you will speak ___English___, too.

More Action!

Internet Option: Assign each of the continents to a group of students. Ask them to find the name of countries that speak in English on their respective continents. Groups can then report back to the class.

A Read.

> *My name is Antonio. I am from Mexico. I am studying English. I am a student at Bayside Adult School. My teacher is Ms. Johnson.*

B Write. (Answers will vary.)

My name is _____ _____.
　　　　　　 first name　　　　　　　　　　 last name

I am from _____. I am studying English. I am a student at
　　　　　　 country

_____. My teacher's name is _____
　　 name of school　　　　　　　　　　　　　　　　　　　　 name

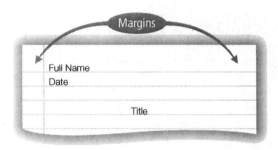

Margins

Full Name
Date

Title

WRITING NOTE
Use margins when you write.

C Sharing Our Stories Read your partner's story. Complete the information below.

1. **Her / His** name is _____ _____

2. **She / He** is from _____.

Hello • **13**

Writing Our Stories: All About Me

A Read.

Have students close their books; then read the passage aloud. Ask: *What's his name? Where does he go to school?* With books open, ask students to look for sentences with the answers.

B Write.

Tell students to fill in the blanks with their own personal information. Call on individuals to share what they've written.

C Sharing Our Stories Read your partner's story. Complete the information below.

Ask students to work in pairs and trade what they've written with their partners. Using their partners' writing, they should fill in the answers to the questions.

More Action!

Ask students to interview each other and ask for personal information. Then, go to the board to write what they've found out. Tell Exercise to use the text from Exercise B as a model but change it to third person. *Her name is _____ She's from _____*

Teaching Tip

Explain what margins are and why they're important. Use a real writing sample to show students examples of margins and other textual features.

English in Action: Understanding Numbers 1–20

  Listen and repeat.
(CD1 • TR12)

• Tell students to look at the chart while they listen to the audio. Have them say each number as they hear it.
• Send a group of students to the board. Dictate numbers out of sequence and ask them to write the correct numerals.

  Listen and write the numbers. (CD1 • TR13)

• Review the pronunciation of all the numbers in the chart. Check comprehension by having students point to the numbers in their charts as you say them in random order.
• Play the recording and have students write their answers to the exercise.
• Provide answers on the board and have students correct their work.

Listen and write the words for the numbers. (CD1 • TR14)

• Play the recording and have students write their answers to the exercise. Remind them that this time they are supposed to write the *words* for the numbers.
• Provide answers on the board and have students correct their work.

English in Action

  Listen and repeat.
CD1•TR12

0	1	2	3	4	5	6	7	8	9	10
zero	one	two	three	four	five	six	seven	eight	nine	ten
11	12	13	14	15	16	17	18	19	20	
eleven	twelve	thirteen	fourteen	fifteen	sixteen	seventeen	eighteen	nineteen	twenty	

 Listen and write the numbers.
CD1•TR13

a. 6
b. 11
c. 0
d. 18
e. 2
f. 15
g. 3
h. 10

i. 17
j. 20
k. 4
l. 9
m. 13
n. 8
o. 12

 Listen and write the words for the numbers.
CD1•TR14

a. ten
b. six
c. eleven
d. three
e. twelve

f. eighteen
g. twenty
h. one
i. seventeen

14 • Unit 1

More Action!

Have each student make a bingo card with three rows of three spaces each. Then they can fill in the spaces with random numbers from 1 to 20. Call out numbers of your choice, from 1 to 20, taking note of the numbers you say. The first student with three numbers in a row (from the numbers you've called out) says *Bingo* and wins. Play several times so there are other winners.

Listen and read.
(CD1·TR15)

What's your telephone number?

301-555-1796?

Thank you.

My telephone number is 301-555-1796.

Yes, that's right.

CULTURE NOTE
In a telephone number, say each number separately.

Listen and write.
(CD1·TR16)

a. 555-3231
b. 555-3080
c. 800-555-4242
d. 201-555-4413
e. 555-3692
f. 555-7548
g. 619-555-7042
h. 813-555-1624

Complete.

A B C

Name _____
Phone _____
Fax _____
Email _____
Address _____

Hello · 15

English in Action: Understanding Telephone Numbers

Listen and read.
(CD1 • TR15)

Ask students to listen to the audio while following the dialogue in their books. Ask if they can remember the telephone number (without looking at the book). In pairs, students should read the dialogue to each other. They may substitute their own telephone numbers but only if they feel comfortable doing so.

Culture Note

Point out that *separately* means *one by one.*

Listen and write.
(CD1 • TR16)

Ask students to listen to the audio, writing the phone numbers they hear. Circulate and check that students' answers are correct.

Complete.

Ask students to fill in the rolodex card with their own information. If they're not comfortable writing their own telephone numbers, tell them to make up phone numbers. Have students work in pairs, exchanging cards.

More Action!

Bring your local yellow pages to class or direct students to the Internet. Explain that the yellow pages are simply a telephone book that lists telephone numbers for local businesses. Have students work in pairs, find local businesses, and ask about their numbers. For example:

A: *What's the number for Jake's Auto Parts?*
B: *It's 555-1234.*

Teaching Tip

Have a few students go to the board. Dictate several telephone numbers and ask the students to write the numbers on the board.

Dictionary: Classroom Objects

  A Listen and repeat.
(CD1 • TR17)

• Ask students about the picture. *Who is in the picture? Where are they?*

• Have students listen to the audio while pointing to the named objects in the picture. Then ask students to point to objects of their choice and name them.

• Students listen to the audio again, repeating the words. Correct any pronunciation problems.

• Point to different objects in the picture at random and call on students to name them.

 A Listen and repeat.
CD1 • TR17

1. a wall
2. a board
3. an eraser
4. a piece of chalk
5. a teacher
6. a desk
7. a computer
8. a printer
9. a student
10. a table
11. a cell phone
12. a backpack
13. a chair
14. a bookcase
15. a map
16. an umbrella
17. a pencil sharpener
18. a door
19. a window
20. a clock

16 • Unit 2

More Action!

Ask a student to walk around the classroom and find an object that is the same as an object in the picture. Ask him or her to name the object. Continue with another student and so forth until all the objects from your classroom that match those in the picture have been named.

Teaching Tip

Some students don't like to be singled out for an activity in front of the class. Sometimes it's best to ask more outgoing students first and then others will follow their examples.

B Listen and repeat.

CD1·TR18

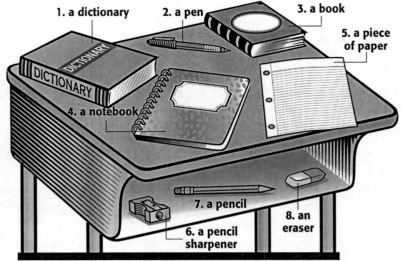

1. a dictionary
2. a pen
3. a book
5. a piece of paper
4. a notebook
7. a pencil
8. an eraser
6. a pencil sharpener

 C **Circle** the items that are in your classroom.
Add to the list. (Answers will vary.)

1. a table	**9.** a white board
2. a chair	**10.** a dictionary
3. a world map	**11.** a window
4. a U.S. map	**12.** a bookcase
5. a clock	**13.** _____
6. a computer	**14.** _____
7. a pencil sharpener	**15.** _____
8. a chalkboard	**16.** _____

WORD PARTNERSHIPS	
erase	a mistake the board
sharpen	a pencil
open	a book
close	a dictionary

The Classroom • **17**

◀)) **B** **Listen and repeat.**
(CD1 • TR18)

• Have students listen to the audio while pointing to the named items in the picture.
• Students listen to the audio again, repeating the words. Correct their pronunciation.
• Point to different objects in the picture at random and call on students to say them.

C **Circle the items that are in your classroom. Add to the list.**

• Ask students to look around the classroom for examples of the words in the list.
• Point to other classroom objects not on the list and ask students to identify them. Have them repeat the words after you. Write the words on the board so students can see the spelling when they add the words to the list.

Word Partnerships

Ask students to make sentences combining verbs and objects in the box. For example: *Please erase the board.*

More Action!

Divide the class into two teams. The first person on Team A holds up or points to an item. The first person on Team B must name the item and spell the word aloud. Then switch so that the second person on Team B holds up an item and the second person on Team A must name and spell it. Every correct answer earns one point. Continue until all available objects have been named. The team with the most points wins.

Teaching Tip

When doing group activities with students of the same language background, make sure that everyone speaks English to each other.

Word Builder

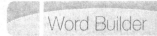

A Write.

• Ask students to name the objects in the drawings before writing them. Go around the class and ask students at random to name an item.

• Ask students to write the words on the lines.

B Listen and complete.

(CD1 • TR19)

• Tell students they will hear five conversations with missing words.

• Have students listen to the audio while looking at the exercise items.

• Students listen again and write in the missing words. Move among them and check spelling.

C Working Together
Work with a group. Find items in your backpack or purse. Put them on the desk. Ask and answer questions.

• Have students work in pairs. Student A holds up an object and asks: *Is this your cell phone?* Student B answers: *Yes, it is. Thank you.*

• Have them reverse roles and use another object. Work around the class until all the assembled objects have been used in dialogues.

A Write.

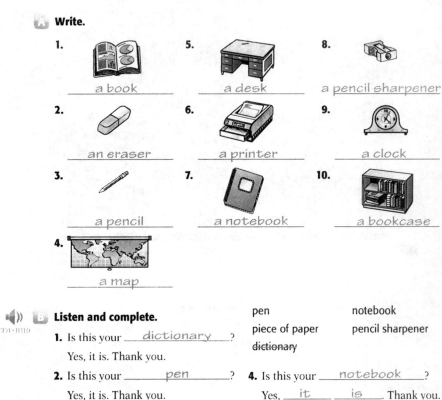

1. a book
2. an eraser
3. a pencil
4. a map
5. a desk
6. a printer
7. a notebook
8. a pencil sharpener
9. a clock
10. a bookcase

B Listen and complete.

CD1 • TR19

pen   notebook
piece of paper   pencil sharpener
~~dictionary~~

1. Is this your _dictionary_?
   Yes, it is. Thank you.

2. Is this your _pen_?
   Yes, it is. Thank you.

3. Is this your _piece of paper_?
   No, it isn't.

4. Is this your _notebook_?
   Yes, _it_ _is_. Thank you.

5. Is this your _pencil sharpener_?
   No, _it_ _isn't_.

C Working Together Work with a group. Find items in your backpack or purse. Put them on the desk. Ask and answer questions.

Is this your cell phone?

Yes, it is. Thank you.

Is this your pen?

No, it isn't.

Teaching Tip

There will be objects in the classroom not mentioned in the text. Discuss the words for these items: *coat hanger, ceiling light, loudspeaker.*

Article	Singular Noun
a	book
	student
an	eraser
	umbrella

Use *a* before a noun that begins with a consonant sound.

Use *an* before a noun that begins with a vowel sound: a, e, i, o, u.

Do not use *a* or *an* with plural nouns.

A Listen and repeat.

(CD1•TR20)

1.

a book   books

2.
a pencil   pencils

3.

a student   students

4.

a man   men

5.

a woman   women

6.

a child   children

B Write *a* or *an*. Write *X* if no article is necessary.

1. _____ a _____ teacher
2. _____ a _____ book
3. _____ a _____ pencil sharpener
4. _____ X _____ Florida
5. _____ an _____ umbrella
6. _____ X _____ Mr. Gonzalez
7. _____ X _____ computers

8. _____ a _____ student
9. _____ X _____ erasers
10. _____ X _____ backpacks

> Do not use *a* or *the* with most proper nouns.
>
> California
> Tom
> Mrs. Smith

Active Grammar: Singular Nouns

- Ask students to look at the chart and the notes. Write a list of vowels on the board and explain that we use *an* before singular words in which the first letter is a vowel: *an eraser, an umbrella.*
- Ask them if they can think of other singular words which use *an.*

Listen and repeat.
(CD1•TR20)

- Have students listen to the audio as they point to the objects and people that are being named.
- Students listen again, repeating the words. Pay attention to their pronunciation of *man/men, woman/women, child/children.*
- Students listen to the audio a third time. Pause after each singular form and call on students to provide the plural form.

Write *a* or *an*. Write *X* if no article is necessary.

- Point out the note box. Ask students to think of other proper nouns that don't take *a* or *the.*
- Ask students to write the answers to the exercise items. Call on them for the correct answers.

Active Grammar: Plural Nouns

Ask students to think of other nouns that have plurals ending in *s*. Review the plural forms of the classroom vocabulary.

🔊 **A Pronunciation: Plural Nouns Listen and circle.** (CD1 • TR21)

Call on students to read aloud the pairs of words. Then have students listen to the audio and circle the word they hear in each pair. Have students listen a second time so they can check their answers.

B Say the words in Exercise A.

Have students work in pairs. Student A says the singular form and Student B says the plural form. Then switch.

C Circle.

Explain to the students that if it's a single object, they should circle the singular form and if there're multiple objects, they should circle the plural form. Walk among them and check their answers.

D Write the plural forms.

• Review the vocabulary orally, saying the singular form for each word and asking individual students for the plural form.
• Have students write the answers to the exercise and walk among them checking the answers.

Plural Nouns
book**s**
student**s**
eraser**s**
umbrella**s**

Irregular Plural Forms	
child	child**ren**
man	m**e**n
woman	wom**e**n

Add *s* to the end of a noun to make it plural. Some plural nouns have an irregular form.

🔊 **A Pronunciation: Plural Nouns Listen and circle.**
CD1 • TR21

1. (a pencil)   pencils
2. a student   (students)
3. a teacher   (teachers)
4. (a man)   men
5. (a map)   maps

6. a dictionary   (dictionaries)
7. (an eraser)   erasers
8. (a notebook)   notebooks
9. a classroom   (classrooms)
10. a woman   (women)

B Say the words in Exercise A.

C Circle.

1.
a table   (tables)

3.
an eraser   (erasers)

5.
a pencil   (pencils)

2.
a clock   clocks

4.
a woman   (women)

6.
a book   books

D Write the plural forms.

1. child ___children___
2. man ___men___
3. desk ___desks___
4. student ___students___

5. dictionary ___dictionaries___
6. umbrella ___umbrellas___
7. woman ___women___
8. clock ___clocks___

20 • Unit 2

Teaching Tip

Pay special attention to the pronunciation of *man/men* and *woman/women*. Students may have trouble hearing the difference.

E Write.

1. pencils

2. books

3. a map

4. a pencil sharpener

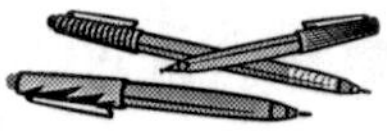

5. pens

6. children

7. a woman

8. a man

F Write *a* or *an*. Write X if no article is necessary.

1. _a_ chair
2. _a_ table
3. _a_ desk
4. _X_ Mr. James
5. _an_ eraser
6. _X_ students
7. _a_ teacher
8. _a_ pen
9. _X_ bookcases
10. _a_ white board
11. _X_ Texas
12. _a_ printer
13. _a_ cell phone
14. _an_ umbrella
15. _a_ dictionary

G Working Together **Work with a group.** Look around your classroom. Write plural nouns. (Answers will vary.)

1. _____
2. _____
3. _____
4. _____
5. _____
6. _____

E Write.
• Review singular and plural forms of the pictured objects. Say the singular, then call on students for the plural. Then do the reverse.
• Ask students to write the answers. Move among them and check spelling.

F Write *a* or *an*. Write X if no article is necessary.
• Review the guidelines for deciding whether a noun takes *a*, *an*, or no article at all.
• Ask students to complete the exercise. Then call on individuals for the correct answers.

G Working Together Work with a group. Look around your classroom. Write plural nouns.
Encourage students to expand on what they've learned by choosing some objects which have not been mentioned in their books, such as *floor, light, bulletin board, drawer, keyboard, mouse, ceiling,* etc.

More Action!

Have students work in pairs. One thinks of an object in the classroom, the other must guess what it is and whether it's singular or plural.
Is it a pencil or pencils?

Teaching Tip

Ask students to study the new vocabulary at home and give a short spelling quiz the next day in class.

Active Grammar:
This / These

Ask students to look at the pictures and the note box. Point to items around the classroom using *this* and *these*. Explain that *this* refers to one object and *these* refers to more than one.

Complete.

- First, review the possessive pronouns that are used in the exercise: *my, your, his, her.*
- Have students write the answers to the exercise. Then call on individuals to read the correct answers aloud.

Ask and answer questions with a partner.

- Choose a student and model the dialogue with him or her. Substitute other classroom items and repeat.
- Select pairs of students to come to the front of the class and act out the individual dialogues. Use the actual objects from the pictures as props.

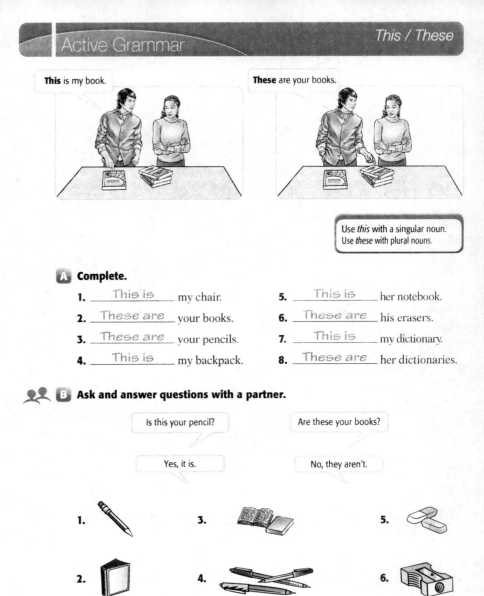

This is my book.

These are your books.

Use *this* with a singular noun.
Use *these* with plural nouns.

A **Complete.**

1. ___This is___ my chair.
2. ___These are___ your books.
3. ___These are___ your pencils.
4. ___This is___ my backpack.
5. ___This is___ her notebook.
6. ___These are___ his erasers.
7. ___This is___ my dictionary.
8. ___These are___ her dictionaries.

B **Ask and answer questions with a partner.**

Is this your pencil?

Are these your books?

Yes, it is.

No, they aren't.

1.
2.
3.
4.
5.
6.

22 · Unit 2

More Action!

Bring to class a variety of items such as a phone book, newspaper, cell phone, radio, globe, or earphones. Display them on a table in front of the room. Say the vocabulary for them and ask students to repeat. Then have pairs of students choose objects and act out the dialogue from Exercise B again.

There	is	a student	in the classroom.
	are	students	

Use *there is* and *there are* to talk about a room, city, or other place.

A Complete.

1. _____There are_____ two students in the classroom.

2. _____There is_____ a student from France in the room.

3. _____There are_____ twenty desks in my classroom.

4. _____There are_____ books in the bookcase.

5. _____There is_____ a dictionary on the desk.

6. _____There is_____ one pencil sharpener in the room.

7. _____There is_____ a woman in the classroom.

8. _____There are_____ five men in the class.

B Listen and (circle) Desk 1 or Desk 2.
CD1·TR22

Desk 1   **Desk 2**

1. (Desk 1)   Desk 2   5. Desk 1   (Desk 2)
2. (Desk 1)   Desk 2   6. (Desk 1)   Desk 2
3. (Desk 1)   (Desk 2)   7. (Desk 1)   Desk 2
4. Desk 1   (Desk 2)   8. Desk 1   (Desk 2)

C Working Together Work with a group. Write three true sentences and three false sentences about your classroom. Then, read your sentences to the class. Your classmates will say, "True" or "False." (Answers will vary.)

> *There are 100 students in this class.*

The Classroom · **23**

More Action!

Have students write statements on the board about themselves and the classroom, using *there is* and *there are*. The statements can be true or false. Ask the class to help you correct any errors in the statements. Call on individuals to say whether each statement is true or false.

Active Grammar:
There is / There are

Model the sentences in the chart. Add other sentences with *there is* and *there are*. Use vocabulary from the school and the community. For example: *There is a desk in the hallway. There are leaves on the sidewalk.*

A Complete.

• Practice orally first, saying examples from the exercise and asking students to choose *there is* or *there are*. For example: **T:** *a student from France.* **S:** *There is.*
• Have students write the answers to the exercise. Move among them checking answers.

B Listen and circle Desk 1 or Desk 2. (CD1 • TR22)

• Ask students to look at the pictures of the two desks and talk about the objects on each desk.
• Have students listen to the audio, pointing to Desk 1 or 2.
• Students listen again, circling the correct desk.
• Students listen a third time, checking their answers.

C Working Together Work with a group. Write three true sentences and three false sentences about your classroom. Then, read your sentences to the class. Your classmates will say, "True" or "False".

Ask students to write their sentences on the board so everyone can read them before deciding if they're true or false.

The Big Picture: The Classroom

A Circle the things you see in this classroom.

- Review vocabulary for all the classroom objects.
- Ask students to talk about the picture. Ask questions to begin the activity. For example: *Who is this? What is this? What is the room number?* Encourage them to make sentences with *there is* and *there are*.
- Ask them to do the exercise. Move among them checking their answers.

B Talk about the people and the things in this classroom.

Introduce vocabulary the students may not know such as *wheelchair, glasses,* etc.

C Listen and look at the picture. (CD1 • TR23)

- Students listen to the audio, pointing to the elements of the picture as they are mentioned.
- Ask students what they remember from the audio.
- Students listen to the audio again, repeating each sentence after the speaker.
- Ask students questions about what the audio said. For example:
Is the classroom on the second floor?
Are there two students from Cambodia?
Is the teacher Mr. Jefferies?

24 · Unit 2

A Circle the things you see in this classroom.

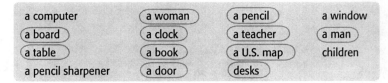

a computer	a woman	a pencil	a window
a board	a clock	a teacher	a man
a table	a book	a U.S. map	children
a pencil sharpener	a door	desks	

B Talk about the people and the things in this classroom.

C Listen and look at the picture.
CD1 · TR23

24 · Unit 2

D Listen and circle.

CD1·TR24

1. True (False)   4. (True) False   7. (True) False
2. True (False)   5. True (False)   8. (True) False
3. True (False)   6. True (False)   9. (True) False

E Listen. If the information is correct, write the sentence. If the information is wrong, put an X.

CD1·TR25

1. __X__

2. __The classroom is in Room 204.__

3. __There are five students from Mexico.__

4. __X__

5. __There are 10 students in this class.__

6. __There is a table for the teacher.__

7. __X__

8. __There is a board in the room.__

F Complete.

clock	clocks	student	students
map	maps	man	men
woman	women	desk	desks

1. There are two ____maps____ on the wall.

2. There is a ____map____ of the world.

3. There are ten ____students____ in the class.

4. There are four ____men____ and six ____women____.

5. There is one ____student____ from India.

6. There are twelve ____desks____ in the classroom.

7. There is a ____clock____ on the wall.

The Classroom · 25

D Listen and circle.
(CD1 • TR24)

• Prepare the students for the listening activity by making up true and false statements about the picture and having them call out *true* or *false*.

• Have students listen to the audio, first just pointing to the part of the picture that will let them know if the statement is true or false.

• Students listen again, this time circling *true* or *false* in the exercise.

• Ask individual students to read out their answers and make corrections.

E Listen. If the information is correct, write the sentence. If the information is wrong, put an X.
(CD1 • TR25)

• Students listen to the audio, first pointing to the part of the picture that will tell them if the information is correct or wrong.

• Students listen again, pausing to write the sentence or X.

• Ask individual students to read out their answers and correct them.

F Complete.

Ask students to complete the exercise on their own. Call on individuals for their answers and make corrections.

Reading: Signs

A. Read the school signs. Ask your teacher about any new signs.

- Ask students to talk about the signs. Introduce vocabulary such as *men's/women's room, alarm, computer lab, tennis club.*
- Point out the icons and drawings on signs that help show their meaning. For example, the books might indicate a classroom or library. Knowing this might help the student recognize the word *library* if he or she has heard the word before, but not seen it in written form. Ask students if they can think of any other drawings on signs they've seen, such as road signs for a hill or curving road.

B. Working Together Work with a group. Walk around your school. Copy three signs that you see.

Encourage students to find signs they don't understand as well as ones they do. Ask students to explain what the signs mean. Ask them where they found them.

A. Read the school signs. Ask your teacher about any new signs.

 MEN　　 WOMEN　　

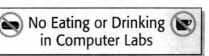 No Eating or Drinking in Computer Labs

 Join The Tennis Club
See Dave Coles
Room 341

 NO SMOKING

LIBRARY HOURS
Monday to Friday　9:00 A.M. to 10:00 P.M.
Saturday　　　　 9:00 A.M. to 5:00 P.M.
Sunday　　　　　 1:00 P.M. to 5:00 P.M.

B. Working Together Work with a group. Walk around your school. Copy three signs that you see.

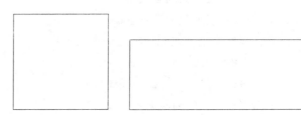

More Action!

- Ask students to bring in copies of signs from the community. Each student should draw his or her signs on the board and ask other students to guess their meaning. Bring some of your own.
- Bring in a copy of the driver's license preparation booklet from your local Division of Motor Vehicles. Make copies of common road signs and hand them out. Ask students to guess their meaning. Write the words on the board. For example: *no passing* or *school crossing.*

A Read.

> I study English at the English Adult School.
> My class is very large. There are 30 students
> in my class. We are from 20 different
> countries. We speak ten different languages.
>   Our classroom is small. There are 30
> small desks. Our teacher, Ms. Garcia, has a large desk for
> her books and her papers. We have many pencils, but we don't
> have a pencil sharpener. We are from many countries, but we
> don't have a map on the wall.
>   We need a larger classroom with a pencil sharpener
> and a map.

WRITING NOTE
Use a period at the end of every sentence.

B Write about your classroom. (Answers will vary.)

I study English at _____. There
name of your school

are _____ students in my class. We are from
number

_____ different countries. We speak _____
number   number

different languages.

Our classroom is _____. There are _____
big / small   number

desks in the classroom. There is _____ _____. There
a / an

_____.

C Sharing Our Stories Read a partner's story. Check for a period at the end of each sentence.

The Classroom · 27

More Action!

Internet Option: Ask students to do a search about class size in various countries. They can enter *class size in schools* for whatever countries they choose. On the board, make a bar graph with names of countries down one side and shaded squares for students in a class alongside each country. Which country has the biggest class size and which has the smallest?

Writing Our Stories: My English Class

A Read.

- Ask students to close their books and read the passage aloud to them.
- Ask them what they remember from the passage.
- Read it again while students follow along in their books.
- Ask comprehension questions. For example: *How many students are in the class? How many languages do they speak?*
- Ask students to take turns reading parts of the passage aloud. Correct pronunciation.

B Write about your classroom.

- Ask students to give you information about the class. One student will have to add up the number of languages spoken. Another student can take a poll on whether the room is too big, too small, too dark, etc.
- Have students complete the composition. Walk among them checking spelling.

C Sharing Our Stories Read a partner's story. Check for a period at the end of each sentence.

English in Action: Understanding Classroom Directions

 **A** **Listen. Write the number of the classroom direction.**
(CD1 • TR26)

• Have students listen to the audio while looking at the pictures.

• Ask them what they remember from the pictures. As they say the words, ask them to imitate the action.

• Students listen to the audio again, pausing to write the number of the action on the appropriate picture.

• Call on students to tell which pictures connect with which numbers.

B **Write each sentence under the correct picture in Exercise A.**

• Read the sentences while the students follow along in their books.

• Call on individual students to read the sentences back to you. Correct pronunciation.

• Have them write the sentences under the appropriate pictures.

C **Working Together Work with a group. Take turns acting out classroom directions. Your classmates will guess the correct action.**

Students can do this in front of the class. At the end, ask: *Who is the best actor/actress?*

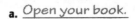 **A** **Listen.** Write the number of the classroom direction.
CD1•TR26

a. *Open your book.*

d. *Put away your cell phone.*

g. *Write on the board.*

b. *Erase your mistake.*

e. *Use the computer.*

h. *1*

c. *Sharpen your pencil.*

f. *Erase the board.*

i. *Close your book.*

B **Write each sentence under the correct picture in Exercise A.**

Erase the board.	Sharpen your pencil.	Close your book.
Use the computer.	Erase your mistake.	Put away your cell phone.
Write on the board.	Open your book.	~~Raise your hand.~~

C **Working Together** **Work with a group.** Take turns acting out classroom directions. Your classmates will guess the correct action.

English in Action

A Listen and repeat.
CD1·TR27

1 one	2 two	3 three	4 four	5 five	6 six	7 seven	8 eight	9 nine	10 ten
11 eleven	12 twelve	13 thirteen	14 fourteen	15 fifteen	16 sixteen	17 seventeen	18 eighteen	19 nineteen	20 twenty
21 twenty-one	22 twenty-two	23 twenty-three	24 twenty-four	25 twenty-five	26 twenty-six	27 twenty-seven	28 twenty-eight	29 twenty-nine	30 thirty

10 ten	20 twenty	30 thirty	40 forty	50 fifty	60 sixty	70 seventy	80 eighty	90 ninety	100 one hundred	1,000 one thousand

B Say the words. Then, write the numbers.

1. twenty-six _26_
2. thirty-three _33_
3. forty-nine _49_
4. one hundred _100_

5. one hundred-ten _110_
6. two hundred-fifty _250_
7. one thousand four hundred _1,400_
8. one thousand ninety _1,090_

C Write.

1. 36 _thirty-six_
2. 51 _fifty-one_
3. 101 _one hundred one_
4. 750 _seven hundred fifty_
5. 300 _three hundred_
6. 1000 _one thousand_

 D Take turns dictating numbers to a partner.

1. Write five large numbers. Read them slowly to your partner.
2. Listen and write the numbers. Then, change roles.

More Action!

Play *Bingo*. Have each student make a bingo card with three rows of three spaces each. Then they can fill in the spaces with any of the numbers from the chart on page 29. Call out numbers of your choice, taking note of the numbers you say. The first student with three numbers in a row from the numbers you've called out says *Bingo* and wins. Play several times so there are other winners.

Teaching Tip

Say pairs of numbers that are either the same or that sound similar. For example: *fourteen/forty, sixteen/sixteen, fifteen/fifty*. Ask students to tell you whether the numbers in each pair they hear are the same or different.

English in Action: Saying Numbers 1–1000

A Listen and repeat.
(CD1 • TR27)

• Have students listen to the audio while following in their books.
• Students listen again and repeat the numbers.
• Students take turns reading the numbers aloud. Correct pronunciation.

B Say the words. Then, write the numbers.

• Call on students to read the words. Make sure they are using correct pronunciation and intonation: *THIR-tee-THREE (33)*.
• Have the students write the numbers while you move among them to correct answers.

C Write.

• Call on students to read the numbers, first correcting pronunciation and intonation.
• Have the students write the numbers while you move among them, checking spelling.

D Take turns dictating numbers to a partner.

• Each student writes five large numbers on a piece of paper. Then he or she reads them to his or her partner. The partner writes them down.
• Partners change roles.

Unit 3

The Family

Dictionary: A Family Tree

 Listen and repeat.
(CD1 • TR28)

• Have students listen to the audio while pointing to the words they hear.
• Ask if there are any words they don't understand. Draw the family tree on the board and explain words such as *nephew, uncle, granddaughter,* etc.
• Students listen to the audio again, this time repeating the words.
• Point out the note box above the Word Partnership box.
Ask: *In your language, what are the words for mother/mom, father/dad.*

 Listen and repeat.
(CD1 • TR29)

• Have students listen to the audio, pointing to each of the three drawings in turn.
• Students listen to the audio again, repeating the words.

3 The Family

Dictionary

  Listen and repeat.
(CD1•TR28)

The Sanchez Family

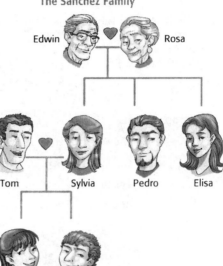

Edwin ♥ Rosa

Tom ♥ Sylvia   Pedro   Elisa

Annie   Eric

The Family

1. husband
2. wife
3. father
4. mother
5. son
6. daughter
7. brother
8. sister
9. grandfather
10. grandmother
11. grandson
12. granddaughter
13. uncle
14. aunt
15. nephew
16. niece

 Listen and repeat.
(CD1•TR29)

1. single   2. married   3. divorced

mother = mom
father = dad
mother + father = parents

WORD PARTNERSHIPS
| an older | brother |
| a younger | sister |

More Action!

Read the words from the list of family terms. If it's a female term, the women students stand up. If it's a male term, the men stand up.

Teaching Tip

Tell students that they will need to bring family photos to class for some of the activities in this unit. If they don't have any photos, they can use pictures from magazines or newspapers to represent members of their families.

Word Builder

A Complete.

Male	Female
son	*daughter*
uncle	*aunt*
grandfather	grandmother
brother	*sister*
husband	wife
grandson	granddaughter
nephew	*niece*
(Answers will vary.)	*(Answers will vary.)*

B Complete.

1. Eric and Annie are *brother and sister*.
2. Edwin and Rosa are *husband and wife*.
3. Rosa and Sylvia are *mother and daughter*.
4. Edwin and Pedro are *father and son*.
5. Pedro and Eric are *uncle and nephew*.
6. Rosa and Annie are *grandmother and granddaughter*.
7. Edwin and Eric are *grandfather and grandson*.
8. Annie and Elisa are *niece and aunt*.

C Listen and (circle) the correct name.

CD1 • TR30

1. (**a.** Tom)	**b.** Pedro	4. **a.** Sylvia	(**b.** Annie)	7. (**a.** Pedro)	**b.** Edwin
2. (**a.** Rosa)	**b.** Sylvia	5. (**a.** Elisa)	**b.** Annie	8. (**a.** Rosa)	**b.** Elisa
3. **a.** Tom	(**b.** Pedro)	6. **a.** Tom	(**b.** Edwin)	9. (**a.** Eric)	**b.** Tom

 Working Together **Draw your family tree.** Tell your partner about your family.

The Family • 31

Word Builder

A Complete.

Do the exercise orally first, saying *son is to daughter as uncle is to aunt*, etc. Then have students fill in the blanks.

B Complete.

Do the exercise orally first. Ask questions: *What are Edwin and Rosa? What are Rosa and Sylvia?* Then have students write the answers.

C Listen and circle the correct name. (CD1 • TR30)

• Have students listen to the audio, pointing to the correct answers in the family tree.
• Students listen again, circling the correct answers.

D Working Together Draw your family tree. Tell your partner about your family.

Have students draw their family trees and share them with their partners, using the tree on page 30 as a model.

More Action!

If students have family photos from home, tell them to place the photos in their family trees. Bring in some of your own family photos and make your own tree on a bulletin board. Ask and answer questions about the trees. *Who's your brother? Who's her niece? Who's my uncle? Who's his son?*

Dictionary: Adjectives

🔊 🅐 **Listen and repeat.**
(CD1 • TR31)

• Have students listen to the audio while pointing to the individual drawings of people described.

• Review the fourteen new vocabulary items on this page. Point to individual drawings and call on students for the new words.

• Students listen to the audio again, this time repeating the sentences.

🔊 🅐 **Listen and repeat.**
CD1 • TR31

1. He's tall. **2.** He's short. **3.** She's heavy. **4.** She's thin.

5. He's young. **6.** He's old.

7. Her hair is long.
She has long hair. **8.** Her hair is short.
She has short hair.

9. Her hair is straight. **10.** Her hair is curly. **11.** Her hair is wavy.

12. He has a beard. **13.** He has a moustache. **14.** He's bald.

More Action!

• Have students bring a variety of magazine and newspaper photos of people to class. There should be a variety of physical types and ages as well as men's and women's hair styles. Display the photos around the room. Call on students to describe them, using the vocabulary on this page. Feel free to include other hair styles. For example: *He has a Mohawk. She has braids.*

• Ask students to make statements about other students in the class and yourself, using some of the new vocabulary.

Teaching Tip

Discourage students from using negative words, such as *fat, bald,* and *old,* when discussing others.

Active Grammar: Adjectives

A **Complete.** (Answers will vary.)

1. I am _____tall_____. (tall / medium height / short)
2. I am _____. (thin / average weight / heavy)
3. I am _____. (young / middle aged / old)
4. My hair is _____. (blond / brown / black / red / gray)
5. I have _____ hair. (short / long / medium-length)
6. My hair is _____. (straight / wavy / curly)

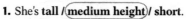

blond

brown

black

red

gray

B **Circle.** (Answers may vary.)

1. She's **tall** / **(medium height)** / **short**.
2. She's **thin** / **(average weight)** / **heavy**.
3. She is **young** / **(middle aged)** / **old**.
4. Her hair is _____black_____. (color)
5. She has **(short)** / **long** hair.
6. Her hair is **straight** / **(wavy)** / **curly**.

C **Circle.** (Answers may vary.)

1. He's **(tall)** / **medium height** / **short**.
2. He's **thin** / **(average weight)** / **heavy**.
3. He is **(young)** / **middle aged** / **old**.
4. His hair is _____black_____. (color)
5. He has **(short)** / **long** hair.
6. His hair is **(straight)** / **wavy** / **curly**.
7. He has a _moustache_.

D **Working Together** **Work with a small group.** Bring in a picture of a famous person from a newspaper or a magazine. Describe the person.

The Family · **33**

Active Grammar: Adjectives

A **Complete.**

Make sure students understand the words for hair color. Go over the vocabulary on page 33 and use some of the photos brought in for the **More Action!** activity from page 32 to illustrate the words for hair color.

B **Circle.**

Review the vocabulary for height and weight and types of hair. Do the exercise orally, calling on individual students. Then, have students circle the correct answers.

C **Circle.**

Do the exercise orally, calling on individual students. Then, have students circle the correct answers.

D **Working Together Work with a small group. Bring in a picture of a famous person from a newspaper or a magazine. Describe the person.**

More Action!

Bring in photographs of world leaders or famous figures. Ask students to describe them. Depending on the interests of the class, consider bringing photos of rock stars, classical performers, sports personalities, or stars of stage and screen.

Active Grammar: Questions with *How old*

Read the sentences in the chart while the students follow along. Then call on individuals to read the sentences. Substitute other pronouns: *I, she, they*.

 Read.

• Ask questions about the photo:
Who is the boy / the girl?
How old is he/she?
• Read the dialogue with a student while the other students follow along.
• Ask students what they remember from the dialogue.
• Assign roles to pairs of students and have them act out the dialogue.
• Point out the **Culture Note**. Ask if this is true in their countries.

 Listen. Number the photographs. Then, listen again and write the relationships and ages. (CD1 • TR32)

• Have students listen to the audio of the first conversation. Pause and ask students what they understood. Do the same with the second and third conversations.
• Students listen again to the three conversations and number the photographs.
• Students listen a third time and fill in the ages and relationships.

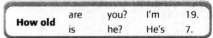
How old	are	you?	I'm	19.
	is	he?	He's	7.

A Read.

Margaret: This is my son, Nico.

Kathy: How old is he?

Margaret: He's 3. And this is my daughter, Alexa.

Kathy: How old is she?

Margaret: She's 7.

Kathy: You have a beautiful family.

> **CULTURE NOTE**
> We ask the ages of children and young people. We do not ask the age of an adult.

B **Listen.** Number the photographs. Then, listen again and write the relationships and ages.
(CD1•TR32)

Relationship	Age
daughter	35
grandson	2

Relationship	Age
daughter	25
son-in-law	28

Relationship	Age
son	3
daughter	6

34 · Unit 3

More Action!

Ask students who have children to bring their photographs to class. Those who don't have children can bring photos of siblings, nieces, nephews, etc. Have student act out the conversations from Exercises A or B using the photographs and inserting their own information. They can refer to the audio script if they need to do so.

Complete.

1. Her first name is ___Emi___ .
2. Her last name is ___Soto___ .
3. Her hair is ___black___ .
4. Her eyes are ___brown___ .
5. Her date of birth is ___7/9/1990___ .
6. She is ___twenty*___ years old.
   * (Answer will vary based on year.)

Complete.

1. His first name is ___Kevin___ .
2. His last name is ___Brooks___ .
3. His hair is ___blond___ .
4. His eyes are ___blue___ .
5. His date of birth is ___5/1/1985___ .
6. He is ___twenty-five*___ years old.
   * (Answer will vary based on year.)

 Ask your partner the questions and complete the student ID card.

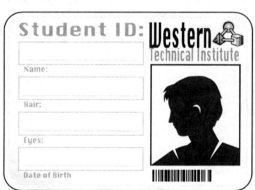

1. What is your first name?
2. What is your last name?
3. What color is your hair?
4. What color are your eyes?
5. What is your date of birth?
   (Answers will vary.)

The Family • 35

ID Cards

Complete.

• Ask students to read the ID card to themselves and then tell you the information they understood.
• Have them work in pairs to fill in the information.

Complete.

• Ask students to read the ID card to themselves and then tell you the information they understood.
• Have them work in pairs to fill in the information.

Ask your partner the questions and complete the student ID card.

• Students work in pairs, interviewing each other and completing the ID card.
• They then switch roles and repeat the procedure.

More Action!

Make a chart about eye color in the class. On the board, write the colors down one side (brown, blue, green, hazel, etc.,) and the first names of the students on the other side. Have each student ask their partner: *What color are your eyes?* They put check marks next to the appropriate colors. Which color is the most common? The least common?

Teaching Tip

Some students may not want to give their real birth dates. They can make up birth dates if they prefer.

Active Grammar:
Yes/No Questions and Answers

Ask pairs of students to study the chart, making questions and answers by substituting other adjectives: *short, thin, young,* etc.

A Write the answer.

• Ask individual students the questions orally.
• Ask students to write the answers about themselves.

◀)) B Listen and write the questions. Ask a partner the questions.
(CD1 • TR33)

• Have students listen first without writing and then listen again and write what they hear.
• Students interview their partners, asking the questions. Then students reverse roles.

Am	I		Yes, you **are**.	No, you **aren't**.
Are	you		Yes, I **am**.	No, I'm **not**.
	he		Yes, he **is**.	No, he **isn't**.
Is	she	tall?	Yes, she **is**.	No, she **isn't**.
	it		Yes, it **is**.	No, it **isn't**.
Are	we		Yes, we **are**.	No, we **aren't**.
	they		Yes, they **are**.	No, they **aren't**.

A Write the answer. (Answers will vary.)

1. Are you tall? _____
2. Are you young? _____
3. Are you from Mexico? _____
4. Is your hair black? _____
5. Is your hair blond? _____
6. Is your teacher from Canada? _____
7. Is he / she short? _____
8. Is he / she married? _____

◀)) B Listen and write the questions. Ask a partner the questions.
CD1 • TR33

1. Are you at school?
2. Are you single?
3. Are you short?
4. Are you from China?
5. Are you young?

More Action!

Using index cards and the questions from Exercise B, write out the questions, one word to a card. Vary the color of markers or pens you use, one color per sentence. Then scramble the word order of each question. Divide the class into two teams. Give one scrambled question to each team. Teams unscramble the questions as quickly as possible. Award points to the fastest group. Then each team scrambles its question and exchanges it with the other group. Continue until all the questions in the exercise have been used.

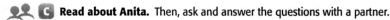

C **Read about Anita.** Then, ask and answer the questions with a partner.

This is my wife, Anita. She is from India. She is 30 years old. She is short and thin. Her hair is black and straight. It's long. I think she is beautiful.

| Is Anita married? | Yes, she is. |

1. Anita / married? Yes, she is.
2. she / from Vietnam?
   No, she isn't.
3. her hair / black?
   Yes, it is.
4. she / tall? No, she isn't.
5. she / 20 years old?
   No, she isn't.
6. she / beautiful?
   Yes, she is.

D **Read about Tony.** Then, ask and answer the questions with a partner.

This is my boyfriend, Tony. Tony is 20 years old. He's from Portugal. He's tall and average weight. He has brown hair. His hair is short and curly. Tony has a moustache. I think Tony is handsome.

| Is Tony old? | No, he isn't. |

1. Tony / old? No, he isn't.
2. he / from Portugal? Yes, he is.
3. Tony / single? No, he isn't.
4. he / short?
   No, he isn't.
5. he / heavy?
   No, he isn't.
6. he / handsome?
   Yes, he is.

E Working Together **Bring in photos of your family.** Talk about your family.

HELPFUL EXPRESSIONS
• That's a nice picture. Is that you?
• Who's that? He's tall.
• Is she your sister?
• Is he married? How old is he?

The Family • 37

C **Read about Anita. Then, ask and answer the questions with a partner.**

• Read the passage to the class while they follow along in their books.
• Ask students what they learned about Anita. Then call on individuals to read the passage aloud.
• Ask students to make questions using the cue words.

D **Read about Tony. Then, ask and answer the questions with a partner.**

• Read the passage to the class while they follow along in their books.
• Ask students what they learned about Tony. Then call on individuals to read the passage aloud.
• Ask students to make questions using the cue words.

E **Working Together Bring in photos of your family. Talk about your family.**

Students can re-use photos they brought for family trees or they can bring new photos. Students should use the sentences and questions in their books as models.

More Action!

Ask students to come to the front of the class and talk about their favorite relative. First, they should tell who he or she is and then describe the relative. Why do they like him or her? Is he or she funny, interesting, wise, talented?

Teaching Tip

Some students may not feel comfortable talking about family members in front of the class. Do this on a voluntary basis.

The Big Picture: A Family Photo

 Work with a partner. Write two adjectives for each person in the picture.

- Describe the picture. Ask students to talk about each person.
- Have students write two adjectives for each picture.

 Listen. Write the names on the picture. (CD1 • TR34)

- Students listen to the audio while looking at the picture.
- Ask students what information they remember.
- Students listen again, writing the missing names on the picture. Move among them, checking that they've named the people correctly.

 Listen again. Write the ages on the picture. (CD1 • TR34)

- Students listen to the audio one more time.
- Ask them what ages they heard on the audio.
- Students listen again, writing the ages on the picture. Move among them, checking answers.

 Work with a partner. Write two adjectives for each person in the picture.

Bob: (Answers may vary.)   tall, bald

Sarah: _____ heavy, old _____

Linda: _____ thin, short _____

Steve: _____ young, heavy _____

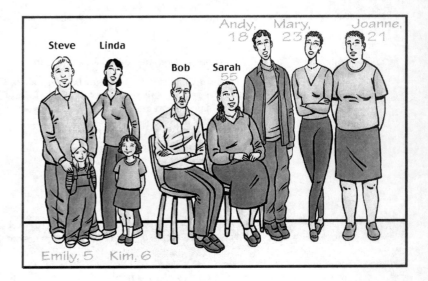

 Listen. Write the names on the picture.
CD1 • TR34

Emily   Kim   Joanne   Mary   Andy

Listen again. Write the ages on the picture.
CD1 • TR34

More Action!

Play a memory game. Line students up in front of the classroom. The first student says his or her name and a sentence to describe himself or herself. For example: *My name is Rita and I have short hair.* The second student repeats the description: *Her name is Rita and she has short hair.* Then the student adds a new line: *My name is José and I'm tall.* Each student must remember all that has been said by others before him or her.

Complete.

1. _____Mary_____ is tall and thin. She has short, curly hair.
2. _____Bob_____ has a moustache, and he's bald.
3. _____Emily_____ is 5 years old. She has long hair.
4. _____Steve_____ is short and heavy. He has blond hair.
5. _____Linda_____ is thin. She has straight, black hair.
6. _____Andy_____ is tall and thin. He has curly hair.
7. _____Joanne_____ is tall and heavy. She has short, curly hair.

Answer the questions. Then, ask and answer questions about the other people in this family.

Andy

1. How old is Andy? 18
2. Is he short? No, he isn't.
3. Is he heavy? No, he isn't.
4. What color is his hair? Black
5. Is it curly? Yes, it is.

Mary

1. How old is Mary? 23
2. Is she single? Yes, she is.
3. Is she tall? Yes, she is.
4. What color is her hair? Black
5. Is it long? No, it isn't.

Pronunciation: Statements and Questions Listen and repeat.
CD1·TR35

Statements

1. He is tall.
2. She is short.
3. It is curly.

Questions

Is he tall?
Is she short?
Is it curly?

Listen and complete. Then, put a period (.) or a question mark (?) at the end of each sentence.
CD1·TR36

1. _____She is_____ old.
2. _____is he_____ young?
3. _____Is it_____ heavy?
4. _____It is_____ tall.
5. _____She is_____ thin.
6. _____Is he_____ tall?
7. _____Is she_____ short?
8. _____He is_____ heavy.

Practice the sentences with a partner.

Complete.

• Look at the picture again and ask students questions about each of the people. For example: *Is Steve tall and thin? Does Bob have curly hair?*
• Ask students to write in the correct names for the descriptions.

Answer the questions. Then, ask and answer questions about the other people in this family.

Call on individual students to answer the questions. Ask students to write the answers.

Pronunciation: Statements and Questions Listen and repeat.
(CD1 • TR35)

• Have students listen to the audio. Point out falling and rising intonation:
He is tall. (falling)
Is he tall? (rising)
• Students listen again and repeat, imitating the falling and rising intonation.

Listen and complete. Then, put a period or a question mark at the end of each sentence.
(CD1 • TR36)

• Point out that falling intonation usually means that the sentence ends with a period. Rising intonation usually means a question.
• Students listen to the audio, adding the correct punctuation. Call on them for answers.

Practice the sentences with a partner.

Reading: Families

A **Discuss.**

- Use the discussion questions as a pre-reading activity. Get students to talk about their families in detail. *Where do they live? What kind of work do their family members do? What kind of food do they like?*
- Ask students to scan the three readings, looking for details such as number of children, ages, marital status, etc.

B **Read.**

- Read *The Soto Family* aloud while the students follow along in their books. Then ask what they learned about the family.
- Call on individual students to read the passage aloud. Have them work in pairs, asking and answering questions about the family.
- Follow the same procedures for *The Park Family* and *The Taylor Family*.

C **Check the information that is true about each family.**

Do the exercise orally, asking students what information is true about each family. Then have them check the boxes.

D **Circle the picture of the writer in each paragraph.**

A **Discuss.**

1. How many people are in your family? What are their names?

2. Tell about the members of your family. Do they have children? Are they married, single, or divorced?

B **Read.**

Three Families

The Soto Family

This is my family. I live with my husband and our three children. My parents live in the same town. We see them every week. My husband's parents live four hours from here. We visit them on holidays and in the summer.

The Park Family

This is my family. I live with my wife and two children. My son is 10 and my daughter is 15. My parents live with us. They are both 70 years old, and they are retired.

The Taylor Family

This is my family. My husband and I are divorced, so I am a single mother. I have two children, a boy and a girl. They live with me, and they see their father every Saturday.

C **Check (✔) the information that is true about each family.**

	Sotos	Parks	Taylors
1. There are three children in this family.	✔		
2. The children live with their parents and grandparents.		✔	
3. The parents are divorced.			✔
4. The children see their grandparents every week.	✔		
5. The children do not see their father every day.			✔
6. There are six people in this family.		✔	

D **Circle the picture of the writer in each paragraph.** *(See arrows above.)*

A **Read.**

> **My Family**
> My name is Liudmila. This is a
> photograph of my family. I am from Cuba.
> I have long, straight hair. My eyes are
> brown. This is my husband, Carlos. He is
> from Ecuador. Carlos is 30 years old. His
> hair is black. It's short and wavy. He is tall and
> handsome. This is our son. His name is Jake. He
> is very friendly. He has brown hair, and his eyes
> are brown, too. I think he looks like my husband.

B **Write about your family.** Bring in a photo. Who are the people in the photo?
Describe what they look like. (Answers will vary.)

My name is _____. This is a picture of _____

_____

_____

_____

C **Sharing Our Stories** **Read your partner's story.**
Complete.

1. My partner is married / single / divorced.

2. My partner is from _____.

> **WRITING NOTE**
> A name begins with a capital letter.
> **Carlos**
> **Marsha**

Writing Our Stories: My Family

A **Read.**
- Ask students to talk about the photo and make predictions about the content of the reading.
- Ask students to scan the reading, picking out details such as *names, hair color,* etc.
- Students listen while you read the passage to them. Call on individuals to read the passage aloud.

B **Write about your family. Bring in a photo. Who are the people in the photo? Describe what they look like.**

Ask students to write about the people in their photos. They should answer all the questions and tell anything else important about their families.

C **Sharing Our Stories Read your partner's story. Complete.**
- Students should ask each other about their stories, based on the facts in them. Then they should reverse roles.
- Then they should complete the information in their books.

English in Action: Talking about Days and Dates

A Listen and repeat.
(CD1 • TR37)

- Have students listen to the audio while looking at the months and days in the text.
- Students listen a second time, repeating the names.
- Correct any pronunciation problems and call on individuals to read the names.

B Listen and repeat.
(CD1 • TR38)

- Have students listen to the audio as they follow the calendar in their books.
- Students listen again, repeating the numbers. Then call on individuals to read the numbers aloud.

C Listen and write.
(CD1 • TR39)

Students listen to the dates the first time. Then have students listen again and write the dates on the lines.

D Practice saying the dates with a partner.

Students work in pairs, reading alternate dates from the exercise to each other.

English in Action — Talking about Days and Dates

A Listen and repeat. CD1 • TR37

Months: January, February, March,
April, May, June,
July, August, September,
October, November, December

Days: Sunday, Monday, Tuesday,
Wednesday, Thursday, Friday, Saturday

B Listen and repeat. CD1 • TR38

Sunday	Monday	Tuesday	Wednesday	Thursday	Friday	Saturday
		1 first	2 second	3 third	4 fourth	5 fifth
6 sixth	7 seventh	8 eighth	9 ninth	10 tenth	11 eleventh	12 twelfth
13 thirteenth	14 fourteenth	15 fifteenth	16 sixteenth	17 seventeenth	18 eighteenth	19 nineteenth
20 twentieth	21 twenty-first	22 twenty-second	23 twenty-third	24 twenty-fourth	25 twenty-fifth	26 twenty-sixth
27 twenty-seventh	28 twenty-eighth	29 twenty-ninth	30 thirtieth	31 thirty-first		

WRITING NOTE

Months and days of the week begin with a capital letter.
January February
Monday Tuesday

C Listen and write. CD1 • TR39

1. January 4, 2005
2. February 11, 1992
3. April 17, 2010
4. July 25, 1990
5. August 18, 2015
6. September 7, 1964
7. November 30, 1999
8. December 25, 2000

D Practice saying the dates with a partner.

42 • Unit 3

More Action!

Ask a student to come to the board and write a date in both numerals and words that is important to him or her. Other students must guess why it's important. *Is it a birthday/holiday? Is it your anniversary?* If they can't guess, the student must tell. Then have another student do the same.

Read and complete.

Date of birth: _9_ / _14_ / _75_
        Month Day Year

Birth date: | 0 | 3 | 0 | 3 | 9 | 4 |
      Month   Day   Year

1. **A:** What's your date of birth?
   B: September 14, 1975.

2. **A:** What's your date of birth?
   B: March 3, 1994.

Complete. (Answers will vary.)

Name: _____ _____ _____
            first   last   middle initial

Status: single married divorced   **Sex:** male female

Telephone: ( )_____

Date of Birth: _____ _____ _____
              month   day   year

NAME (Last, First, Middle)

MARITAL STATUS	SEX	
Single Married Divorced	☐ Male	☐ Female
TELEPHONE NUMBER (include Area Code) ( )	BIRTH DATE Month / Day / Year _____/_____/_____	

Answer the questions with a partner.

1. Your aunt was born in 1980. How old is she? ___She is 30.___

2. Your mother was born in 1962. How old is she? ___She is 48.___

3. How old is your grandfather? He was born in 1940. ___He is 70.___

4. Your father is 40 years old. What year was he born? ___1970___

5. Your brother is 18. What year was he born? ___1992___

(All answers above will vary based on the current year.)

The Family • **43**

Read and complete.

Students work in pairs, asking and telling their dates of birth. Move among them, correcting pronunciation and intonation.

Complete.

Ask students to fill in the two forms, using their own personal information. Then they can exchange the forms with a partner and ask and answer questions about the information.

Answer the questions with a partner.

Figuring out these items requires simple arithmetic and should give the students no problems. Students may want to know some of the terms in English, such as *subtract*, *add*, and *multiply*.

More Action!

Internet Option: Have students search for birthdays of famous people living today. They write the person's birthday on the board and ask other members of the class to tell how old they are as of this year. For example:
S1: *Madonna's birthday is August 16, 1958. How old is she?*
S2: *She's __ years old this year.*

Teaching Tip

Before doing Exercise F, review the words *married*, *single*, and *divorced* and explain what each one means. Discuss any other items in the forms that students may not understand.

At Home

Dictionary: Rooms, Furniture, and Appliances

🔊 **A** **Listen and repeat.**
(CD1 • TR40)

Rooms

- Ask students to listen to the audio while they look at the pictures of rooms.
- Ask students to listen again and repeat the words after the audio.
- Call on individuals to read the words below the pictures.

Furniture and Appliances

- Ask students to listen to the audio while they look at the pictures of furniture and appliances.
- Ask students to listen again and repeat the words after the audio. Correct pronunciation and intonation.
- Call on individuals to read the words below the pictures or have students cover the words and try to identify each picture.

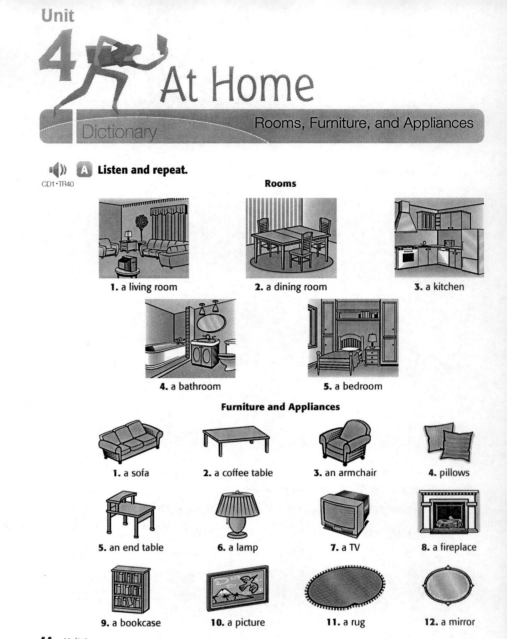

🔊 **A** **Listen and repeat.**
CD1 • TR40

Rooms

1. a living room **2.** a dining room **3.** a kitchen

4. a bathroom **5.** a bedroom

Furniture and Appliances

1. a sofa **2.** a coffee table **3.** an armchair **4.** pillows

5. an end table **6.** a lamp **7.** a TV **8.** a fireplace

9. a bookcase **10.** a picture **11.** a rug **12.** a mirror

44 • Unit 4

More Action!

Make a copy of the two pages of pictures. Then cut out individual drawings and tape them on flashcards. Use these for warm up and review throughout this unit.

13. a bed

 14. a dresser

 15. a night table

16. a desk

 17. a window

 18. a dining table

 19. a chair

20. a cabinet

 21. a stove

 22. a sink

 23. a microwave

24. a refrigerator

 25. a closet

 26. a toilet

 27. a bathtub

 28. a shower

WORD PARTNERSHIPS	
make	the bed
take	a bath a shower
turn on turn off	the TV the lamp the microwave the washer

• Continue the process described on page 44 for all of the vocabulary items on this page.

Word Partnerships

• Ask students to look at the word partnership box. Explain that we use certain words with some of the items.

• Ask them to repeat the word partnerships after you. Then call on individuals to read them.

• Ask students to write other common word partnerships with other pictures. For example: *flush the toilet, turn on the water, go to bed.*

• Point to pictures on pages 44 and 45 that have partnerships and ask the students to say the correct phrases.

More Action!

Ask student volunteers to act out the word partnerships in front of the class, such as *make the bed, set the table*, etc. Ask others to guess the action that is being performed.

Word Builder

Word Builder

A **Look at the floor plan. Complete the sentences.**

- Ask students to work in pairs as they look at the floor plan. One student chooses a room, points to a piece of furniture or appliance, and the other student names the item. If the item is part of a word partnership, the student should say the word partnership. Then the students exchange roles.
- Ask students to complete the exercise and then call on individuals for the correct answers.

B **Write four more sentences about the floor plan.**

- First, have students make sentences about the floor plan orally. Call out the name of one of the rooms, such as *kitchen*. Students should answer: *There is a stove in the kitchen.* Continue through all the rooms in the floor plan.
- Have students write four sentences of their choice about the items in the floor plan, beginning with *there is* or *there are.*

Working Together Draw a floor plan of your home. Talk about your home.

A **Look at the floor plan.** Complete the sentences.

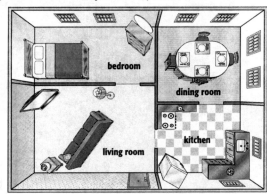

bedroom
dining room
living room
kitchen

1. There is a sofa in the ___living room___.
2. There is a bed in the ___bedroom___.
3. There are four chairs in the ___dining room___
4. There is a TV in the ___living room___.
5. There is a refrigerator in the ___kitchen___.

B **Write four more sentences about the floor plan.** (Answers will vary.)
1. There is an end table in the living room.
2. There is a table in the dining room.
3. There is a sink in the kitchen.
4. There is a dresser in the bedroom.
5. There is a stove in the kitchen.

 **Working Together Draw a floor plan of your home.** Talk about your home.

| I have a TV in my bedroom. | There is a TV in my bedroom, too. |

More Action!

Ask students to draw floor plans of their ideal homes. Introduce terms such as *swimming pool, media room, family room, gym, tennis court,* etc. Display the pictures around the room and have students describe their homes.

Teaching Tip

Floor plans of houses or apartments in students' native countries may differ from floor plans in the U.S. Ask students to compare and contrast floor plans of houses or apartments in different countries.

A Listen and repeat.

The book is **on** the chair.
The lamp is **next to** the chair.

The book is **under** the chair.

The window is **in back of** the chair.
The chair is **in front of** the window.

The book is **between** the chair and the desk.

The book is **in** the desk.

The picture is **above** the chair.
The picture is **over** the chair.

B Complete.

1. book

2. mirror

3. picture

4. lamp

5. night table

6. picture

1. The book is ___under___ the coffee table.
2. The mirror is ___over / above___ the dresser.
3. The picture is ___on___ the desk.
4. The lamp is ___between___ the armchair and the sofa.
5. The night table is ___next to___ the bed.
6. The picture is ___in___ the closet.

At Home • **47**

Active Grammar: Prepositions of Location

A Listen and repeat.

(CD1 • TR41)

• Have students listen to the audio while looking at the pictures.
• Ask them to listen again, repeating the sentences.
• Ask them to read the sentences under the pictures.
• Ask questions about the pictures and have the students answer. For example: *Where is the lamp? Where is the window?*

B Complete.

Have students ask and answer the questions orally before they fill in the blanks.

More Action!

Ask students to use prepositions of location to describe the contents of their backpacks, briefcases, or purses. They can use sentences such as the following:
The keys are on the key ring.
The money is in the wallet.
The paperclip is on the homework.
The cell phone is in its case.

Active Grammar: *Where* Questions

- Point out the contracted forms *it's* and *they're*. Ask students to repeat them.
- Tell students to look at the drawing of the living room and to ask and answer questions using the contracted forms.

🔊 **A Listen and write each question. Then, look at the picture and write the answer.**
(CD1 • TR42)

- Have students listen to the questions while looking at the picture of the living room.
- They listen again, pausing to write the questions.
- Have students look at the picture and answer the questions.

👥 **B Working Together Work in a group. Put objects on a desk. Talk about their location. Then, move the objects around. Talk about their new location.**

If possible, set up a table or desk in front of the classroom. Have the first group come to the front. One student takes an object, such as a cell phone, and moves it on, under, over, behind, or in front of the table, while the other students make sentences to describe the locations. Then, do the same with the next group until all the groups have had a chance to practice.

Where	is	the book?		It	is	on the desk.
	are	the books?		They	are	

| It is = It's |
| They are = They're |

🔊 **A Listen and write each question.** Then, look at the picture and write the answer.
CD1·TR42

1. Q: _Where is the end table?_
   A: _It's next to the armchair._

2. Q: _Where are the books?_
   A: _They're on the bookcase._

3. Q: _Where is the lamp?_
   A: _It's between the sofa and the armchair._

4. Q: _Where is the rug?_
   A: _It's under the coffee table._

5. Q: _Where are the pillows?_
   A: _They're on the sofa._

6. Q: _Where is the mirror?_
   A: _It's over the armchair. / It's above the armchair._

👥 **B Working Together Work in a group.** Put objects on a desk. Talk about their location. Then, move the objects around. Talk about their new location.

> The cell phone is on the table.

> Now the cell phone is under the table.

More Action!

Make a pie chart. Ask one student to draw a large circle on the board and then ask students to hold up their hands if their homes have one, two, three, or more rooms. Have the student divide the pie chart accordingly.

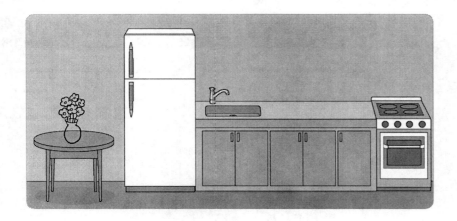

Working Together **Draw the following objects in your kitchen.** Write eight questions. Ask your partner each question. *(Answers will vary.)*

window   clock   cabinets   flowers

cups   pot   glasses   toaster

1. *Where is the window?*
2. _____
3. _____
4. _____
5. _____
6. _____
7. _____
8. _____

Working Together Draw the following objects in your kitchen. Write eight questions. Ask your partner each question.

• Tell students that today they are going to be artists. Point out the drawing of the kitchen and explain that they're going to draw objects in that kitchen.

• Pair off students. Both students should draw the items listed in the text.

• Student A asks Student B about the objects in his or her kitchen, using questions such as the following:
Is there a toaster in your kitchen? Where is it?
When Student B answers, Student A should find the location of the item in the kitchen. Continue until Student A has found all of Student B's items in the kitchen.

• Reverse roles, using the same question forms until Student B has located all of Student A's objects in his or her kitchen.

More Action!

Design the perfect kitchen. Ask students to bring to class pictures of kitchen appliances and décor from magazines or newspapers. Teach words for other common kitchen items, such as *plates, blender, dishwasher,* etc. Have students draw plans for the kitchen and place the pictures of objects where they'd like them. Each student can tell the class about his or her plan.

Active Grammar: *Yes/No* Questions and Answers

- Read the questions and answers in the charts to students.
- Have students ask each other questions and give short answers. For example: *Is the lamp next to the computer?* Students should give short answers like those in the chart.

Look at the picture. Answer.

Have students fill in the correct answers to the questions. Move among them and check their answers.

| Is | the pillow | on the sofa? | Yes, it is. | No, it isn't. |
| Are | the pillows | | Yes, they are. | No, they aren't. |

A **Look at the picture.** Answer.

1. **A:** Is the computer on the desk? **B:** _Yes, it is._

2. **A:** Is the lamp next to the armchair? **B:** _No, it isn't._

3. **A:** Are the books on the coffee table? **B:** _Yes, they are._

4. **A:** Is the end table between the sofa and the armchair? **B:** _Yes, it is._

5. **A:** Is the desk under the window? **B:** _No, it isn't._

6. **A:** Is the armchair next to the end table? **B:** _Yes, it is._

7. **A:** Are the pillows on the armchair? **B:** _No, they aren't._

8. **A:** Is the coffee table in front of the sofa? **B:** _Yes, it is._

50 · Unit 4

More Action!

Using the plans students made for their ideal kitchens, have each student present his or her plan to the class. The class can ask questions about the plans and the student must reply with a short answer.

Teaching Tip

If students are shy about talking in front of the class, pair them off so that more confident students can help the less confident.

B **Work with a partner.** Ask and answer questions about the people and things in the picture.

1. the flowers   3. the window   5. the woman

2. the cat   4. the man   6. the sofa

 C **Look at the picture on page 50 and listen to the conversation.** Write the missing questions.

CD1·TR43

Tom: Where is my cell phone?

Sara: *Is it on the coffee table?*

Tom: No, it isn't.

Sara: *Is it on the desk?*

Tom: No, it isn't.

Sara: *Is it on the floor?*

Tom: Yes, here it is!

 D **Listen.** Write the missing questions.

CD1·TR44

Tom: Where are my keys?

Sara: *Are they under the coffee table?*

Tom: No, they aren't.

Sara: *Are they on the sofa?*

Tom: No, they aren't.

Tom: Are they on the desk?

Sara: Yes, here they are!

 E Working Together **Work with a partner.** Look at page 50. Act out a conversation with these items: glasses, camera, and cat.

At Home · **51**

More Action!

Tell students to role-play a phone conversation. They've left something in a friend's house. They must call and ask about the item and ask a *yes/no* question. They can begin like this:

Caller: *Hello, Juan? This is Giorgos.*

Friend: *Hello Giorgos.*

Caller: *Is my notebook on your table?*

 Work with a partner. Ask and answer questions about the people and things in the picture.

 Look at the picture on page 50 and listen to the conversation. Write the missing questions. (CD1 • TR43)

• Have students listen to the audio and follow the conversation in their books.

• Ask them what they remember from the conversation.

• Ask them to listen again, this time filling in the missing questions in the exercise.

 Listen. Write the missing questions. (CD1 • TR44)

• Have students listen to the audio and follow the conversation in their books.

• Ask them what they remember from the conversation.

• Ask them to listen again, this time filling in the missing questions in the exercise.

Working Together Work with a partner. Look at page 50. Act out a conversation with these items: glasses, camera, and cat.

The Big Picture: A Messy Bedroom

A Write the name of each object.

• Ask students to study the detailed picture. Make sure they understand all of the vocabulary. Point to objects in the room and ask: *What's this?*

• Tell them to look at the numbers in the picture. Then in the exercise, have them write the correct word next to the corresponding number. Ask individuals to read out their answers.

B Listen. (CD1 • TR45)

• Ask students to listen to the audio while looking at the picture.

• Ask them to listen again, pointing to the objects as they are mentioned. Ask: *Is Kathy telling the truth?*

A Write the name of each object.

bed	CDs	dresser	computer	night table	printer
TV	clothes	bookcase	remote	stereo	telephone

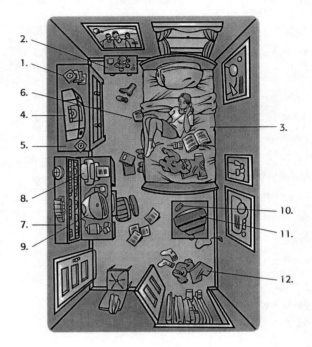

1. ___CDs___
2. ___night table___
3. ___bed___
4. ___stereo___

5. ___dresser___
6. ___telephone___
7. ___bookcase___
8. ___printer___

9. ___computer___
10. ___remote___
11. ___TV___
12. ___clothes___

B Listen.
CD1 • TR45

More Action!

Ask students to describe their bedrooms. Are they messy or neat? They can tell what objects are in their bedrooms. The class can ask questions about location of objects and students can answer using the correct prepositions.

Teaching Tip

Continue the discussion by asking students to talk about other rooms in their homes.

C **Listen to the questions.** Write the number of the question next to Kathy's answer.

CD1 • TR46

3 **a.** "Mom, my clothes are in the closet."

5 **b.** "Mom, my books and papers are on the desk."

2 **c.** "Yes, Mom. My room is perfect."

1 **d.** "Yes, I have a lot of homework."

4 **e.** "They're in the closet."

D **Complete each sentence with the correct preposition.**

1. The pillows are ___on___ the bed.
2. The stereo is ___on___ the dresser.
3. The CDs are ___next to___ the stereo.
4. The computer is ___on___ the desk.
5. The printer is ___next to___ the computer.
6. Some clothes are ___in___ the closet.
7. The telephone is ___under___ the bed.

E **Ask and answer the questions.**

1. Is the desk next to the bed? No, it isn't.
2. Is the window over the bed? Yes, it is.
3. Are the pillows on the floor? No, they aren't.
4. Is the TV on the dresser? No, it isn't.
5. Are the shoes under the bed? Yes, they are.
6. Are the clothes on the bed? Yes, they are.
7. Is the remote under the chair? No, it isn't.
8. Is Kathy on her bed? Yes, she is.

Yes, it is.
No, it isn't.
Yes, they are.
No, they aren't.
Yes, she is.
No, she isn't.

F **Ask and answer questions about things in Kathy's room.**

Where are her shoes?

They're under the bed.

More Action!

Describe another room in your home (not the bedroom or kitchen). Each student describes it to the class, telling where everything is. For example: *The television is on the end table.* Others can ask questions. *Are there pictures on the wall?*

C Listen to the questions. Write the number of the question next to Kathy's answer.

(CD1 • TR46)

• Ask students to listen to the questions while looking at the answers.
• Ask them to listen again, this time writing the correct question numbers. Call on individuals for their answers.

D Complete each sentence with the correct preposition.

• Review prepositions by having students ask and answer questions about the picture. For example:

S1: *Are the clothes in the closet?*

S2: *No, they aren't. They're on the floor.*

• Have students write the correct prepositions in the exercise. Call on individuals for the correct answer.

E Ask and answer the questions.

Tell the students to ask questions about the picture on page 52 and choose the appropriate short answers from the box.

F Ask and answer questions about things in Kathy's room.

At Home • 53

Reading: Classified Ads

A Discuss.

Ask students to bring copies of their local newspapers to class. Show them how to find the classified ad section of each one. Help them locate ads for garage and yard sales. Ask if they've ever gone to a garage sale. *What did you buy there? Do you like garage sales? Have you ever had a garage sale of your own?*

B Read.

• Look at the ads on this page. Encourage students to scan for details. Assign each student an item and ask them to find the item without reading all of the ads thoroughly.
• Make sure all new vocabulary in the ads is understood. Introduce any other new terms such as *rain or shine*.

C Circle these items in the ads.

After students have done the exercise, have them look for additional items from the ads such as *twin bed, dryer, bookcase*, etc.

D Working Together
Go online and look at a website with classified ads. Or, bring in the classified section of your local newspaper. Circle the garage sales that you want to visit.

A Discuss.

1. What is the name of your local newspaper?
2. Where is the classified ad section?

B Read.

Garage Sales

In your local newspaper, you can find ads for garage sales, yard sales, or tag sales in your area. At these sales, you can buy furniture, electronic equipment, children's items, clothing, and kitchen items at very good prices.

C Circle these items in the ads. *(See circled answers above.)*

1. a refrigerator	**3.** a TV	**5.** kitchen items	**7.** bedroom furniture
2. baby items	**4.** a sofa	**6.** a printer	**8.** a microwave

D Working Together **Go online and look at a website with classified ads.** Or, bring in the classified section of your local newspaper. Circle the garage sales that you want to visit.

More Action!

Write classified ads for garage sales. Tell students to pretend they are moving to another city and have many objects they want to sell. Using the ads on this page as a model, they should write ads of their own. Put some of them on the board.

Teaching Tip

Students may be reluctant to try scanning readings because they may think they will miss something important if they don't read every word. Point out that we use scanning only when we are looking for key pieces of information. Explain that because this skill helps them pick out the information they need and skip over the information they don't need, scanning can save them time.

A   Read.

I live in an apartment in San Diego. My wife and children are in Poland, so I live alone. My apartment has a bedroom and a small kitchen. There is a refrigerator, a microwave, and a table in the kitchen. I have an armchair and a TV! I have a bed and a dresser. My apartment is small but it's the right size for me.

I live in a house in Chicago. It has six rooms. There are three bedrooms and two bathrooms. The living room is on the first floor. There is a TV and a computer in the living room. My house is very big and it has a backyard. I need a big house because I have three children.

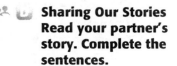
WRITING NOTE
The names of cities begin with capital letters:
San Francisco

B   Check the information that is true for you.

☐ I live in a house.   ☐ There are _____ rooms.

☐ I live in an apartment.   ☐ I have a small _____.

☐ I live alone.   ☐ I have a large _____.

☐ I live with _____   ☐ There's a TV in my bedroom.

C   Write about your home. (Answers will vary.)

_____

_____

 D   **Sharing Our Stories**   **Read your partner's story.**   Complete the sentences.

My partner lives in _____. It has _____ rooms.

Writing Our Stories: My Home

A   Read.

- Read the first story aloud to the students while they follow in their books.
- Ask students to scan the reading for details such as the number of rooms and the objects in them.
- Call on individuals to read sentences from the story aloud. Correct pronunciation.
- Repeat this process with the second story.

B   Check the information that is true for you.

Discuss the kinds of housing in the area of the school. What are the percentages of houses, apartments, or condominiums?

C   Write about your home.

Students can either write about their homes here or in their own countries. They should describe the area, the type of housing, the number of rooms, and whether they live alone, or with a roommate or family members.

D   Sharing Our Stories Read your partner's story. Complete the sentences.

More Action!

Take a poll. How many students live in apartments? Houses? Mobile homes? Condominiums? Make a bar graph. List the types of housing down one side and put a shaded square next to each type for each student who lives in that housing. In what type do most students live? The least?

English in Action: Understanding Addresses

A Read.

• Read the conversation aloud while students follow in their books.
• Ask students to role-play the conversation. They can substitute their own addresses but only if they're comfortable doing this.

B Listen to each address and repeat. (CD1 • TR47)

• Have students listen to the audio while they look at the pictures of the buildings at those addresses.
• Have them listen again, repeating each address.

C Listen. Complete the addresses. Then, repeat the addresses with a partner. (CD1 • TR48)

Dictate additional addresses and have students write them. Choose addresses from a local phone directory. Check the spelling of place names.

D Working Together Interview three students. Complete the chart.

Students interview other students who are sitting in front of, to the side of, or behind them. They use the questions in the chart. Then they can report to the class.

A Read.

A: What's your address?
B: 419 South Avenue.
A: And the town?
B: Cranford.
A: What's your zip code?
B: 07016.

South Avenue

B Listen to each address and repeat.
CD1 • TR47

a. Main Street   c. Second Street   e. Park Avenue

b. Maple Street   d. Central Avenue   f. North Avenue

C Listen. Complete the addresses. Then, repeat the addresses with a partner.
CD1 • TR48

a. _73_ North Avenue   d. _861_ Park Avenue
b. _66_ Maple Street   e. _9924_ Second Street
c. _143_ Central Avenue   f. _3285_ Main Street

D Working Together Interview three students. Complete the chart.

	What's your name?	What's your address?	What's your zip code?
1.			
2.			
3.			

More Action!

Have students write their own addresses (or ones they make up) on the board. Ask other students to read them to the class.

A **Read.** What information is on each line?

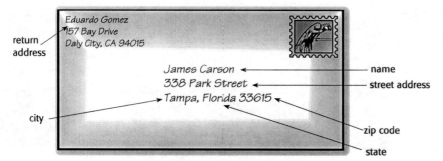

return address

Eduardo Gomez
157 Bay Drive
Daly City, CA 94015

James Carson ← name
338 Park Street ← street address
→ Tampa, Florida 33615 ←

city

zip code

state

B (Circle) the problems.

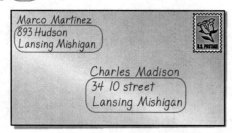

Marco Martinez
893 Hudson
Lansing Mishigan

Charles Madison
34 10 street
Lansing Mishigan

C **Address this envelope to the President of the United States.** The address is 1600 Pennsylvania Avenue NW, Washington, D.C. 20500. Remember to write your return address.

Return address will vary.

President of the United States
1600 Pennsylvania Avenue NW
Washington, D.C. 20500

At Home • 57

English in Action: Addressing an Envelope

A **Read. What information is on each line?**

Ask students to read the address on the envelope. Call on individuals to ask and answer questions about it.

B **Circle the problems.**

Students should identify the following errors with the envelope:

Return Address:
• *Street* should added to address
• Commas are needed between city and state
• *Mishigan* is spelled incorrectly (*Michigan*)
• Zip code is missing

Address:
• Capitalize *street*
• Commas are needed between city and state
• *Mishigan* is spelled incorrectly (*Michigan*)
• Zip code is missing

C **Address this envelope to the President of the United States. The address is 1600 Pennsylvania Avenue NW, Washington, D.C. 20500. Remember to write your return address.**

More Action!

Ask students if they more often write letters or use e-mail. Ask them to find out how much it costs to send a half-ounce letter to another state or country. How long does it take to get there?

Unit 5

I'm Talking on the Phone

Dictionary: Actions

 Listen and repeat.
(CD2 • TR1)

- Have students listen to the audio while looking at the pictures and the captions.
- Students listen again, repeating the sentences.
- Point to individual pictures and ask students to read the corresponding sentence.
- Say the sentences at random and ask students to point to the corresponding picture.

Dictionary

  Listen and repeat.
CD2 • TR1

1. He is eating. **2.** She is washing the car. **3.** She is listening to music. **4.** They are studying.

5. He is cooking. **6.** She is sleeping. **7.** He is reading. **8.** She is drinking.

9. They are talking. **10.** They are watching TV. **11.** He is doing his homework. **12.** She is cleaning the house.

13. She is driving. **14.** They are walking. **15.** She is making lunch. **16.** He is doing the laundry.

58 • Unit 5

More Action!

Ask students to come to the front of the class and mime the actions pictured on this page. The other students will guess the actions.

Teaching Tip

When asking students to do something in front of the class, it's best to ask more outgoing students first. Shyer students may feel encouraged by the examples of others.

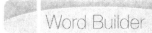

A Complete.

| is reading | is talking | are watching | ~~is cooking~~ | is sleeping |
| are studying | am writing | is drinking | is eating | are listening |

1. She _____ is cooking _____ dinner.

2. She _____ is reading _____ the newspaper.

3. I _____ am writing _____ in my notebook.

4. They _____ are watching _____ a movie.

5. The students _____ are studying _____ English.

6. He's in bed. He _____ is sleeping _____ .

7. She _____ is drinking _____ a cup of coffee.

8. They _____ are listening _____ to the stereo.

9. He _____ is talking _____ on the telephone.

10. He _____ is eating _____ a hamburger.

WORD PARTNERSHIPS	
make	dinner
	the bed
	a phone call
	homework
do	the dishes
	the laundry

B Working Together Act out an activity. The class will guess the action.

| You are eating. | You are dancing. |

C Write six new actions on the lines. (Answers will vary.)

1. _____   3. _____   5. _____

2. _____   4. _____   6. _____

D Write three more sentences about the people in your family. What is each person doing now? Read your sentences to another student.

1. My mother is working. _____

2. (Additional answers will vary.) _____

3. _____

4. _____

I'm Talking on the Phone · **59**

Word Builder

A Complete.

• Go over the exercise orally first. Have students repeat the present continuous actions.

• Ask students to write the correct answers. Then call on individuals to read them aloud.

Word Partnerships

Say the collocations aloud and ask students to repeat after you. Then ask them to make sentences using the collocations and the present continuous tense.

B Working Together Act out an activity. The class will guess the action.

Encourage students to come up with completely new actions (actions that were not used on page 58).

C Write six new actions on the lines.

If students thought up new actions for Exercise B, they can use those actions in this exercise.

D Write three more sentences about the people in your family. What is each person doing now? Read your sentences to another student.

Make some suggestions to get the students started. Write a few cues on the board:

• feeding the baby
• driving to work
• listening to music
• getting dressed

Active Grammar: Present Continuous Statements: Affirmatives

A Complete the sentences.

- Tell students to use the short sentences that come first as clues for completing the longer sentence. Do the exercise orally first, calling on individuals.
- Have students write the answers. Move among them and make corrections.

B Pronunciation: Contractions
Listen and repeat the sentences. (CD2 • TR2)

- Have students listen to the audio while looking at the long forms and contracted forms listed.
- Students listen again, repeating the sentences.
- Provide the long form and have students provide the contracted form.
- Provide the contractions and have students provide the long forms.

C Listen and circle the form you hear. (CD2 • TR3)

- Before asking students to circle their answers, read pairs of similar sentences aloud. Tell students that you will read pairs of similar statements. If they hear identical statements (*He's reading. / He's reading.*) they should call out *Same!* If they hear different sentences (*He is reading. / He's reading.*) they should call out *Different!*
- Have students listen to the audio and circle the forms they hear.

60 • Unit 5

I	am	
He	is	study**ing**.
We	are	

A Complete the sentences.

1. I'm at school. I ___am studying___ English. (study)
2. Maria is at the store. She ___is buying___ a notebook. (buy)
3. The students are at the library. They ___are studying___ for a test. (study)
4. The baby is in his bedroom. He ___is sleeping___. (sleep)
5. You are on the phone. You ___are talking___ to your friend. (talk)
6. Jason is in the kitchen. He ___is making___ dinner. (make)
7. Larry is in his car. He ___is driving___ to work. (drive)
8. We ___are sitting___ in the classroom. (sit)

B Pronunciation: Contractions Listen and repeat the sentences.
CD2 • TR2

Long Forms	Contractions
1. I am studying.	I'm studying.
2. She is reading.	She's reading.
3. He is sleeping.	He's sleeping.
4. We are talking.	We're talking.
5. They are eating.	They're eating.
6. You are cooking.	You're cooking.

C Listen and circle the form you hear.
CD2 • TR3

1. **(a.)** He is walking.
   b. He's walking.
2. a. She is cleaning.
   (b.) She's cleaning.

3. a. I am making lunch.
   (b.) I'm making lunch.
4. a. You are driving.
   (b.) You're driving.

5. **(a.)** They are watching TV.
   b. They're watching TV.
6. **(a.)** We are studying.
   b. We're studying.

60 • Unit 5

D **Read.** Underline the verbs in the present continuous.

It is Saturday morning, and everyone in the Lee family is busy. Jenny is in the bathroom. She's <u>taking</u> a shower. Jenny is <u>getting</u> ready for work. David is in his bedroom. He's <u>sitting</u> at his desk and <u>studying</u> for a test on Monday. Mrs. Lee is in the living room. She's <u>cleaning</u>. Right now, she's <u>vacuuming</u> the rug. Mr. Lee is in the kitchen. He's <u>cooking</u> lunch for the family. Carla is <u>helping</u>. She's <u>washing</u> the dishes. Grandma Lee is in the kitchen, too. She's <u>doing</u> the laundry.

E **Match.**

_d_	**1.** Where is Jenny?	**a.** She's in the living room.
_f_	**2.** What is she doing?	**b.** He's cooking lunch.
_a_	**3.** Where is Mrs. Lee?	**c.** He's studying.
_e_	**4.** What is she doing?	**d.** She's in the bathroom.
_g_	**5.** Where is Mr. Lee?	**e.** She's cleaning.
_b_	**6.** What is he doing?	**f.** She's taking a shower.
_h_	**7.** Where is David?	**g.** He's in the kitchen.
_c_	**8.** What is he doing?	**h.** He's in his bedroom.

I'm Talking on the Phone • **61**

 Read. Underline the verbs in the present continuous.

• Read the passage aloud while the students follow along in their books. Ask comprehension questions about the reading. For example: *What day is it? What is Jenny doing? What is David doing?*
• Read the passage again. When students see a verb in the present continuous tense, have them raise their hands.
• Have students read the passage to themselves and underline the present continuous verbs.

 Match.

• Do the first few items in the exercise orally, calling on students to give the correct answers.
• Ask students to write the correct answers while you move among them, checking their answers.

More Action!

Have a spelling bee using the vocabulary words from this unit. Make a list of new vocabulary from this unit. Ask each student to stand and spell one word (or write the word on the board). If he or she spells correctly, he or she is still in the bee. When a student makes a mistake, he or she must sit down and the word passes to the next student. The students still standing at the end of the bee are the winners.

More Action!

After you finish Exercise E with the class, have pairs of students use the exercise as a model for conversation practice. One person asks questions about the people from the reading and the other answers. Then students change roles.

Active Grammar: Present Continuous Statements: Negatives

Ask students to look at the grammar chart. Point out that these sentences have the same meaning: *He is not studying. = He isn't studying.*

They are not studying. = They aren't studying.

A **Use the words to talk about yourself and your class. Some sentences are affirmative and some sentences are negative.**

• First, ask students to make some true statements about their class and then to make some negative ones.
• Go through the exercise orally, calling on individuals for answers.

B **Complete the sentences. Some sentences are negative and some are affirmative.**

• Ask students to look at the pictures and talk about what the people are doing.
• Then ask them to complete the sentences, deciding which should be negative and which affirmative.

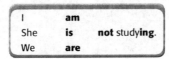
I	am	
She	is	not studying.
We	are	

A **Use the words to talk about yourself and your class.** Some sentences are affirmative and some sentences are negative. *(Answers will vary.)*

1. I / study / French
2. I / talk / on my cell phone   I'm not studying French.
3. We / sit / in class
4. I / look at / page 25
5. We / watch / TV
6. I / wear / a hat
7. The teacher / drink / a cup of coffee
8. The students / sit / at their desks

B **Complete the sentences.** Some sentences are negative and some are affirmative.

1. Mariana _isn't studying_ at home. (study)
2. She _is studying_ in the library. (study)
3. She _isn't drinking_ a cup of coffee. (drink)
4. She _isn't writing_ in her notebook. (write)

5. They _are doing_ the dishes. (do)
6. They _aren't doing_ the laundry. (do)
7. They _aren't watching_ TV. (watch)
8. They _are talking/ aren't talking_ about school. (talk)

62 · Unit 5

More Action!

Play a true or false game. Each student makes up a sentence about what they or another student are doing right now. The sentences should use the present continuous and can be true or false. For example:
I'm doing laundry.
Sally is writing in her notebook.
The other students must say if the sentence is true or false and respond:
It's false. You aren't doing laundry now.
It's true. Sally is writing in her notebook.

Teaching Tip

Give students some additional examples to help them make true and false sentences. For example:
ironing a shirt
going to the movies
drinking a cup of coffee
Discourage students from making up sentences that might embarrass another student.

Questions	Short Answers	
Are you work**ing**?	Yes, I **am**.	No, **I'm not**.
Is she work**ing**?	Yes, she **is**.	No, she **isn't**.
Are they work**ing**?	Yes, they **are**.	No, they **aren't**.

A Answer the questions with a partner.

Yes, she is.

1. Is she cleaning her house?

2. Is she washing her car? No, she isn't.

3. Is she listening to music? Yes, she is.

4. Is she doing the laundry? No, she isn't.

B Answer the questions with a partner.

1. Are they sitting on the sofa? Yes, they are.

2. Are they eating dinner? No, they aren't.

3. Are they watching TV? Yes, they are.

4. Are they talking? Yes, they are.

C Work with a partner. Ask and answer the questions. (Answers will vary.)

1. Are you sitting in class?

2. Are you writing?

3. Are you drinking a soda?

4. Are you talking?

5. Are you listening to music?

6. Are you speaking English?

D Complete with *is* or *are*.

1. ___Is___ the student sleeping?

2. ___Are___ the boys playing soccer?

3. ___Are___ the students walking to school?

4. ___Is___ Michael reading a book?

5. ___Is___ Serena writing a letter?

6. ___Are___ the men working?

7. ___Is___ your sister studying English?

8. ___Are___ you doing your homework?

I'm Talking on the Phone · 63

Active Grammar: Short Questions and Answers

Ask students to look at the note box and recite the short answers, using the correct intonation. For example: *Yes, I AM.* *No, I'm NOT.*

A Answer the questions with a partner.

Ask students to discuss what is happening in the picture. Have students take turns asking and answering the questions.

B Answer the questions with a partner.

Follow the same process as in Exercise A.

C Work with a partner. Ask and answer the questions.

• Discuss all the things you and the students are doing at the moment.
• Students work in pairs to ask and answer the questions. Exchange roles.

D Complete with *is* or *are*.

Point out that it is important to determine whether the subject of each sentence is singular or plural. Ask students to choose correct form of *be*.

I'm on the phone.

I'm on the phone.

A Listen and complete.
(CD2 • TR4)

- Ask students to listen to the audio while looking at the conversation in the book.
- Ask them to listen again and write the missing sentences.

B Listen and complete.
(CD2 • TR5)

Follow the same process as in Exercise A.

C Working Together Choose one of the pictures. Write a conversation with a partner. Act out your conversation for the class.

Pairs of students should come to the front of the class to act out each conversation. They shouldn't tell the class which picture they've chosen. Let the class guess.

A Listen and complete.
CD2•TR4

A: Hello.

B: Hi, Jenny. It's Sarah. Where are you?

A: <u>I'm at home. I'm in the kitchen</u>.

B: What are you doing?

A: <u>I'm cooking dinner</u>.

B: Okay. I'll call you later.

> When making a phone call, say your name.
>
> "Hi. This is Maria."
> "Hi. It's Maria."

B Listen and complete.
CD2•TR5

A: Hello.

B: Hi, Alex. It's Ben. <u>Where are you</u>?

A: I'm at work.

B: <u>Are you busy</u>?

A: Yeah. I'm writing a report.

B: Okay. I'll call you later.

C Working Together **Choose one of the pictures.** Write a conversation with a partner. Act out your conversation for the class. *(Answers will vary.)*

A: Hello. _____ _____

B: Hi, _____. It's _____. Where are you?

A: _____.

B: What are you doing?

A: _____.

B: Okay. I'll call you later.

64 • Unit 5

More Action!

Write on the board good and bad reasons for calling in sick. Discuss the reasons. Then students work in pairs and practice calling in sick.
For example:
S1: *Hello. Millie's Boutique.*
S2: *This is Lisa Gomez. I can't come to work today. I have the flu.*
S1: *Thank you for letting us know, Lisa. Get better soon.*
S2: *Goodbye.*
S1: *Goodbye.*

A Working Together

In a group, look at the picture of this family. Name each person and write about them. Where are they? What are they doing?

B Working Together

Work in a group. Choose two places from the locations below. What are people doing? Write four sentences. Use your imagination.

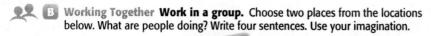

park cafeteria student lounge airplane

computer lab bus office car

Example: car

1. A man is driving.

2. A woman is listening to the radio.

3. A driver is stopping at the red light.

4. A man is talking on his cell phone.

(Answers will vary.)

What are they doing?

A Working Together
In a group, look at the picture of this family. Name each person and write about them. Where are they? What are they doing?

- Divide the class into small groups. Each group will write a story about the picture, frame by frame. One person in each group can be the secretary and write down the story as the group makes it up. Each group should begin by making up names for all the characters.
- Each group should choose one person to read its story to the rest of the class. The class should ask questions about each story, using the present continuous tense.

B Working Together
Work in a group. Choose two places from the locations below. What are people doing? Write four sentences. Use your imagination.

Each group will write a four-sentence story using two of the locations from the list. Each group should have a secretary to write down the story as the group makes it up. Then each group should choose one person to read the story to the class.

The Big Picture: Mom's on the phone!

Listen to the conversation between Tommy and his mother. (CD2 • TR6)

- Before listening to the audio, ask students to talk about the picture. Where is the family? What is each member of the family doing? What time of day is it? Where is the woman on the phone? What do you think she's saying?
- Have students listen to the audio while looking at the picture. Explain any new vocabulary such as *video games*.
- Students listen to the audio again. Ask comprehension questions about the conversation.

Listen again and write the names on the picture. (CD2 • TR6)

While the students are listening and writing, move among them to make sure they are naming the characters correctly.

Complete.

Make sure students remember the names of the rooms in a house. Then ask them to write the correct answers.

**Listen to the conversation between Tommy and his mother.**

Listen again and write the names on the picture.
CD2 • TR6

Mom   Tommy   Brian   Katie   Dad

Complete.

1. Tommy is in the _kitchen_
2. Brian is in the _living room_
3. Katie is in her _bedroom_
4. Dad is in the _living room_
5. Mom is at _work_

More Action!

Divide the class into two teams. Cut two copies of the conversation between Tommy and his mother into strips, one sentence each. Scramble the conversation. Give one set to each team. The team that assembles the conversation correctly and the fastest wins.

Listen and write short answers.

1. No, she isn't.
2. Yes, she is.
3. No, he isn't.
4. No, he isn't.
5. Yes, he is.
6. No, he isn't.
7. No, she isn't.

> Yes, he is.
> No, he isn't.
> Yes, she is.
> No, she isn't.

Match.

_b_ **1.** Where is Tommy?   **a.** No, he isn't.

_d_ **2.** What is he doing?   **b.** He's in the kitchen.

_e_ **3.** Is Tommy playing video games?   **c.** He's playing video games.

_f_ **4.** Is Tommy talking to his mother?   **d.** He's watching TV.

_g_ **5.** Where is Brian?   **e.** No, he isn't.

_c_ **6.** What is he doing?   **f.** Yes, he is.

_a_ **7.** Is Brian sleeping?   **g.** He's in the living room.

Answer.

1. Where is Dad? He's in the living room.
2. Is he cooking dinner? No, he isn't.
3. What's he doing? He's sleeping.
4. Where is Katie? She's in her bedroom.
5. What's she doing? She's talking to her boyfriend.
6. Is she doing her homework? No, she isn't.

Working Together **Work with another student.** Write a conversation between the mother and the father.

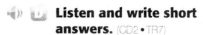

Listen and write short answers. (CD2•TR7)

- Students listen to the audio questions while looking at the picture again.
- Students listen again, pausing to write the short answers to the questions they hear. Call on individuals for the correct answers.

Match.

Tell students to follow the example. Ask individuals to write the correct questions and answers on the board.

Answer.

Ask the questions and call on individuals to answer. Then have students write the answers.

Working Together Work with another student. Write a conversation between the mother and the father.

- Discuss some of the possibilities for the conversation:

Does the mother want the father to cook the dinner?

Does she want him to stop Brian from playing video games?

Should Katie be talking on the phone or doing her homework?

- In pairs, Student A should write the mother's lines and Student B should write the father's lines.
- Ask each pair of students to act out their conversation.

Reading: Cell Phones

A Read.

- Ask students to scan the reading, looking for details such as the first country to have cell phones or the names of countries with more cell phones than people.
- Read the passage to the students while they follow in their books. Pause to explain any unknown vocabulary, such as *company, billion,* etc.
- Ask students comprehension questions about the passage, such as: *What do people use cell phones for other than for talking? Why don't teachers like cell phones?*
- Call on individuals to read parts of the passage aloud. Correct pronunciation.

B Match.

Do the exercise orally first and then ask students to write the answers.

 C Talk about the rules for using cell phones at your school. What is the policy in your school? Can you bring cell phones to your class?

A Read.

Everybody's Talking

On the street, people are walking and talking on their cell phones. In cars, people are driving and talking. In offices, people are working and talking on the phone.

Finland was the first country in the world with cell phones. The largest cell phone company in the world is in Finland. Now, there are more than four billion cell phones in the world. China has more cell phones than any other country. In many countries, there are more cell phones than people. For example, there are more cell phones than people in Hong Kong and Portugal. Many people have two cell phones, one for home and one for work. People use their cell phones for many things. They play games, listen to music, take photographs, and use the Internet. In Japan, people are using cell phones to learn English.

Teachers are not happy about cell phones. When they are teaching, cell phones ring. Sometimes, students text message each other. They text message one another during tests! In many schools, students cannot bring their cell phones to class. In other schools, students must turn off their cell phones before class.

B Match.

_d_	**1.** Finland	**a.**	This country has more cell phones than any other country.
_c_	**2.** Portugal	**b.**	Many people in this country get English lessons on their phones.
_a_	**3.** China	**c.**	This country has more cell phones than people.
_b_	**4.** Japan	**d.**	This country is the home of the largest cell phone company.

 C Talk about the rules for using cell phones at your school. What is the policy in your school? Can you bring cell phones to your class?

68 • Unit 5

More Action!

Have students do an internet search about *cell phone dangers*. Students should collect information on cell phone use by drivers and pedestrians. Have student report back to the class.

Teaching Tip

Do students understand why cell phones can be a problem? Ask them to discuss their ideas and give examples of improper cell phone usage.

A Read.

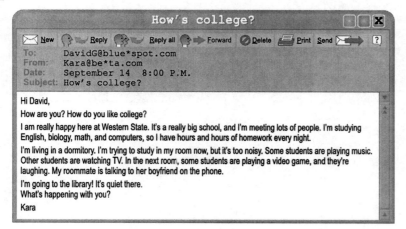

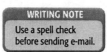

WRITING NOTE
Use a spell check before sending e-mail.

B Write an e-mail to a friend. What are you doing now?

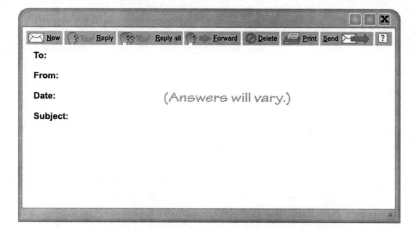

(Answers will vary.)

More Action!

Take a poll. How many e-mails do class members send a day, a week, a month, and a year? Write the names of students in a vertical list on the board with numbers per day, week, month, and year. Who sends the most? The least?

Writing Our Stories: What's Happening?

A Read.

- Ask students to scan the e-mail looking for details, such as what the sender is studying. Why is it noisy?
- Read the e-mail aloud to the students while they follow in their books. Ask comprehension questions, such as: *What is the sender doing now? Where is she going to go?*
- Call on individuals to read parts of the passage aloud.

B Write an e-mail to a friend. What are you doing now?

- Encourage students to brainstorm before writing. Ask: *What kind of information will interest your friend? What are you thinking now? What are you feeling at the moment? What are you looking at now?*
- Ask students to write the messages and then call on individuals to read what they have written to the class.
- Make sure students understand the general e-mail commands: *reply all, forward, delete,* etc.

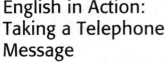

English in Action: Taking a Telephone Message

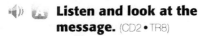

A Listen and look at the message. (CD2 • TR8)

- Have students listen to the audio while looking at the message.
- Students listen again, pausing to repeat key expressions, such as:
  Can I speak with. . .
  Can I take a message?
  Please repeat that.
- Ask students to role-play the conversation.

B Listen to two phone calls. Take the messages. (CD2 • TR9)

- Have students listen to the audio of the first call. Ask what they understood. What was the name of the caller? Of the person called? What was the phone number of the caller?
- Students listen again and then write the message. Ask individuals to write their messages on the board.
- Students listen to the second call and repeat the process above.

C Working Together Work with a partner. Write and practice leaving a message. Act out your conversation for the class.

D Working Together Take your cell phone outside the classroom. Call another student in class and leave a short message.

Tell students to be sure to spell their names, tell what time it is when they're phoning, and leave their phone numbers.

70 · Unit 5

A Listen and look at the message.
CD2·TR8

Call
Steve Carson
555-8341

TELEPHONE EXPRESSIONS
This is _____.
May I speak to _____?
Can I take a message?
Please ask him/her to call me.
Please repeat that.

B Listen to two phone calls. Take the messages.
CD2·TR9

Maya:
Call Mary Lyons
555-6672

Mr. Pano:
Call Adam Madison
555-9143

C Working Together Work with a partner. Write and practice leaving a message. Act out your conversation for the class. (Answers will vary.)

D Working Together Take your cell phone outside the classroom. Call another student in class and leave a short message. (Answers will vary.)

70 · Unit 5

Teaching Tip

When arranging students for pair work, it's often a good idea to pair a more fluent student with a less fluent student. The less fluent student is able to benefit from the guidance they receive, while the more fluent student gets extra practice with spoken and written English.

179   Palmer – Park

A	Palmer David 177 Central Av Cranford..............555-1483	Pannullo T 46 Sussex St Plainfield..............555-4316
B	Palmer Emily 43 Grand St Cranford..............555-1234	Panosh John 336 Forest Ave Westfield..............555-8274
C	Palmer R 34 Broad St Essex..............555-5477	Pantagis Stephen 3 Chester Ave Essex..............555-8682
D	Palmer William 6 Linden L Fanwood..............555-6134	Pantagis Susan 200 Broad St Fanwood..............555-8833
E	Palmieri Ann 45 Grove St Fanwood..............555-5579	Pantano N 59 Maple St Plainfield..............555-7604
F	Palmieri Fred 114 Maple T Essex..............555-9966	Pantoja R 80 Prospect St Essex..............555-9038
G	Palumbo Ed 110 South Ave Warrenville..............555-1024	Paoli P 621 Sunny Drive Plainfield..............555-8652
H	Palumbo George 110 South Av Essex..............555-6403	Paolo Stephen 56 Davis Rd Plainfield..............555-0294
I	Palumbo Henry 184 Second St Essex..............555-4403	Paone Joan 44 Harding St Essex..............555-5657
J	Palumbo L 23 Coles Way Fanwood..............555-7761	Papa's Pizza 77 Main St Plainfield..............555-2534
K	Palumbo P 650 Brant Crt Cranford..............555-7463	Papen Chris 204 Euclid Av Plainfield..............555-8541
L	Palusci Ellen 67 Main St Warrenville..............555-9832	Papen George 399 Glen Road Fanwood..............555-2538
M	Palusci Martin 173 First St Essex..............555-4411	Papen Theresa 75 Glen Road Fanwood..............555-7520
N	Panagos Cleaners 43 South Ave Essex..............555-7764	Papik B 34 Hazel Court Warrenville..............555-6852
O	Panagos H 65 Rahway Rd Fanwood..............555-0102	Pappas John and Marge 12 Lake Ave Essex..............555-6427
P	Panagos Joseph 76 Third Av Fanwood..............555-2310	Pappas S 216 State St Plainfield..............555-0208
Q	Panarese B 876 Park Av Warrenville..............555-8525	Parada Juan 169 Sunset St Plainfield..............555-7314
R	Panarese Brad 9 Willow Ave Cranford..............555-0113	Parada Ricardo 14 Forest Ave Essex..............555-6291
S	Panarese C 453 Rogers Way Essex..............555-7509	Parada Teresa 90 South Av Cranford..............555-7326
T	Panasik Craig 65 Davis Road Fanwood..............555-8029	Paradise Ed 501 Martin St Fanwood..............555-6491
U	Panek Darren 431 Coles Way Essex..............555-7435	Paradise H 36 Grant Av Essex..............555-2509
V	Panek Katherine 107 Charles St Fanwood..............555-1128	Pardo Charles 153 Glen Road Fanwood..............555-8574
W	Panek Bakery 54 Center St Cranford..............555-7039	Pardon R 54 Paulis St Warrenville..............555-2530
X	Panera Richard 87 Route 22 Cranford..............555-2085	Parente A 591 Hort St Warrenville..............555-0203
Y	Pang Hang 43 Grove Av Fanwood..............555-6965	Parente E 88 Broad St Westield..............555-8637
Z	Pang J 44 Thomas St Plainfield..............555-7413	Parisi L 71 Francis Av Plainfield..............555-8630
	Pang Y 87 Woods Way Plainfield..............555-8530	Parisi M 490 Kent Place Plainfield..............555-3250
	Pango L 866 Baker St Plainfield..............555-2527	Park In-Chui 937 North Av Fanwood..............555-7831
	Pannone 60 Davis Rd Fanwood..............555-4682	Park Jeong 503 Lake Av Cranford..............555-1509

A   Write the phone numbers.

Emily Palmer _555-1234_   John and Marge Pappas _555-6427_

Y Pang _555-8530_   Henry Palumbo _555-4403_

Juan Parada _555-7314_   Charles Pardo _555-8574_

B   Write the addresses.

Papa's Pizza _77 Main Street, Plainfield_

Panagos Cleaners _43 South Avenue, Essex_

Jeong Park _503 Lake Avenue, Cranford_

I'm Talking on the Phone • **71**

English in Action: Using the Phone Book

A   Write the phone numbers.

• Before students look up the numbers, have them alphabetize the list of names so they know in what order they'll find the numbers on the page. If they haven't done this before, explain that when the first letters of two names are the same, we have to look at the second letters, and so forth.

• Ask a group of students to come to the front of the class and alphabetize themselves in a row by their last names.

• Point out the use of head words as a guide on the phone book page.

B   Write the addresses.

Explain that in most phone books, businesses, community centers, and local government offices are in a different section (or a different phone book) than private residences.

More Action!

Ask students to bring real phone books to class. They can work in pairs. One student chooses a name or business and asks: *What's the number for George Benson?* The other student looks it up and answers. Then one student simulates phoning the other student and leaves a message. For example:

S1: *Hi. May I speak to Carlos?*

S2: *I'm sorry. He's not here. Can I take a message?*

S1: *This is George Benson. My number is. . .*

Listen and repeat.
(CD2 • TR10)

- Have students listen to the audio of the adjectives while pointing to the corresponding pictures in their books.
- Students listen again, repeating each adjective.
- Say the adjectives at random, asking students to point to the corresponding pictures.
- Ask students to read the adjectives. Correct their pronunciation.
- Ask students to make up sentences for each adjective, based on the corresponding picture. For example: *They're walking on a safe street.* (Picture #9)

Unit

6 My City

Dictionary   Adjectives, Locations, Weather

  Listen and repeat.
CD2•TR10

Adjectives

1. large

2. small

3. quiet

4. noisy

5. busy

6. clean

7. dirty

8. fun

9. safe

10. dangerous

11. beautiful

12. ugly

13. cheap

14. expensive

15. interesting

16. boring

More Action!

Write these headings on the board: *People, Places, Things.* Divide the class into three groups, one for each of the three headings. Each group must look at the adjectives on pages 72 and 73 and decide if they are used to describe a person, place, or thing. One student should come to the board and write the appropriate adjectives under the correct heading. The first group to get them all wins. Note that some adjectives fit more than one heading. For example: *quiet* is for *People* and *Places*.

Teaching Tip

Ask students to make present continuous statements about each picture. What are the people doing in each picture? *She's covering her ears.* (Picture #4: noisy)

17. heavy

18. light

19. friendly

20. unfriendly

🔊 **B Listen and repeat.**
CD2·TR11

Locations

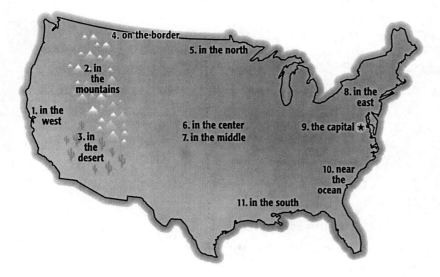

4. on the border
5. in the north
2. in the mountains
1. in the west
8. in the east
3. in the desert
6. in the center
7. in the middle
9. the capital ★
10. near the ocean
11. in the south

🔊 **C Listen and repeat.**
CD2·TR12

Weather

1. wet / rainy **2.** dry **3.** humid **4.** hot **5.** cold / snowy

My City · **73**

🔊 **B Listen and repeat.**
(CD2 • TR11)

• Have students listen to the audio while looking at the map and pointing to the areas described.
• Students listen again, repeating along with the audio.
• Say the locations and ask students to indicate the correct places on the map. If you have a classroom map, point to the areas and ask the students for the correct locations.
• Ask students to make sentences with the locations. For example: *There's snow in the mountains. This city is on the border.*

🔊 **C Listen and repeat.**
(CD2 • TR12)

• Have students listen to the audio while looking at the pictures.
• Students listen again, repeating along with the audio.
• Point to locations on the map, say one of the weather adjectives, and ask a student to make a sentence. Point to the mountains and say: *snowy.* Student should answer: *It's snowy in the mountains.* Point to the south and say: *humid.* Answer: *It's humid in the south.*

More Action!

Ask students to bring to class maps of their native countries, if they have them. Each student can show his or her map to the class and talk about the weather in various locations. For example: *It's dry in the middle of Spain, but humid near the ocean.*

Word Builder

A Match the opposites.

- As a preliminary activity, have students look again at the adjectives on pages 72 and 73. Tell them to find the opposites, such as: *large/small, quiet/noisy, clean/dirty,* etc.
- Have students do the exercise orally in pairs, one reading the listed adjective and the other providing the opposite.
- Have students make the matches. Move among them, checking their answers.

B Circle the adjectives.

- Ask students questions about the neighborhood the school is in, using the adjectives in the exercise.
- Ask students to complete the exercise and call on them for their answers.

Word Builder

A Match the opposites.

h	**1.** busy	**a.** ugly
g	**2.** wet	**b.** expensive
i	**3.** clean	**c.** unfriendly
f	**4.** quiet	**d.** boring
b	**5.** cheap	**e.** light
a	**6.** beautiful	**f.** noisy
d	**7.** interesting	**g.** dry
j	**8.** small	**h.** quiet
c	**9.** friendly	**i.** dirty
e	**10.** heavy	**j.** large

B Circle the adjectives. *(Answers will vary.)*

1. The city where I live is **beautiful / ugly**.
2. It is **interesting / boring**.
3. My building is **small / large**.
4. My neighborhood is **busy / quiet**.
5. The streets are **clean / dirty**.
6. The traffic near my house is **heavy / light**.
7. The people are **friendly / unfriendly** to visitors.
8. Today the weather is **hot / cold / and wet / dry**.

WORD PARTNERSHIPS	
a busy	neighborhood
a convenient	
a friendly	neighbor
a helpful	

More Action!

Ask students to sketch a map of their neighborhoods or a favorite place in their neighborhood and to show the map to the rest of the class. They can describe the streets, the buildings, the parks, the traffic, the shops, the people, the pets, etc. The class should ask questions about the map using the adjectives in this unit.

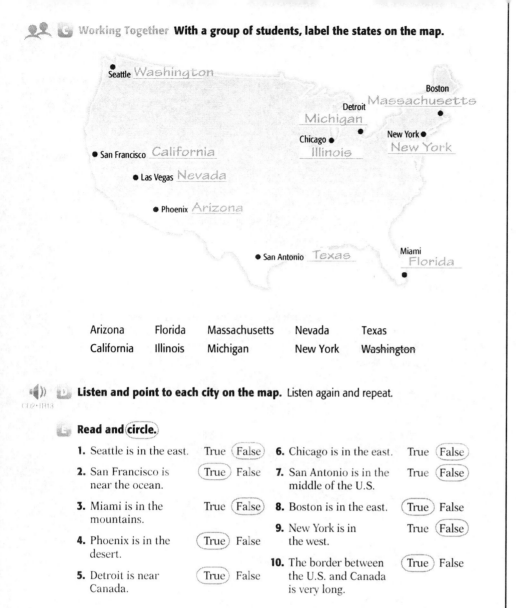

Seattle Washington

Boston

Massachusetts

Detroit

Michigan

Chicago • New York •

Illinois New York

• San Francisco California

• Las Vegas Nevada

• Phoenix Arizona

Miami

• San Antonio Texas Florida

| Arizona | Florida | Massachusetts | Nevada | Texas |
| California | Illinois | Michigan | New York | ~~Washington~~ |

Listen and point to each city on the map. Listen again and repeat.

CD2•TR13

 Read and circle.

1. Seattle is in the east. True (False)
2. San Francisco is near the ocean. (True) False
3. Miami is in the mountains. True (False)
4. Phoenix is in the desert. (True) False
5. Detroit is near Canada. (True) False

6. Chicago is in the east. True (False)
7. San Antonio is in the middle of the U.S. True (False)
8. Boston is in the east. (True) False
9. New York is in the west. True (False)
10. The border between the U.S. and Canada is very long. (True) False

My City • 75

Working Together With a group of students, label the states on the map.

• Before starting the exercise, make sure students can locate where you are on the map. Ask: *What state are we in? Where is it on the map?*
• Ask students to work in groups, writing in the states.
• Ask them to say the names they've written in, correcting pronunciation.

Listen and point to each city on the map. Listen again and repeat. (CD2•TR13)

• Students listen to the audio, looking at the map.
• Students listen a second time, repeating the place names and pointing to the locations.

Read and circle.

• Do the exercise orally first, asking students to look at the map and then calling on individuals for the answers.
• Ask students to circle the correct answers. Move among them and check their answers.

More Action!

Assign a state to each student. Ask the students to do research to find information about the state, such as where it is, what its population is, and what it's famous for. Each student should describe his or her state to the class. Would he or she like to visit his or her assigned state? Why or why not?

Active Grammar:
Or Questions

A Ask and answer questions about the city where you study.

Explain that *or* questions ask us to choose between two things: *hot or cold, clean or dirty*. Ask students to look at the grammar chart. Substitute other cities for New York.

B Working Together Work with a partner. Ask and answer questions about your hometown.

Practice the sample dialogue with a student. Ask pairs of students to practice asking and answering questions about their hometowns using the adjectives in the boxes. Then, ask students to change places with their partners and repeat the dialogues. They can substitute adjectives of their own if they wish.

C Dictation Work with a partner.

Ask Student 1 to dictate to Student 2. Then, have students switch roles.

A Ask and answer questions about the city where you study.
(Answers will vary.)

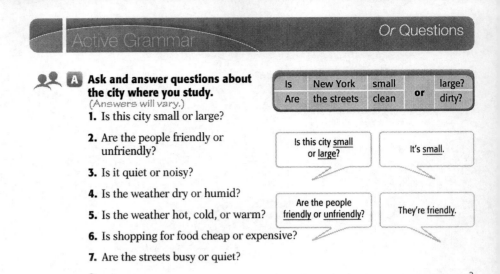

Is	New York	small	or	large?
Are	the streets	clean		dirty?

1. Is this city small or large?
2. Are the people friendly or unfriendly?
3. Is it quiet or noisy?
4. Is the weather dry or humid?
5. Is the weather hot, cold, or warm?
6. Is shopping for food cheap or expensive?
7. Are the streets busy or quiet?
8. _____?

Is this city small or large? · It's small.

Are the people friendly or unfriendly? · They're friendly.

B Working Together **Work with a partner.** Ask and answer questions about your hometown.

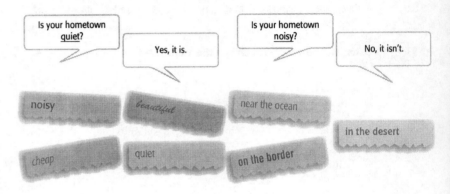

Is your hometown quiet? · Yes, it is.

Is your hometown noisy? · No, it isn't.

noisy   beautiful   near the ocean   in the desert

cheap   quiet   on the border

C Dictation **Work with a partner.**

Student 1: Turn to page 226 and read Questions 1–6 to your partner.

Student 2: Listen and write your answers. Then, turn to page 227 and read Questions 7–12 to your partner.

Active Grammar

A **Listen and complete.**

CD2·TR14

> I want to visit Beijing **because** it's interesting.
> They want to visit Brazil **because** the beaches are beautiful.

A: What city do you want to visit?

B: I want to visit _____ Miami _____.

A: Why do you want to go there?

B: I want to visit Miami because it's ____ sunny and beautiful ____

A: Well, *I* want to visit ____ New York City ____.

B: Why do you want to go there?

A: Because it's _____ exciting _____. There are so many things to do!

B **Working Together** **Talk about a city you want to visit.** Agree on a place to go.

> Where do you want to go?

> I want to visit Paris.

> Really? Why do you want to go there?

> I want to see Paris because it's a beautiful city.

My City · **77**

More Action!

Ask one student to go to the board and make a chart with these categories: *people, places to visit.* Down one side write the names of the students. Ask students to name a place, city, or country that they have always wanted to visit. Are there any students who want to visit the same place?

Teaching Tip

Point out that *because* sentences usually tell the reason for something. Give more examples: *I'm late <u>because</u> I have no watch. She's happy <u>because</u> she's going to Paris.*

Active Grammar: *Because*

A **Listen and complete.**
(CD2 • TR14)

• Have students listen to the dialogue while following in their books.
• Students listen again, pausing to fill in the missing information in the dialogue.

B **Working Together Talk about a city you want to visit. Agree on a place to go.**

• Ask pairs of students to read the dialogue in the speech balloons as a role play. Go around the room until most students can say the dialogue without looking at their books.
• Use the dialogue as a guide and have students repeat the dialogue, this time substituting other cities and reasons.

Active Grammar: Adjectives

Point out the note about word order and the example sentences. Put a number of other adjectives and nouns on the board in no particular order. Mix singular and plural words. Ask students to arrange them in the right order, pointing out the grammar note that we don't make adjectives plural.

Complete the sentences. Use a singular or plural noun.

Call on individuals for the answers to the items.

Working Together With your group, complete the sentences. Use an adjective.

Each group should work independently at first; then, one person from each group should read that group's answers. They will vary from group to group.

Put the adjective before the noun.

This is a **large city**.

New York is a **large city**.

Boston and Chicago are **large cities**.

Tampa is near a **beautiful beach**.

Miami is near **beautiful beaches**.

Do not put an 's' on an adjective.

Miami is near beautifuls beaches.

A Complete the sentences. Use a singular or plural noun. (Answers may vary.)

1. There are friendly _____students_____ at our school.
2. There is an old _____computer_____ in our classroom.
3. There are cheap _____restaurants_____ in this city.
4. There is an interesting _____museum_____ in this city.
5. There is a fun _____playground_____ in this city.
6. There are noisy _____trains_____ in this city.
7. There is an ugly _____building_____ in this city.

B Working Together With your group, complete the sentences. Use an adjective.

1. We are _____ students.
2. We have _____ books.
3. We study in a / an _____ classroom.
4. English is a / an _____ language.
5. We have _____ desks.
6. Our school is in a / an _____ area.
7. We have a / an _____ teacher.
8. We like the _____ weather in our city, but we don't like the _____ weather.

(Answers will vary.)

> We are friendly students.

Write the sentences in the correct order.

1. there / beaches / in this city / beautiful / are
   There are beautiful beaches in this city.

2. fun / is / a / there / park / in my area
   There is a fun park in my area.

3. is / on this street / museum / there / interesting / an
   There is an interesting museum on this street.

4. buildings / there / in New York / are / tall
   There are tall buildings in New York.

5. large / in the east / are / there / businesses
   There are large businesses in the east.

6. weather / in the mountains / there / cold / is / and snowy
   There is cold and snowy weather in the mountains.

 Working Together **Make a short presentation. Stand in front of the class. Talk about your hometown. Give the following information.** *(Answers will vary.)*

1. I am from _____ , _____ .
   city   country
2. My city **is / is not** the capital of the country.
3. _____ is in the _____ of the country.
   city   location
4. The weather is _____ .

My City • 79

More Action!

Have students sit in a circle. Give the students the first line of a story: *There is a large animal outside the window.* The first student in the circle continues the story by adding another sentence that uses an adjective and a noun. Take turns moving around the circle as each student adds a new sentence to the story. Have one student record the story and then read the completed story aloud to the class.

Teaching Tip

Give students guidelines for speaking in front of a group.
• Maintain eye contact with members of the audience.
• Project your voice strongly so it can be heard clearly in the back of the room.
• Make a few notes on index cards about what you want to say. Glance at the cards occasionally while you are speaking but do not read from them.

 Write the sentences in the correct order.

• Give students some guidelines for this kind of activity. Explain what the subject and the main verb are and tell students that they should first look for these in any scrambled sentence. Tell students that each sentence contains *there is* or *there are* and this can help them figure out the main verb.

• Ask individuals to come to the board and unscramble the sentences in writing. Let the rest of the class correct any mistakes.

 Working Together Make a short presentation. Stand in front of the class. Talk about your hometown. Give the following information.

In addition to the four topics mentioned as talking cues, ask students to show the locations of their towns on a map. They might also want to bring photographs, mementos, or other items which are characteristic of the area.

The Big Picture: Chicago, Illinois

A Can you identify these people and places?

• As a pre-reading activity, ask students what they already know about Chicago, if anything. They may associate windy weather, the Chicago Cubs baseball team, or Barack Obama with the city.

• Ask students to look at the photographs and match them with the people and places in the answer box. Call on individuals to point to the pictures and say the names.

B Listen. (CD2•TR15)

• Have students listen to the audio of the first two paragraphs. Ask them what information they understood. Explain new vocabulary, such as *Midwest, downtown, Art Institute, blues musicians,* etc.

• Students listen to the rest of the audio. Again, ask them what they understood and review new vocabulary, such as *professional teams, zoo,* etc.

• Students listen to the whole audio. Then, ask comprehension questions: *Where is Chicago? What are the summers and winters like? What are some interesting places to visit?*

C Match.

Do the exercise as a class activity. Call on individuals for the answers.

A Can you identify these people and places?

The Brookfield Zoo	Barack Obama	a blues club
The Art Institute of Chicago	Oprah Winfrey	Wrigley Field
Lake Michigan		

Oprah Winfrey

Lake Michigan

a blues club

The Art Institute of Chicago

Wrigley Field

Barack Obama

B Listen.
CD2•TR15

C Match.

c	**1.** paintings	**a.**	blues clubs
a	**2.** musicians	**b.**	Wrigley Field
g	**3.** Oprah Winfrey	**c.**	The Art Institute of Chicago
b	**4.** baseball	**d.**	The Brookfield Zoo
d	**5.** animals	**e.**	President of the United States
e	**6.** Barack Obama	**f.**	a large lake in the north
f	**7.** Lake Michigan	**g.**	a TV talk show host

D Listen again and (circle.)

CD2·TR15

1. Chicago is in the south of the United States.　True　(False)
2. Chicago is next to water.　(True)　False
3. Spring is a good time to visit Chicago.　(True)　False
4. Chicago's summers are hot.　(True)　False
5. There are many opportunities to see art and listen to music.　(True)　False
6. Chicago has one professional sports team.　True　(False)
7. Oprah Winfrey is a popular blues musician.　True　(False)
8. Barack Obama is originally from Chicago.　True　(False)

E Work with a partner. Ask and answer the questions.

1. Is Chicago in the midwest or in the south?
   It's in the Midwest.
2. Are the winters in Chicago warm or cold?
   Winters are cold.
3. Is Chicago near a lake or an ocean?
   It's near a lake.
4. Is Chicago famous for rock music or blues music?
   It's famous for blues music.
5. Is Wrigley Field a baseball field or a football field?
   It's a baseball field.
6. Is the Brookfield Zoo interesting or boring for children?
   It's interesting.
7. Is downtown Chicago quiet or busy?
   It's busy.

> Is Chicago a city or a state?

> It's a city.

F Complete with *is, isn't, are,* or *aren't.*

1. It ___is___ fun to see professional sports in Chicago.
2. Lake Michigan ___is___ a large, beautiful lake.
3. Winters in Chicago ___aren't___ hot and humid.
4. Downtown Chicago ___is___ busy.
5. The Art Institute of Chicago ___isn't___ a boring museum.
6. The Brookfield Zoo ___is___ fun for children.
7. Chicago's blues clubs ___are___ exciting and fun.

D Listen again and circle. (CD2 • TR15)

• Students listen to the entire audio again, listening for the sentences that contain the information they need for the exercise.
• Students do the True/False exercise as a group in class. Call on individuals and ask students to correct each other.

E Work with a partner. Ask and answer the questions.

Divide the class into pairs. Student A asks Student B the questions. Then, they reverse roles.

F Complete with *is, isn't, are,* or *aren't.*

Ask students to write in the answers on their own and then check their answers with a partner.

More Action!

Write the first six lines of the Carl Sandburg poem *Chicago* on the board:
> Hog Butcher for the World,
> Tool Maker, Stacker of Wheat,
> Player with Railroads and the
> Nation's Freight Handler;
> Stormy, husky, brawling,
> City of the Big Shoulders...

Explain the vocabulary to students. Then, ask them what kind of feeling they get about Chicago from this poem. Is Chicago presented the same way in the Sandburg poem as it is in the audio (CD2, Track 15)?

Teaching Tip

Tell students that Sandburg published this poem in 1916. Ask them to discuss or research how Chicago has changed since then.

"Chicago" from CHICAGO POEMS by Carl Sanburg, copyright 1916 by Holt, Reinhart and Winston and renewed 1944 by Carl Sanburg, reproduced by permission of Houghton Mifflin Harcourt Publishing Company.

Reading:
Seattle, Washington

A Discuss. Then read.

• Ask students what they know about the state of Washington. Explain the difference between Washington State and Washington, D.C.

• Ask them to find Seattle on the map on page 244. What geographical features can they see? Mountains? Ocean?

• Ask students to scan the reading, looking for facts, such as population, weather conditions, etc.

• Ask students to read the first paragraph to themselves and then talk about unknown vocabulary, such as *seaport, western*, etc. Follow this procedure with the other paragraphs.

B Circle the answer.

Have students answer the questions on their own. Check answers by doing the exercise orally as a group. Then, make up other True/False statements about Seattle, such as: *Seattle is near the Pacific Ocean. Seattle is the capital of the United States.*

C Underline the adjectives in the reading.

A Discuss. Then read.

1. Look at the U.S. map on page 75. Where is Seattle, Washington?

2. Is Seattle near the mountains? Is it near an ocean?

Seattle

Seattle is the largest city in Washington State. The population of Seattle is 594,210. It is in the northwest of the United States. It is in a <u>beautiful</u> location near the Pacific Ocean and Canada. Seattle is a <u>busy</u> seaport. Boats come and go to many other seaports in the world.

Seattle is a <u>beautiful</u> city, but it is a <u>wet</u> city. It gets 36.2 inches (92 cm.) of rain every year. Between October and May, it is <u>cloudy</u> almost every day. When the weather is clear, you can see the <u>famous</u> volcano, Mount Rainier.

Many people know Seattle because of the Space Needle. You can take an elevator to the top and see the whole city. You can see the University of Washington and the seaport.

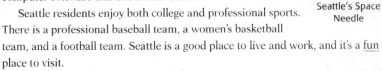

Seattle's Space Needle

There are many <u>large</u> companies in Seattle. One makes computer software and one makes coffee.

Seattle residents enjoy both college and professional sports. There is a professional baseball team, a women's basketball team, and a football team. Seattle is a good place to live and work, and it's a <u>fun</u> place to visit.

B Circle the answer.

1. Seattle is a large city.	(True)	False
2. Seattle is in the southwest of the United States.	True	(False)
3. Seattle has warm, sunny weather all year.	True	(False)
4. Many large companies are in Seattle.	(True)	False
5. Seattle is a good place for a vacation.	(True)	False

C <u>Underline</u> the adjectives in the reading. *(See underlined answers above.)*

82 · Unit 6

More Action!

Internet Option: Assign other U.S. cities to students. Have them find facts about the cities and report back to the class.

Teaching Tip

Make a list on the board of adjectives that describe Seattle. Ask students to point out the sentences that made them choose these adjectives.

Read.

My name is Steven Lee. I am from Taipei, Taiwan. The population of my city is about 7,700,000. It is the capital of my country. Taipei is in the north of the country. There are mountains and rivers in Taiwan. My city is big and interesting. There are many famous places in my city. The National Palace Museum is an art museum. The people in my city are busy and friendly.

> **WRITING NOTE**
> Use a comma between the name of a city and the name of a country.
> Puebla, Mexico

Write about your hometown. *(Answers will vary.)*

My name is _____. I am from

_____, _____. The population of my
      city   country

city is about _____. It **is / is not** the capital city of my

country. _____ is in the _____ of the
          city   location

country. There are _____ in my city. My city is

_____ and _____. There are **many /**
      adjective   adjective

a few famous places in my city. _____

_____

Sharing Our Stories **Share your story with a partner.** Complete. *(Answers will vary.)*

1. My partner is from _____, _____
                              city   country

2. The population of **his / her** city is _____.

3. My partner's city is _____ and _____.
                        adjective   adjective

My City • **83**

Writing Our Stories: My City

Read.

- Preview the reading by asking students what they know about Taiwan. Where is it? Can they find it on a map? Are there any students from Taiwan in the class?
- Ask students to read the passage to themselves, underlining any words they don't know. Explain the words they underlined.
- Ask them what they remember about what they've read. Ask comprehension questions about the reading.

Write about your hometown.

- Ask students to read through the structured composition before they begin writing. Ask what they intend to write in the blanks.
- Have them complete the composition by filling in the blanks.

Sharing Our Stories Share your story with a partner. Complete.

Tell students to trade their compositions with their partners, read them, and then answer the questions. Call on individuals to tell the class what they found out about their partners.

Teaching Tip

Expand on the **Writing Note** by putting a list of cities, states or provinces, and countries from around the world. Ask students to put in the commas.

English in Action: Reading State Maps

A Look at the map and complete the sentences.

• Ask students to look at the cities on the map. Where are they in relation to each other? Elicit sentences, such as: *Los Angeles is south of San Francisco.*

• Ask students to answer the questions about the California cities.

 B Working Together In a group, draw a map of your city and state. Show the capital and three other important cities. Share your map with the class.

Each large group should divide into two teams: one to draw a map of the city, the other of the state. If they live in several different towns or cities, they should work individually on the maps of towns and cities, and work together on the state map.

A Look at the map and complete the sentences.

Sacramento
San Francisco
San José
Los Angeles
San Diego
Nevada
Arizona
Mexico
Oregon
Pacific Ocean

1. The capital of California is ___Sacramento___ .
2. Three other important cities are ___San Francisco___ , ___San Diego___ , and ___Los Angeles (or San José)___
3. The state to the north is ___Oregon___ .
4. The states to the east are ___Nevada___ and ___Arizona___ .
5. The country to the south is ___Mexico___ .
6. The ___Pacific Ocean___ is to the west.

 B **Working Together In a group, draw a map of your city and state.** Show the capital and three other important cities. Share your map with the class.

More Action!

Internet Option: Learn about California. Ask students to enter some of the city names from the map in their search engines and find information about them. Others can find general information about the state, such as area climates, level of income, history of the state, etc. Students should report back to the class.

A Listen and repeat.
CD2•TR16

1. Miami, Florida: 409,719
2. Atlanta, Georgia: 519,145
3. Las Vegas, Nevada: 552,539
4. Washington, D.C.: 588,292
5. Detroit, Michigan: 916,952

6. San Antonio, Texas: 1,328,984
7. Philadelphia, Pennsylvania: 1,449,634
8. Houston, Texas: 2,208,180
9. Oakland, California: 397,067
10. New York, New York: 8,274,527

B Listen and write the population.
CD2•TR17

> 594,210 = five hundred ninety four thousand, two hundred and ten

1. Seattle, Washington __594,210__
2. Phoenix, Arizona __1,552,259__
3. San José, California __939,899__
4. Boston, Massachusetts __590,763__
5. Chicago, Illinois __2,836,658__
6. Honolulu, Hawaii __371,657__
7. Dallas, Texas __1,240,499__
8. Greensboro, North Carolina __258,671__

C Pronunciation: Large Numbers **Work with a partner.** Follow the directions.

Student 1: Read world population numbers 1–4 to Student 2.

Student 2: Cover the page with a piece of paper. Listen to Student 1. Write the numbers. Now, change and read the population numbers 5–8 to Student 1.

Student 1: Cover the page. Listen and write the numbers.

1. Seoul, Korea: 10,421,780
2. Tokyo, Japan: 8,731,000
3. Shanghai, China: 13,481,600
4. Cairo, Egypt: 6,758,581

5. Mexico City, Mexico: 8,836,045
6. Moscow, Russia: 10,452,000
7. Bogotá, Colombia: 7,155,052
8. Mumbai, India: 13,922,000

My City • 85

English in Action: Reading City Populations

A Listen and repeat.
(CD2•TR16)

• Have students listen to the audio, paying attention to the way the numbers are spoken.
• They listen again, this time repeating the numbers they hear.
• Without the audio, they say the numbers, reading them from the page.

B Listen and write the population. (CD2•TR17)

• Students listen to the numbers the first time, repeating them after the audio.
• Students listen again, writing the numbers they hear.

C Pronunciation: Large Numbers **Work with a partner. Follow the directions.**

Divide the class into pairs. One student reads the first half of the list while the other student writes the numbers. Then, they reverse roles and repeat the exercise with the second half of the list. Move among them, checking answers.

Teaching Tip

Before starting the listening exercises, write numbers in the hundreds (such as 375, 291, and 465) on the board. Have students repeat the numbers after you. Build up to numbers in the thousands, such as 2,461. Ask students to write numbers of their own on the board and call on others to read them.

Unit 7

Downtown

Dictionary: Stores and Other Places Downtown

  Listen and repeat.

(CD2 • TR18)

- Have students listen to the words for **Stores** while looking at the corresponding pictures.
- Students listen again, this time repeating the words after the audio.
- Have students close their books while you point to individual pictures and ask students to name them.
- Repeat this same procedure for the vocabulary words in **Places Downtown.**

Unit 7 Downtown

Stores and Other Places Downtown

 Listen and repeat.

CD2 • TR18

Stores

1. a bank   2. a bakery   3. a bookstore   4. a coffee shop

5. a laundromat   6. a shoe store   7. a supermarket   8. a drugstore

Places Downtown

9. City Hall   10. a library   11. a police station   12. a park

13. a post office   14. a hospital   15. a parking lot

More Action!

Ask students to make word associations with each picture. For example: *bread in a bakery.* Ask what else you can buy or find in a bakery and the other locations pictured.

Other possibilities are:
- *books in a bookstore.*
- *shoes and sandals in a shoe store.*
- *coffee and doughnuts in a coffee shop.*
- *groceries in a supermarket.*
- *ATM in a bank.*
- *clean shirts in a laundromat.*

Teaching Tip

Make a copy of the pictures and then cut them out and tape them to index cards to make vocabulary flash cards. Use them for review as you work through the unit.

Complete.

1. I mail letters at the _____ post office _____.
2. I borrow books at the _____ library _____.
3. I buy food at the _____ supermarket _____.
4. I buy books at the _____ bookstore _____.
5. I wash my clothes at the _____ laundromat _____.
6. I deposit money at the _____ bank _____.
7. I fill my prescriptions at the _____ drugstore _____.
8. I walk in the _____ park _____.
9. I buy sneakers at the _____ shoe store _____.

 Working Together Work in a group. Write the name of a store or location in your community. *(Answers will vary.)*

1. park: _____
2. hospital: _____
3. supermarket: _____
4. drugstore: _____
5. bakery: _____
6. coffee shop: _____
7. bank: _____
8. bookstore: _____
9. music store: _____
10. movie theater: _____
11. shoe store: _____

WORD PARTNERSHIPS		
take out		
check out	a book	from the library
	a DVD	
borrow		

Downtown • **87**

More Action!

Using the Word Partnerships box, ask students what else they can do at the public library. Ask students to go to the library and apply for cards (or refer them to the public library card application on page 92).

Teaching Tip

Bring copies of the local phone directory to class for Exercise B in case students aren't familiar with local businesses.

Word Builder

 Complete.

• Review the goods and services that are available at the stores and places downtown.
• Ask students to complete the exercise. They can check their answers with a partner.

Working Together Work in a group. Write the name of a store or location in your community.

• Students should brainstorm these answers. One of them may know the name of a local bank but not a local bakery, etc.
• When groups have completed the exercise, ask one student to represent each group and compare answers with students representing the other groups. All answers are correct as long as they are actual stores or places in the local community.

Word Partnerships

Ask students to make sentences from the partnerships in the box. Ask them to make similar sentences concerning the other stores and places on page 86.

Active Grammar: Prepositions of Location

 A **Listen and repeat.**
(CD2 • TR19)

- Have students listen to the audio while looking at the drawings of locations around the bank.
- Students listen again, repeating after each sentence. Say the prepositional phrases only and have them repeat: *in front of, across from,* etc.
- Say the sentences out of order and ask students to point to the correct pictures.

 B **Listen and complete the map.** (CD2 • TR20)

- Review pronunciation of places in the box. Then, students listen to the audio.
- Students listen to the audio a second time and label the map.
- Students exchange work with a partner and listen to the audio a third time as they check each other's work.

Active Grammar

 A **Listen and repeat.**
CD2•TR19

1. The bank is **on the corner of** First Street and Main Street.

2. Mr. Garcia is **in front of** the bank.

3. Mr. Garcia is **in back of / behind** the bank.

4. Mr. Garcia is **next to** the bank.

5. Mr. Garcia is **across from** the bank.

6. Mr. Garcia is **between** the bank and the coffee shop.

 B **Listen and complete the map.**
CD2•TR20

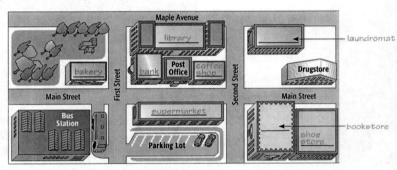

| bakery | shoe store | library | coffee shop |
| supermarket | bookstore | bank | laundromat |

88 • Unit 7

Teaching Tip

Use a chair to demonstrate the prepositional phrases. Stand *behind, next to,* or *in front of* the chair to show the location. Stand between your desk and the chair and say: *I'm standing between the desk and the chair.*

Reading a City Map

 A Working Together **Give the location of the places on the map.**

The bookstore is next to the bakery.

The parking lot is behind the school.

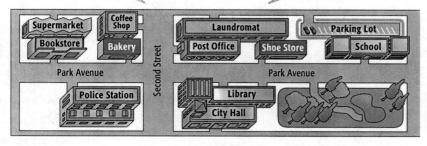

Supermarket
Coffee Shop
Bookstore
Bakery
Park Avenue
Second Street
Laundromat
Post Office
Shoe Store
Parking Lot
School
Park Avenue
Police Station
Library
City Hall

B **Look at the map and write the locations of five buildings.** (Answers will vary.)

1. The supermarket is in back of the bookstore.
2. _____
3. _____
4. _____
5. _____
6. _____

CD2·TR21

 C Pronunciation: Checking Information **Listen and repeat the conversations.**

1. A: Where's the shoe store?
   B: It's on Park Avenue.
   A: On Park Avenue?
   B: Yes.

2. A: Where's the parking lot?
   B: It's behind the school.
   A: Behind the school?
   B: That's right.

3. A: Where's the park?
   B: It's next to the library.
   A: Next to the library?
   B: Yes.

4. A: Where's the bakery?
   B: It's across from the police station.
   A: Across from the police station?
   B: That's right.

D Working Together **Practice the conversations in Exercise C with a partner.**
Use different buildings and locations.

Reading a City Map

A **Working Together Give the location of the places on the map.**

Ask students to look at the map and talk about it. Name a building and ask them to make a sentence. For example: *The Post Office is next to the shoe store.*

B **Look at the map and write the locations of five buildings.**

Students can write down five of the sentences they made in Exercise A.

C **Pronunciation: Checking information Listen and repeat the conversations.**
(CD2·TR21)

• Have students listen to the audio of the four conversations.
• Students listen again, repeating the conversations.

D **Working Together Practice the conversations in Exercise C with a partner. Use different buildings and locations.**

• Have pairs of students practice each conversation. Students should switch roles and repeat the conversations again.
• For the new conversation, tell students either to place themselves in other locations on the map or in actual locations in their community. For example:
S1: *Where's the coffee shop?*
S2: *It's next to the bakery.*

Understanding and Giving Directions

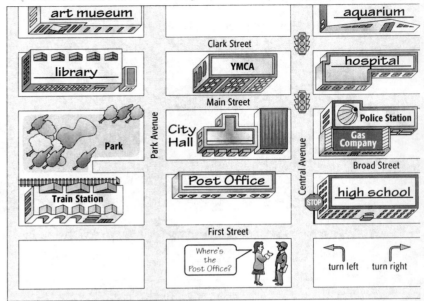

Understanding and Giving Directions

(Answers here are for Activity A below and Activity C on page 91.)

Working Together Read the conversations. Follow the directions and write the locations on the map.

Working Together
Read the conversations.
Follow the directions and write the locations on the map.

• Say the new words and phrases and ask students to repeat them after you: *traffic light, stop sign, turn left, three blocks,* etc.
• Ask students to trace each route on the map with a finger as you read each dialogue.
• Then, ask students to read the dialogues to themselves and complete the activity.

1. A: Where's the library?

B: Walk three blocks to the first traffic light.

Turn left.

The library is two blocks up on your right.

2. A: Where's the art museum?

B: Walk four blocks to the second traffic light. That's Clark Street.

Turn left.

The art museum is about two blocks up on your right.

3. A: Where's the high school?

B: Walk one block to the first stop sign. That's First Street.

Turn right.

The high school is on your left.

traffic light

stop sign

90 · Unit 7

More Action!

Make a very general map of your community. Label only a few streets and the locations of a few buildings. Leave everything else blank. Tell students to take the maps and go out into the community in small groups. They will need to ask people on the street or in shops to find out the names of the streets and buildings and how to get to each one. With this information, they fill in their maps. When the groups return to the classroom, they can compare maps and make one big master map.

More Action!

Use the map on page 90 or a community map. Tell students to pretend they are tour guides who are showing the important parts of the community to visitors. Have students role-play conversations between a tour guide and a visitor. What are the most interesting places to see? How do you get there from here?

B **Look at the map on page 90.** Read and complete the directions.

traffic light	right	Clark	Broad
stop sign	left	Main	First

1. **A:** Where's the gas company?

   B: Walk two blocks to _____Broad_____ Street.

   Turn _____right_____.

   The gas company is on your _____left_____.

2. **A:** Where's the train station?

   B: Walk one block to the first _____stop sign_____.

   That's _____First_____ Street.

   Turn _____left_____.

   The train station is two blocks up on your _____right_____.

3. **A:** Where's the park?

   B: Walk two blocks to _____Broad_____ Street.

   Turn _____left_____.

   The park is about two blocks up, in front of you.

C **Listen and write the locations on the map on page 90.**

1. City Hall   2. post office   3. hospital   4. aquarium

D **Working Together** **Write the directions to each of the locations.** Then, tell the directions to another student. Can he or she follow your directions?

1. City Hall   2. police station   3. aquarium

Walk _____ blocks.

Walk _____ blocks to the first _____.

That's _____ Street.

Turn right.

Turn left.

The _____ is on your right / left.

Directions may vary.

1. Walk two blocks to Broad Street. Turn left. City Hall is on your right.
2. Walk three blocks to the first traffic light. Turn right. The police station is on your right.
3. Walk four blocks to the second traffic light. That's Clark Street. Turn right. The aquarium is on your left.

Downtown • **91**

Teaching Tip

Before beginning Exercise D, ask students to use the locations in Exercise C to give directions orally.

B **Look at the map on page 90. Read and complete the directions.**

- Ask students to look at the map, the labels on the buildings, the street names, and other markers, such as traffic lights or stop signs. Practice basic directions once more: *turn right, turn left, go straight ahead three blocks*, etc.
- Ask students to complete the exercise, trading papers with a partner and comparing answers.

C **Listen and write the locations on the map on page 90.** (CD2 • TR22)

- Have students listen to the audio while looking at the map.
- Students listen a second time pausing to label the four locations. Move among them, checking answers.

D **Working Together Write the directions to each of the locations. Then, tell the directions to another student. Can he or she follow your directions?**

After each student has given directions to his or her partner, they should read the directions to another pair of students. Do all directions make sense? Why or why not?

The Public Library

A **Complete these sentences about your local library.**

If students don't know much about the local library, make sure you have all information on hand so they can answer the questions.

B **Complete.**

Ask students to fill in their own information on the application form. If they'd rather not use personal information, such as phone numbers, they can make it up.

A **Complete these sentences about your local library.** (Answers will vary.)

1. The library is on _____.

2. The telephone number of the library is _____.

3. I **have / don't have** a library card.

4. I can take out _____ from the library.

5. I can also borrow _____ and _____.

B **Complete.** (Answers will vary.)

Public Library Card Application

_____ _____ _____ ___/___/___
Last name   First name   MI   Today's date

☐ Adult ☐ Child _____-____-_____   _____
                  Social Security Number (If child, signature of parent/guardian)

_____
Address

_____ _____ _____
City   State   Zip Code

Telephone: (_____) _____-_____

92 · Unit 7

More Action!

Most libraries give out bookmarks or flyers with information about their services. Bring these to class and pass them out. Ask students: *How can the library help you learn English? Does the local library offer free English classes? Does it have materials that students can borrow? What other opportunities are available there?* Have students discuss these questions as a class.

Teaching Tip

Before doing Exercise A, you might want to discuss other items that can be found in a library: *an atlas, a volume of an encyclopedia, magazines and newspapers,* etc.

C Look at the picture on page 92. Complete the sentences.

1. The maps are _____next to_____ the dictionaries.

2. The videos are _in back of/behind_ the circulation desk.

3. Edward is standing _____next to_____ Theresa at the circulation desk.

4. The periodicals are _____in/on_____ the bookcase.

5. The newspapers are _in front of_ the circulation desk.

6. The computers are _____on_____ a long table. The table is ___across from___ the circulation desk.

7. Josh is sitting ___in front of___ a computer.

8. The children's section is (downstairs)/ upstairs.

9. The maps and dictionaries are downstairs /(upstairs.)

 D Ask and answer the questions. *(Students should answer in complete sentences.)*

1. Where are the librarians?
   circulation desk
2. What is Theresa doing?
   scanning a book
3. Is she reading a book?
   No.
4. Where is Edward?
   circulation desk
5. What is he doing?
   working on the computer
6. Is he reading a newspaper?
   No.
7. Where is Josh?
   at the computer
8. What is he doing?
   typing
9. Where is Amy?
   near the bookcase
10. Is she looking at the periodicals?
    No.
11. What is she looking at?
    new books
12. Where is Sara going?
    to the children's section.

E Working Together Go to the library or other place in your school. Write about the location of items or people. *(Answers will vary.)*

Example: *The periodicals are next to the newspapers.*

1. _____
2. _____
3. _____
4. _____
5. _____

C Complete the sentences.

• Before doing the exercise, review prepositional phrases with the class: *above, behind*, etc. Demonstrate these locations using a chair and a desk.
• Then, call on individuals for the answers to the exercise.

D Ask and answer the questions.

• Tell students to look at the picture again. Make sure they have all the vocabulary necessary for the exercise: *periodicals, circulation desk*, etc.
• Have students work in pairs. One student asks the questions, and the other answers them. Then, they switch roles.

E Working Together Go to the library or other place in your school. Write about the location of items or people.

If there is no school library, students can go to the public library. Or they can write about the school front office or another public area that is easily accessible.

More Action!

Ask students with a library card to go to the library and check out one item, bring it to class, and tell why they chose the item. Encourage students who don't have library cards to apply for a card.

Teaching Tip

Be sure to present libraries in a positive light, as interesting and useful places. Encourage students to use them regularly.

The Big Picture: Downtown

  Listen and point to each person in the story. (CD2 • TR23)

• First, ask students to talk about the picture. Ask questions, such as: *What happened to the truck? What is the policeman doing?*
• Have students listen to the audio while looking at the picture. Ask students what they remember from the audio.
• Students listen again, pausing to work out vocabulary and pronunciation.

  Listen and circle.
(CD2 • TR24)

• Have students listen to the audio while looking at the picture.
• Students listen a second time, circling the correct answers.
• Students exchange papers with a partner and listen for a third time, checking each other's answers.

The Big Picture

  Listen and point to each person in the story.
CD2 • TR23

 Listen and circle.
CD2 • TR24

1. **a.** Elena is.   **b.** Jane is.   **c.** Mrs. Lee is.

2. **a.** Michael is.   **b.** Luisa is.   **c.** Michael and Luisa are.

3. **a.** Officer Ortiz is.   **b.** Mr. Thomas is.   **c.** Mark is.

4. **a.** Officer Ortiz is.   **b.** Jane is.   **c.** Mrs. Lee is.

5. **a.** Mark is.   **b.** Joseph is.   **c.** Jane is.

6. **a.** Joseph is.   **b.** Jane is.   **c.** Luisa is.

7. **a.** Joseph is.   **b.** Officer Ortiz is.   **c.** Michael and Luisa are.

8. **a.** Mr. Thomas is.   **b.** Mrs. Lee is.   **c.** Officer Ortiz is.

94 • Unit 7

More Action!

Ask students to describe a downtown area from their own countries. It can be from a small town or city. What kind of stores are there? Restaurants? Coffee houses? Sidewalk vendors? If they have photographs, ask them to bring them to class.

Teaching Tip

Encourage students to rephrase one-word answers or incomplete sentences in full sentence form.

Circle and complete.

1. The playground is _____on_____ Smith Street.
   a. across from   **b.** on   c. between
2. City Hall is _____next to_____ the playground.
   a. across from   **b.** next to   c. on the corner of
3. The coffee shop is _____next to_____ the bakery.
   a. next to   b. between   c. behind
4. The parking lot is _____across from_____ the laundromat.
   a. across from   b. behind   c. between
5. Jane and Joseph are sitting _____in front of_____ the coffee shop.
   a. behind   **b.** in front of   c. next to
6. The police station is _____across from_____ City Hall.
   a. across from   b. behind   c. on
7. Officer Ortiz is standing _____next to_____ Mrs. Lee's car.
   a. next to   b. on   c. in front of

Write the location of the people in the picture.

1. Joseph and Jane _____are sitting in front of the coffee shop_____
2. Michael and Luisa _____are standing in front of City Hall_____
3. Mr. Thomas _is on the corner of Smith St. and North Main St_
4. Officer Ortiz _____is in the parking lot_____
5. Elena _____is sitting in the park_____

Complete.

watch   read   sit   ~~talk~~   work   play   get

1. Mr. Thomas _____is talking_____ to the other driver.
2. Elena _____is watching_____ the children.
3. The children _____are playing_____ in the park.
4. Joseph and Jane _____are sitting_____ at tables.
5. Joseph _____is reading_____ a newspaper.
6. Mark _____is working_____ at the coffee shop.
7. Michael and Luisa _____are getting_____ married.

Downtown • 95

Circle and complete.

• Ask students to talk about locations in the picture: *City Hall is across from the police station.*

• Ask students to look at the picture again and complete the exercise.

• Call on individuals for the correct answers.

Write the location of the people in the picture.

Each student completes the sentence and his or her partner checks the answers.

Complete.

• Review the present continuous tense for actions going on now or at this moment. Ask what the individual people in the picture are doing right now.

• Ask students to choose the correct verb from the answer box and use it in the present continuous to complete the sentences. Ask individuals to come to the board and write the correct answers.

More Action!

Ask pairs of students to create dialogues for the people in the picture on page 94: Michael and Luisa, Officer Ortiz and Mrs. Lee, Mr. Thomas and the other driver, Mark and Joseph, Mark and Jane, or Elena and the children. Students should include the present continuous tense and discuss what the people are doing right now.

For example:

Mrs. Lee: *Stop, stop! What are you doing?*

Officer Ortiz: *I'm writing you a parking ticket.*

Mrs. Lee: *Oh, no. Please!*

Officer Ortiz: *You're too late. Please pay at City Hall.*

Reading: The Library

A **Read.**

- Ask students to scan the reading for facts, such as what day they go to the library, what time Story Time is, etc.
- Read the first two paragraphs while students follow in their books. Explain any unknown vocabulary.
- Have students read the rest of the story to themselves. Ask students what they remember from it. Ask comprehension questions, such as: *What does he read after class?*
- Call on individuals to read parts of the story to the class. Correct pronunciation.

B **Circle *True* or *False*.**

- Make up other true or false statements and use them as a warm-up to the exercise. For example:
  He and his son live in a large house.
  His computer class is upstairs.
- Ask students to complete the exercise and call on individuals for the correct answers.

A **Read.**

My Local Library

Every Saturday morning, my son and I go to the public library. The library is only four blocks from our apartment. We can walk there.

My son and I have library cards. We go to the children's section, and he takes out books and videos about animals. He can borrow books for one month, but he can only borrow a video for three days.

Story Time is at 10:00. He stays downstairs and listens to the librarian read stories. I go upstairs and take a computer class. I don't have a computer at home. I am learning how to use the Internet and how to send e-mail to my family.

At the library, I can use the computer for free. After my class, I stop in the reference section and read a newspaper from my country for a few minutes.

The library is a wonderful place for both me and my son. And best of all, it's free!

B **Circle *True* or *False*.**

1. He drives to the library.　　　　　　　　　　True　(False)
2. His son has a library card.　　　　　　　　　(True)　False
3. His son likes books about animals.　　　　(True)　False
4. They can borrow videos for a month.　　　True　(False)
5. He stays with his son at Story Time.　　　True　(False)
6. He is learning how to use a computer.　　(True)　False
7. He has a computer at home.　　　　　　　　True　(False)
8. Newspapers are in the reference section.　(True)　False
9. He likes to read the news from his country.　(True)　False

Teaching Tip

As a reading strategy, show students how they can use context clues to figure out the meaning of an unknown word. To figure out the word *borrow*, a student can look at the words that come after it: *books for one month* and *a video for three days*. So *borrow* means to take for some time and then to bring back. Ask them to use this strategy with other unknown words, such as *section*. Note the context clues *children's* and *reference*.

A Read.

I am a student at Union County College in Elizabeth, New Jersey. Our school is on West Jersey Street. West Jersey Street is a busy street. The traffic is heavy and noisy all day. There are many stores and buildings on West Jersey Street. Our school is between a small parking lot and the gas company. There is a large clothing store across the street. Our school is convenient to transportation. The train station is across the street, and the bus stop is on the corner. We have one problem. Because our school is in a city, it is difficult to find a parking space.

B Working Together **Work in a group.** Draw and label a map of the area around your school. Talk about the locations of different places.

C Write about the location of your school. Use your map. (Answers will vary.)

I am a student at _____ in _____.

Our school is on _____

_____

_____

D Sharing Our Stories **Work with a partner and compare your paragraphs.** Which stores or buildings did you both write about?

WRITING NOTE

Check the prepositions in your story.

<u>on</u> Market Street

<u>in</u> San Francisco

Downtown • **97**

Writing Our Stories: Our School

A Read.
• Ask students to scan for facts, such as names of streets, kind of traffic, location of transportation, etc.
• Call on individuals to read the story aloud, one student per sentence.
• Ask them what they remember about the story.

B Working Together
Work in a group. Draw and label a map of the area around your school. Talk about the locations of different places.

Pass out large sheets of paper and markers or have groups work at sections of the board. In each group, one student can draw and label the streets, another draws the buildings, another the stores, parking lots, etc. When groups present their maps to the class, each speaker should be sure to use the correct prepositional phrases.

C Write about the location of your school. Use your map.
Ask students to write a paragraph using the paragraph from Exercise A as a model.

D Sharing Our Stories
Work with a partner and compare your paragraphs. Which stores or buildings did you both write about?

Ask students to trade paragraphs with their partners. Each student should underline all of the prepositions in the other's paragraph.

Downtown • **97**

English in Action: Getting Directions on the Internet

A   Discuss.

Use the discussion questions to stimulate conversation about Internet use. Do students prefer to ask others for directions or to get them online? Why? Do online directions always work? Encourage students to relate experiences about their use of online directions.

B   Read.

Are these the kind of symbols students are familiar with? Are there any others they wish to mention? Ask students to put any other symbols on the board. Where did they find them?

C   Complete the directions.

• First review basic direction-giving vocabulary: *turn left, straight ahead, take Exit 6,* etc.
• Tell students to look at the pictures as they fill in the directions. Ask students to exchange papers.

D   Look at the directions in Exercise C and answer the questions.

Expand the discussion by asking students to describe the person's trip, to describe trips they have taken, and Internet directions they have used in the past.

A   Discuss.

1. How do you get directions to somewhere new?
2. Do most people give clear directions?
3. Do you use the Internet to get directions?

B   Read.

| START | Go straight. | End. | Take exit. | Turn right. | Get onto Route. | Turn left. |

C   Complete the directions.

START	1. ___Start___ at 12 Park Place.	0.0 miles
→	2. ___Turn right___ onto River Road.	2.5 miles
←	3. ___Turn left___ onto Summit Avenue.	0.5 miles
ROUTE	4. ___Get onto___ Route 68 South.	10.4 miles
EXIT	5. ___Take Exit___ 12.	0.1 miles
←	6. ___Turn left___ on Davis Road.	1.5 miles
→	7. ___Turn right___ onto Morris Avenue.	0.2 miles
END	8. ___End___ at 52 Morris Avenue.	

Distance: 15.6 miles   Drive time: 35 minutes

D   Look at the directions in Exercise C and answer the questions.

1. Where is this driver starting?
   12 Park Place.
2. Where is she going?
   52 Morris Avenue
3. How far is she driving?
   15.6 miles.
4. What is the drive time?
   35 minutes.

Teaching Tip

You may have students in the class who have not used the Internet for directions or who do not have cars. Make sure they don't feel excluded from the activity. Partner them with students who have more experience in this area.

Working Together **Work in a group.** Write directions from your school to a place in your city or state.

 Complete the Internet directions form. Write the address of your school and the location from Exercise E. *(Answers will vary.)*

MAP | **DIRECTIONS** | NEW INFO

I am starting at:
Location
_____

Street Address
_____

City _____ State __ Zip Code _____

I am going to:
Location
_____

Street Address
_____

City _____ State __ Zip Code _____

 Use the Internet to check your directions.

1. Find a map site on the Internet.
2. Click *Directions*.
3. Fill in the information from Exercise F.
4. Print the directions.
5. Compare your directions from Exercise E and the directions from the map website.

Downtown · **99**

More Action!

Ask students to do other Internet searches for directions to places they'd like to visit in the area. If possible, they can visit the locations and report back to class about them.

 Working Together Work in a group. Write directions from your school to a place in your city or state.

Do this activity at the board with the participation of the class. Ask someone to provide a destination and then elicit the step-by-step directions to get there, keeping in mind that there are often several ways to get to the same place. Do this several times with different destinations so everyone has a chance to participate.

Complete the Internet directions form. Write the address of your school and the location from Exercise E.

Ask students to choose one or more of the destinations they used in Exercise E and to fill out the form accordingly. Encourage students to use a variety of directions.

Use the Internet to check your directions.

Ask students to go online and follow the directions in the activity. They should bring a printout of the directions to class and compare them to the directions they worked out in groups. Which sets of directions give the most direct routes in the shortest periods of time?

Unit 8

Money

Dictionary: Coins and Bills

  A Listen and repeat.
(CD2 • TR25)

- Have students listen to the audio while pointing to the pictures of currency in their books.
- Students listen again, repeating after the audio.
- Point to individual types of currency and ask students to read the denominations below the pictures. Then, ask them to cover the words and to name the coins or bills you are pointing to.

Money

  A Listen and repeat.
CD2•TR25

Coins

a penny	a nickel	a dime	a quarter
one cent	five cents	ten cents	twenty-five cents
$.01	$.05	$.10	$.25

> **CULTURE NOTE**
>
> From 1999 to 2009, the United States issued a new series of fifty quarters. Each quarter honors a different state. Do you have any quarters in your pocket? Which state's name is on the back?

Bills

a dollar
$1.00

five dollars
$5.00

ten dollars
$10.00

twenty dollars
$20.00

100 • Unit 8

More Action!

Point out the **Culture Note.** Ask students to take out any quarters they have and to tell what states are on the backs. Ask what symbols are used for each state. For example, Abraham Lincoln is on the Illinois quarter. What's on the back of the quarter for the state you're in? Can the class collect quarters for all 50 states?

Teaching Tip

Explain that we rarely use the word *one* with the word *dollar.* We say *a dollar* or *a dollar and twenty-five cents.*

Teaching Tip

Point out that the words and numbers under the coins and bills are said the same way.

Word Builder

 A **Listen and repeat.**
CD2·TR26

a. 4¢	$.04		**f.** 50¢	$.50
b. 10¢	$.10		**g.** 62¢	$.62
c. 25¢	$.25		**h.** 75¢	$.75
d. 30¢	$.30		**i.** 85¢	$.85
e. 35¢	$.35		**j.** 99¢	$.99

> There are three ways
> to write cents:
>
> ten cents
> 10¢
> $.10

B **Write the amount.**

a.

35 ¢ / $.35

b.

11 ¢ / $.11

c.

41 ¢ / $.41

d.

31 ¢ / $.31

e.

36 ¢ / $.36

C **Working Together** **Work in a group.** Take out your change and count it together.
Write the amount. Who has the most change? (Answers will vary.)

 D **Listen and write the amount.**
CD2·TR27

a. $.02 / 2 ¢	**d.** $.25 / 25¢	**g.** $.50 / 50¢
b. $.10 / 10¢	**e.** $.38 / 38¢	**h.** $.69 / 69¢
c. $.17 / 17¢	**f.** $.49 / 49¢	**i.** $.98 / 98¢

WORD PARTNERSHIPS	
	credit card
pay by	check
	cash

Money · **101**

Word Builder: Coins

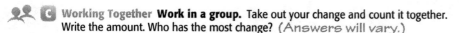 **A** **Listen and repeat.**
(CD2·TR26)

• Have students listen to the audio while looking at the numbers in their books.
• Students listen again, repeating the amounts.
• Have students read the amounts, making sure they understand that the two amounts on each line are the same and are said the same way.

B **Write the amount.**

Ask students to do this orally first: *A quarter and a dime equal thirty-five cents.* Or *Twenty-five cents and ten cents equal thirty-five cents.* Then, ask them to write the amounts.

C **Working Together**
Work in a group. Take out your change and count it together. Write the amount. Who has the most change?

Each student can first count his or her own change and write the amount. Then the group, as a whole, can pool their change and add it up. Make sure each student gets his or her correct amount back.

D **Listen and write the amount.** (CD2·TR27)

Students listen to the audio twice, the second time while writing the correct amounts.

Teaching Tip

Introduce the terms *decimal point, dollar sign, cent sign.* Point out that when a dollar sign is followed immediately by a decimal point, the amount is in cents.

Word Builder: Bills

  Listen and repeat.
(CD2 • TR28)

• Make sure that students understand that if the decimal point follows a number, the amount is more than a dollar.
• Students listen to the audio while reading the amounts in their books. Students listen again and repeat the amounts.
• Call on individuals to read the amounts.

  Listen and write the amount. (CD2 • TR29)

• As a warm-up activity, send students to the board and ask them to write the numerals for amounts you give them. Ask the class for corrections.
• Students listen to the audio without writing and then listen once again and write the numerals.

  Pronunciation: Numbers Listen and repeat the numbers.
(CD2 • TR30)

• Students listen to the audio twice, repeating after it the second time through.
• Make sure students stress the first syllable of the teens: *SIXteen, SEVenteen,* etc.

 Circle the number you hear. (CD2 • TR31)

Students listen to the audio twice, circling the correct numbers the second time. They should trade books with a partner and listen a third time, making corrections.

102 · Unit 8

Word Builder

> **Dollars and Cents**
>
> $ 2.50 = two dollars and fifty cents = two fifty
> $10.99 = ten dollars and ninety-nine cents = ten ninety-nine
> $498.79 = four hundred and ninety-eight dollars and seventy-nine cents
> = four ninety-eight seventy-nine

  Listen and repeat.
CD2•TR28

a. $1.00	**d.** $4.99	**g.** $127.98
b. $1.50	**e.** $17.49	**h.** $249.99
c. $2.75	**f.** $59.50	**i.** $629.77

> **CULTURE NOTE**
> The dollar is the monetary unit of the United States. What is the monetary unit in your country?

  Listen and write the amount.
CD2•TR29

a. $1.00	**d.** $3.75	**g.** $157.62
b. $1.25	**e.** $15.08	**h.** $230.99
c. $2.50	**f.** $79.25	**i.** $457.24

  **Pronunciation: Numbers** **Listen and repeat the numbers.**
CD2•TR30

13	14	15	16	17	18	19
30	40	50	60	70	80	90

Circle the number you hear.
CD2•TR31

a. (13) 30	**f.** ($18) $80	**k.** $14.40 ($14.14)
b. 14 (40)	**g.** ($19) $90	**l.** ($17.20) $70.20
c. (15) 50	**h.** ($13) $30	**m.** ($16.16) $60.16
d. 16 (60)	**i.** ($15) $50	**n.** ($18.75) $80.75
e. 17 (70)	**j.** ($19) $90	**o.** ($10.50) $10.15

102 · Unit 8

More Action!

Look at the **Culture Note** on page 102. Ask students to bring samples of money from their own countries, including bills and coins. Each student can show his or her money to the class and estimate its approximate value in dollars and cents. They can also compare prices of items from their native countries with prices in the United States.

Working Together **Talk about the places you like to shop.** (Answers will vary.)

1. I shop at _____ for clothes.
2. I shop at _____ for food.
3. I shop at _____ for toys.
4. I shop at _____ for shoes.
5. I shop at _____ for school supplies.
6. I shop at _____ for electronic equipment.
7. I stop at _____ for gas.
8. I stop at _____ for a cup of coffee.
9. I stop at _____ for the newspaper.
10. _____ is a convenience store in my area.

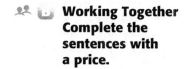 Working Together **Complete the sentences with a price.** (Answers will vary.)

1. A first-class stamp is _____.
2. The local newspaper is _____.
3. A cup of coffee is _____.
4. A gallon of regular gas is _____.
5. A bottle of water is _____.
6. A DVD is _____.
7. A video rental is _____.
8. A movie ticket is _____.
9. A round-trip plane ticket to my country is _____.
10. A laptop computer is about _____.

Working Together **Bring in sales circulars.** Discuss.

1. Where is the sale? When is the sale?
2. List four items on sale. What is the regular price? What is the sale price?

Money · **103**

Stores and Prices

**Working Together
Talk about the places
you like to shop.**

• Go over vocabulary
in advance, introducing
items, such as *department
store, supermarket, gas
station, office supply
store,* etc.
• Ask students to fill
in the statements with
actual stores in their
communities.

**Working Together
Complete the
sentences with
a price.**

Encourage students to
brainstorm about their
shopping habits and
prices. They should
come to the board and
write the prices they
decided on for each
item. What other items
do they regularly shop
for and what are their
prices?

**Working Together
Bring in sales
circulars. Discuss.**

Discuss the circulars and
explain any unknown
words. Point out the
discounts, how long
the sale lasts, and other
information you can find
in a circular.

Teaching Tip

Students may be interested in
learning simple mathematical
terms in English, such as *add,
subtract, multiply, divide, percentage,*
etc. Demonstrate these by putting
their appropriate symbols on the
board.

Active Grammar: Questions with *How much*

Ask students to talk about the picture. *What is the cashier doing? What is the customer buying? Where are the notebooks, folders, computers, and printers?*

👥 **A** **Write the names of items you can buy at an office supply store.**

In addition to the items in the picture, elicit some of the following items from the students: *paper clips, ink cartridges, mouse, planner, pens and pencils, briefcase, tape dispenser, printer paper, account books, stapler and staples, etc.*

👥 **B** **Ask and answer questions about the price of each item.**

• Ask students to take turns saying the basic conversation in the speech balloons.
• Pairs of students can role-play the dialogue, substituting the other items and prices.

| **How much is** a map? | **It's** $9.00. |
| **How much are** the markers? | **They're** $3.50. |

👥 **A** **Write the names of items you can buy at an office supply store.** (Answers will var

1. _____   4. _____   7. _____

2. _____   5. _____   8. _____

3. _____   6. _____   9. _____

👥 **B** **Ask and answer questions about the price of each item.**

How much is this map?

It's $9.00.

1. a map   3. a ruler   5. a shredder

2. a stapler   4. a calculator   6. a printer

104 • Unit 8

More Action!

Ask students to bring to class advertisements from newspapers or magazines for items they'd like to buy. Have students cover the prices. Each student should show his or her ad to the class and ask the others to guess the price. The student who guesses the correct price wins that round. The student who guesses the most correct (or nearly correct) prices wins the game.

C Ask and answer questions about the price of each item.

$5.39
1. batteries

99¢
3. crayons

$1.29
5. envelopes

How much are
the batteries?

They're $5.39.

$3.99
2. scissors

$16.50
4. markers

59¢
6. paper clips

D Complete the questions and answers.

1. How much ___is___ this stapler?   ___It's___ $5.99.

2. How much ___is___ the calculator?   ___It's___ $16.50.

3. How much ___are___ the batteries?   ___They're___ $5.39.

4. How much ___are___ the envelopes?   ___They're___ $1.29.

5. How much ___is___ a ruler?   ___It's___ 99¢.

6. How much ___is___ a shredder?   ___It's___ $24.95.

7. How much ___are___ the paper clips?   ___They're___ 59¢.

E Working Together **Work with a partner and figure out your change.**

1. Buy a box of paper clips for 59¢. Give the cashier $1.00. $.41 / 41¢

2. Buy a pair of scissors for $3.99. Give the cashier $5. $1.01

3. Buy a stapler for $5.99. Give the cashier $10. $4.01

4. Buy a shredder for $24.95. Give the cashier $30. $5.05

5. Buy a map for $9.00 and a pack of batteries for $5.39. Give the cashier $20. $5.61

Money • 105

C Ask and answer questions about the price of each item.

• Go over words for containers in an office supply store: *a box of, a package of, a pair of.*
• Ask pairs of students to role-play the dialogues. Tell students that paying attention to singular and plural nouns will help them decide to use either *how much is* or *how much are.*

D Complete the questions and answers.

• Do the exercise orally first, reviewing the use of *is/are* and *it's/they're.*
• Ask students to write the answers. Then, students should trade papers and correct answers.

E Working Together Work with a partner and figure out your change.

Tell students to make change by counting out coin change up to the nearest dollar and then give dollar change. Ask students to role-play the dialogue.

More Action!

Students stand in a line. The first says: *I'm buying (item) ____ for $____.*
The next student says: *She/He is buying ____ for $____, and I'm buying...*
Each student must remember all the items and prices before adding a new item.

Teaching Tip

Bring play money from any board game to class for use in Exercise E.

Active Grammar: Giving Instructions

Point out the grammar note. Explain that we use this imperative form to tell someone to do something: *Open your book, Close the window,* etc.

Check the machines that you use.

Encourage students to think of other machines where they have to pay and follow a procedure: *public fax machine, storage locker,* etc.

Working Together Practice giving directions. Act out the directions.

Encourage each group to act out the directions in sequence, one student per direction. Then, each group can perform the directions in front of the class while the others call out the direction line that a student is demonstrating.

Complete the directions for using a vending machine.

First, ask students to put the words in the answer box in the correct sequence. Then, they can complete the exercise.

A Check (✓) the machines that you use .

_____ copy machine   _____ vending machine

_____ gas pump   _____ parking lot meter

_____ self-checkout machine   _____ washer / dryer

> For instructions, use the simple form of the verb.
>
> **Insert** your cash.
> **Push** the button.
> **Take** your change.

B Working Together **Practice giving directions.** Act out the directions.

Directions

1. Open the cover.
2. Place your document on the glass, face down.
3. Close the cover.
4. Insert your money in the coin slot.
5. Press "Copy."
6. Take your copy from the side of the copy machine.
7. Open the cover and take your original.

C Complete the directions for using a vending machine.

take   ~~choose~~   take   insert   press

1. _____*Choose*_____ the item you want.
2. _____*Press*_____ the correct numbers.
3. _____*Insert*_____ the money.
4. _____*Take*_____ your item.
5. _____*Take*_____ your change.

106 · Unit 8

More Action!

Discuss what to do if a machine gives you a wrong item or the incorrect change. Has this happened to anyone in the class?

D **Put the directions for using an ATM machine in order.**

    _3_   Select *Withdraw Cash*.

    _5_   Take your cash.

    _1_   Insert your ATM card.

    _6_   Take your receipt.

    _2_   Put in your PIN number.

    _7_   Don't forget to take your ATM card!

    _4_   Choose the amount you want.

E **Write the directions for using an ATM machine.**

First, insert your ATM card. Next,
put in your PIN number. Then, select
Withdraw Cash. Next, choose the
amount you want. Then, take your
cash. Finally, take your receipt.

> **Words to give order to directions**
>
> First,
> Next,
> Then,
> Finally,

Working Together **Talk about how to use the self-checkout in a store.**
Write the steps. (Answers will vary.)

Money · **107**

The Big Picture:
I Need a Desk

Ask students to talk about the picture. *What is each individual doing (Katrina, Fabio, Raul, Sonia)? Where are they in relation to each other? What room are they in? Describe the room and the people in it.*

🔊 **A** **Listen to the conversation. Complete the sentences.** (CD2 • TR32)

• Have students listen to the audio while looking at the picture. Ask them what they remember from the audio.
• Students listen again. Then, ask them comprehension questions: *Why can't Katrina study? What's wrong with the bedroom? Where are she and Fabio going tomorrow?*
• Students listen a third time, completing the sentences in the exercise. Move among them and correct answers.

🔊 **A** **Listen to the conversation.** Complete the sentences.

CD2•TR32

1. Katrina can't study because _____ *it's too noisy* _____.
2. She is going to study in the _____ *bedroom* _____.
3. Katrina and Fabio are going to go to the _____ *office supply store* _____.
4. She is going to buy a _____ *desk* _____, a _____ *chair* _____, and a _____ *light* _____.
5. She also needs _____ *folders* _____.
6. Fabio is going to look at a _____ *shredder* _____.

108 • Unit 8

 B **Listen to the conversation.** Then, write the items that Katrina and Fabio buy. Write the prices.

CD2·TR33

1.	a desk	$119
2.	a chair	$69
3.	a lamp	$19
4.	a shredder	$20
5.	folders	$4

C **Write the total amount for all the items.**

$231

 D **Listen and write the responses.**

CD2·TR34

1. **A:** This desk is nice. **B:** It's too big .
2. **A:** How about this desk? **B:** It's too small .
3. **A:** This one is the right size. **B:** Yes, I like that one .
4. **A:** Do you like this chair? **B:** It's too big for me .
5. **A:** How about this one? **B:** It isn't comfortable .
6. **A:** How about this one? **B:** I like it. And it's a good price .
7. **A:** How much is this lamp? **B:** It's on sale for $19 .

Money • **109**

More Action!

Bring in catalogs or flyers from office supply stores. Ask students to choose items they want to purchase. Write these cues on the board and ask students to role-play:

S1: *How much is this____?*
S2: *The price is $_____.*
S1: *Sounds good. I'll take it. Here's my credit card.*
S2: *That's $____ with tax. Please sign here. Have a good day.*

Teaching Tip

Explain that cashiers may ask if customers have a store discount card. With a discount card, they may get cheaper prices. Stress that these discount cards are different from store credit cards.

Teaching Tip

When doing a dictation, students may find it useful to repeat the dictated words to themselves (silently) before writing.

Ask students to look at the picture and talk about it. Where are Katrina and Fabio? What is Katrina looking at? What is Fabio pushing? What's in the cart?

B **Listen to the conversation. Then, write the items that Katrina and Fabio buy. Write the prices.** (CD2 • TR33)

• Have students listen to the conversation. Ask them what they remember about it.
• Students listen again, pausing to work on vocabulary, such as *size, drawer, comfortable, shredder.*
• Students listen a third time, writing the prices in the exercise.

C **Write the total amount for all the items.**

Put the list of prices on the board and ask students to add orally, like this: *Three nines make twenty-seven plus four makes thirty-one. Write the one and carry the three,* etc.

D **Listen and write the responses.** (CD2 • TR34)

• Students listen the first time without writing. Ask them to repeat the responses.
• Students listen again, pausing to write the responses. Move among them, checking their answers.

Reading: My Favorite Store

Read.

- Ask students to look at Mimi's story and underline any words they don't understand. They may underline *mall*, *department*, or *coupon*, among others. Tell them to look for context clues to explain the meanings. The word *stores* should be a context clue for *mall*. The words *kitchen*, *bedroom*, and *bathroom* are clues for *department*. The term *20% off* is a clue for *coupon*.
- Call on individual students to read the story sentence by sentence. Then, ask comprehension questions, such as: *What is Mimi's favorite department?*
- Repeat this same process with Carla's story.

Check.

Do the exercise orally first, asking questions, such as: *Who has a credit card for her favorite store?* Then, ask students to check the correct person.

Talk about your favorite stores.

Encourage students to talk about the stores they visit most often. *Why do you like them? What are the best things about them? Do you pay cash or do you pay by credit or check? What is the best way to pay?*

Read.

I like houseware stores. There is a beautiful houseware store in the mall near my house. It sells kitchen, bedroom, and bathroom items. My favorite department is the kitchen department. I buy something there every month, such as glasses or a new pot. The store sends ads and catalogs to my home. Every month, the store gives me a coupon for 20 percent off any item.

Mimi

There is a bookstore in my city that is as big as a supermarket. It has a small café. People order tea or coffee and look at books. The store has every kind of book. I speak Spanish, and it has a section with many books in Spanish. I can buy Spanish newspapers and magazines, too. I love cookbooks. Every month, I buy a new cookbook. I have a special credit card for that store, and I get 30 percent off every book I buy.

Carla

Check (✓).

	Mimi	Carla
1. She has a credit card for her favorite store.		✓
2. She receives store coupons.	✓	
3. She gets a 30 percent discount on the things she buys.		✓
4. She checks store ads.	✓	
5. She buys something at her favorite store every month.	✓	✓
6. She receives catalogs from the store.	✓	
7. She gets 20 percent off one item every month.	✓	

Talk about your favorite stores. *(Answers will vary.)*

1. What is your favorite store?
2. Where is it?
3. Is it large or small?
4. How often do you shop there?
5. Do you have a credit card for the store?
6. Do you look for sales?

More Action!

Ask students to bring to class any coupons they can find in newspapers, ads, shopping flyers, etc. Distribute the coupons and ask each student to talk about one. For example: *Home Office is taking 15% off all $500 laptops. So the price of a laptop is now $425 with the coupon.*

Read.

> My favorite store is an electronics
> store. There is an electronics store on
> the highway near my house. It sells TVs,
> computers, printers, cameras, telephones,
> and other equipment. I go there almost
> every week. I have a laptop computer and
> a digital camera. I like to take pictures of
> my family and friends. I want a photo
> printer. It's about $99. When there is a
> sale, I'm going to buy one.

Complete the information. Then, write about your favorite store. (Answers will vary.)

1. My favorite store is _____.

2. It is **near / far from** my home.

3. It sells _____, _____, and
   _____.

4. I go there _____.

Sharing Our Stories Read your story to a partner. Complete these sentences.

1. My partner's favorite store is _____.

2. My partner likes to buy _____.

3. I **never / sometimes / often** go to my partner's favorite store.

WRITING NOTE

Use capital letters for the
name of a store:

Best Electronics
Sweet Things Bakery

Money • **111**

Writing Our Stories: My Favorite Store

Read.

- As a pre-reading activity, ask students to talk about electronics stores in their area. Do they ever visit them? Where are they? What have they bought there?
- Ask students to read the story to themselves. Can they figure out any unknown vocabulary from context clues?
- Ask comprehension questions, such as: *Where is the electronics store? What items does it sell?*
- Ask students to read sentences from the story aloud. Correct pronunciation and intonation.

Complete the information. Then, write about your favorite store.

First, ask students to complete the information and link the sentences into a paragraph. If they wish to add other information about the store not covered by the statements, they should feel free to do so.

Sharing Our Stories Read your story to a partner. Complete these sentences.

Pairs of students should ask and answer questions about each other's stories before completing the sentences.

Teaching Tip

Tell students to make sure to indent the first line of a paragraph a few spaces. They can also give their stories titles, such as *My Favorite Store.*

English in Action: Understanding a Store Receipt

Ask students to look at the sample receipt and help them to read it. Ask: *What's the name and address of the store? What's the date of the receipt? How many items is it for? What is the difference between subtotal and total? How much is the tax? Why does the credit card number have x's in it?*

A **Look at the store receipt and complete the sentences.**

Ask students to complete the sentences and then exchange papers with a partner. Are the answers on both papers the same?

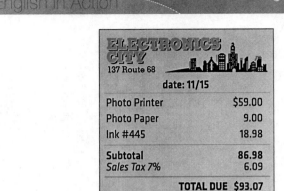

ELECTRONICS CITY
137 Route 68

date: 11/15

Photo Printer	$59.00
Photo Paper	9.00
Ink #445	18.98
Subtotal	86.98
Sales Tax 7%	6.09
TOTAL DUE	**$93.07**
CREDIT CARD	*$93.07*
xxxx-xxxx-xxxx-1234	

A **Look at the store receipt and complete the sentences.**

1. The name of the store is ___ Electronics City ___
2. The date of the sale was ___ 11/15 ___
3. This person bought ___ three ___ items.
4. The photo printer was $ ___ 59.00 ___
5. The photo paper was $ ___ 9.00 ___
6. The cost of all three items was $ ___ 86.98 ___
7. In this state, the sales tax is ___ 7 ___ %.
8. The sales tax for these items was $ ___ 6.09 ___
9. The total for everything was $ ___ 93.07 ___
10. This person paid by ___ credit card ___

Keep your receipt.
1. You can use receipts to check your credit card statement.
2. You might need the receipt to return an item.

More Action!

- Ask students to bring receipts for purchases to class. They can be for groceries, office supplies, electronics, or anything else they've purchased. Ask each student to present a receipt to the class. He or she can tell about the purchases, prices, tax, and total. He or she can also explain how he or she paid (by cash, credit or debit card, or check). Was he or she happy about the item(s) purchased?
- Point out the note box. Ask students if they've ever returned anything to a store. What was wrong with it? Did the store replace it or return the money?

Teaching Tip

If complete credit card numbers are on the receipts the students bring to class, ask them to cover them or black them out.

Ask students to look at the advertisement. Do they understand all the vocabulary, such as *GPS Navigational System* or *Mini Camcorder*? How many of these items do they own? Where did they buy them?

A **In a small group, answer these questions.**

Students should ask and answer the questions in their group.

 A **In a small group, answer these questions.**

1. What is the name of this store? Electronics City

2. When is the sale? July 3rd, 4th, and 5th

3. What time is the store open? 8:00A.M. to 10:00P.M.

4. How much will you save on the laptop computer? $400

5. What is the original price of the TV? How much is the sale price? What size is the TV? $2,000/ $1,399/ 42"

6. How much is the digital camera? $199

7. Are cell phones on sale? Yes.

8. Is this a good sale? (Answers may vary.)

Money • 113

More Action!

Internet Option: Ask students to search for online catalogs for their favorite brands, print out some product listings, and bring them to class. Each student should tell the class about what he or she brought. Why do they like these brands? Are there sale prices for any of the items? What percentage off is advertised? Is this a good bargain? What are the advantages of Internet shopping? What are the disadvantages?

More Action!

Give students large pieces of poster paper and some markers and ask them to design an ad for a product of their own choosing. What information should be included or excluded? What sales message will persuade customers to buy the product? Should there be a discount? How much? Each student should present his or her ad to the class.

Unit 9

Transportation

Dictionary: A Busy Street

• Ask students to look at and talk about the picture. You can ask these questions: *What are Ahmed and Briana doing? What is Briana carrying? What's the number of the bus? What does the sign outside the bus say? What's Carrie doing? Who's getting out of the taxi? What's the name of the woman getting into the taxi? How many cars are stopped at the red light? Where are Frank and Joni? What's Harry doing? What's Ivan carrying?*

• Have students work in pairs, asking and answering questions about the picture.

 Listen and repeat.
(CD2 • TR35)

• Ask students to listen to the audio while pointing to the corresponding items and people in the picture. Ask them to listen again, repeating the words.

• Point to parts of the picture and ask students to identify items and people.

Word Partnerships

Using the two-word verbs in the box, ask students to make sentences about the picture. For example: *Briana is getting on the bus.*

 Listen and repeat.
CD2 • TR35

1. a car	**6.** a taxi	**11.** a street
2. a driver	**7.** a bicycle	**12.** a sidewalk
3. a bus stop	**8.** a helmet	**13.** a traffic light
4. a bus	**9.** a truck	**14.** a shopping bag
5. passengers	**10.** an airplane	**15.** a briefcase

WORD PARTNERSHIPS	
get on	a bus
get off	a train
get into	a car
get out of	a taxi

114 • Unit 9

Complete.

1. The boy on the bicycle is wearing a red ___helmet___.
2. Two people are crossing the street. The ___traffic light___ is red.
3. Two ___passengers___ are getting on the bus.
4. The man with the briefcase is walking on the ___sidewalk___.
5. A woman is getting on the bus. She's carrying a ___shopping bag___.

Working Together Complete the sentences with a partner. You can use the same name more than once.

1. ___Elena___ is getting into the taxi.
2. ___Ivan___ is carrying a briefcase.
3. ___Frank___ and ___Joni___ are crossing the street.
4. ___Harry___ is riding a bicycle.
5. ___Ahmed___ and ___Briana___ are getting on the bus.
6. ___Carrie___ is running for the bus.
7. ___Harry___ is wearing a helmet.
8. ___Briana___ is carrying a shopping bag.
9. ___David___ is getting out of the taxi.
10. ___Harry___ is wearing a backpack.

Working Together Complete. Then talk about your answers. (Answers will vary.)

1. I live _____ miles/km from school.
2. **I drive / don't drive.**
3. **I walk / drive / take the bus / take the train / take the subway** to school.
4. I live _____ miles/km from work.
5. **I walk / drive / take the bus / take the train / take the subway** to work.
6. The **bus / train / subway** is $ _____.
7. A gallon of gas is $ _____.

Transportation • 115

Word Builder

Complete.

Tell students that the vocabulary they need for the exercise is in the list on page 114. Then, ask them to complete the exercise orally before writing.

Working Together Complete the sentences with a partner. You can use the same name more than once.

Review the names of the people in the picture. Then, have students fill in the blanks with the correct names. Check answers orally.

Working Together Complete. Then talk about your answers.

What are the advantages and disadvantages of travel to school or work by bus, subway, train, driving, or walking? Which is the most expensive? The least expensive?

More Action!

Have students report the distance they travel and the mode of transportation they use to get to school (car, bus, subway, bicycle, walking). Total the numbers and make two pie charts on the board. In one chart, section the pie in slices corresponding to modes of transportation. For example: 10% for walking, 40% for driving. Do the same with the other chart, sectioning it for distance: 14% travel under one mile, 24% travel 2-5 miles, etc. Make sure that the slices in each chart total 100%.

Active Grammar: Review of Present Continuous Statements

Ask students to describe what they're doing now (at this moment). Then, they can describe what others in the class are doing. Ask them to predict what friends or relatives outside the class are doing, thinking, or eating at this moment.

 A **Working Together Answer these questions with a partner. Do not look back at the picture on page 114.**

• Students can test their memory for detail. Students should alternate asking and answering questions.
• When they've asked and answered all the questions, they can look back at the picture to check their answers. Who had the better memory?

 B **Look at the picture on page 114. Talk about what the people are doing.**

Emphasize the two-word verbs in this exercise: *get on, get out of, get in/into, run for, walk along,* etc. Ask students to do the exercise orally.

 C **Working Together Work with a group. Look around your class. In your notebooks, write five sentences about what students are doing now.**

If most students are doing the same thing, encourage students to do something different, such as raise their hand or sharpen a pencil.

116 · Unit 9

 A **Working Together Answer these questions with a partner.** Do not look back at the picture on page 114.

> I **am studying** English.
> The teacher **is looking** at her book.
> The students **are talking**.

1. Who is running for the bus? *Carrie*
2. How many people are getting on the bus? *Two people*
3. What is Ivan carrying? *A briefcase*
4. Is Ivan talking on his cell phone? *No, he isn't.*
5. Is the woman getting into the taxi? *Yes, she is.*
6. How many people are crossing the street? *Two people*
7. Is the boy on the bike wearing a helmet? *Yes, he is.*

 B **Look at the picture on page 114.** Talk about what the people are doing.

> Ahmed and Briana are getting on the bus.

1. get on the bus
2. get out of the taxi
3. run for the bus
4. walk along the sidewalk
5. cross the street
6. carry a shopping bag
7. get into the taxi
8. carry a briefcase
9. ride his bicycle

 C **Working Together Work with a group.** Look around your class. In your notebooks, write five sentences about what students are doing now.

> *Carlos is sharpening his pencil. Maya is walking into the classroom. She's late today.*

(Answers will vary.)

D Answer the questions.

Picture 1

Picture 2

Picture 1

1. Where are these people?

They're at the bus stop.

2. How many people are waiting for the bus?

Four people are waiting for the bus.

3. What are the men carrying?

They're carrying briefcases.

4. What is the woman on the right doing?

She's reading a newspaper.

Picture 2

1. Where is the man?

He's at the train station.

2. What is he doing?

He's waiting for the train.

3. What is he looking at?

He's looking at his watch.

4. What is he holding?

He's holding his computer / laptop.

Transportation • **117**

D Answer the questions.

• Ask students to talk about the first picture. They should describe each person, their location, and their clothing.
• Then, they should write the answers to the questions. Move among them and check their answers.
• Repeat the same process for the second picture.

More Action!

Bring to class a variety of photographs from magazines, newspapers, or online sources. Bring more photographs than there are students and choose photographs which are busy and complicated. Put five of these face down on a table and ask five students to each choose one photograph. Students should not show the photo to anyone else. They should study the photos and then describe them to the class using the present continuous tense. Then, collect the photos and display them on the board. Other students must correctly identify the photo that each student described. Repeat this until all students have had a chance to participate.

Teaching Tip

Encourage students to use contracted forms while speaking casually:
She's writing.
He's getting into the taxi.
They're taking a walk.
We're singing a song.
You're riding a bike.

Active Grammar: Yes/No Questions and Answers

Ask students to look at the sentences in the chart. Say the affirmative and negative responses and ask the students to repeat after you.

 Answer the questions.

- Do a warm-up before the exercise by asking a series of questions with short answers. Ask questions that will prompt an affirmative response, such as: *Are you sitting in class now?* Ask questions that will prompt a negative response, such as: *Are you climbing a tree? Are you singing an opera? Are you dancing a tango?*
- Students should write the answers to the questions. Call on individuals for their answers.

👥 **Working Together Ask and answer the questions about the picture on page 114.**

The student who is answering the questions should look closely at the detailed picture while the other student asks the questions. Then, they can change roles.

Questions	Affirmative Answer	Negative Answer
Are you **driving?**	Yes, I **am.**	No, **I'm not.**
Is he **walking** to work?	Yes, he **is.**	No, he **isn't.**
Are they **taking** the bus?	Yes, they **are.**	No, they **aren't.**

 Answer the questions.

1. Are you sitting in class now? — *Yes, we are. / Yes, I am.*
2. Are you studying English? — *Yes, we are. / Yes, I am.*
3. Are you talking with a partner now? — *Yes, I am. / No, I'm not.*
4. Are you writing in your book? — *Yes, I am. / No, I'm not.*
5. Is your teacher sitting? — *Yes, he/she is. or No, he/she isn't.*
6. Is your teacher writing on the board? — *Yes, he/she is. or No, he/she isn't.*
7. Is your teacher wearing a sweater today? — *Yes, he/she is. or No, he/she isn't.*
8. Are the students taking a test now? — *No, they aren't. / No, we aren't.*
9. Are the students looking at their books? — *Yes, they are. / No, we aren't.*

👥 **B Working Together Ask and answer the questions about the picture on page 114.**

1. Are Ahmed and Briana getting on the bus?
2. Is Ahmed carrying a briefcase?
3. Is Carrie running for the bus?
4. Is David getting into the taxi?
5. Is Elena driving the taxi?

6. Are Frank and Joni crossing the street?
7. Are Frank and Joni talking?
8. Is Harry riding his bicycle to school?
9. Is Ivan crossing the street?
10. Is Ivan going to work?

1. Yes, they are.
2. No, he isn't.
3. Yes, she is.
4. No, he isn't.
5. No, she isn't.

6. Yes, they are.
7. Yes, they are.
8. Yes, he is.
9. No, he isn't.
10. Yes, he is.

118 · Unit 9

More Action!

Ask one student to come to the front of the class. The student should say: *Guess what I'm thinking about right now?* Seated students can ask questions: *Are you thinking about the summer holiday?* The student should respond in the affirmative or negative: *Yes, I am* or *No, I'm not.* When a seated student guesses correctly, he or she goes to the front of the class. Or, set a time limit and have students switch roles when time is up.

Write questions and answers about the picture.

1. Is he talking on the phone?   Yes, he is.

   talk on the phone

2. Is he wearing a headset?   Yes, he is.

   wear a headset

3. Is he using his GPS?   Yes, he is.

   use his GPS

4. Is he wearing sunglasses?   No, he isn't.

   wear sunglasses

5. Is it snowing?   No, it isn't.

   snow

6. Is he drinking a cup of coffee?   Yes, he is.

   drink a cup of coffee

7. Is he wearing his seat belt?   Yes, he is.

   wear his seat belt

 Working Together **Draw a picture of a person performing an action.** The other students will guess what the person is doing. (Answers will vary.)

| Is he washing the dishes? | No, he isn't. | Is he doing the laundry? | Yes, he is. |

 Write questions and answers about the picture.

• Ask students to look carefully at the picture. *What is the man doing? Is he doing too many things at the same time? Is he a good driver?*

• Ask students to do the exercise orally first and then to write the answers.

Working Together Draw a picture of a person performing an action. The other students will guess what the person is doing.

Students don't need to know how to draw well to do this exercise. In fact, if the drawing is very rough, it will work better because it will be more difficult for students to guess the right answer, giving everyone more practice. Tell students to use the conversation in the speech balloons as a model.

More Action!

Ask students to think about their hobbies or other free-time activities. Each student can demonstrate the activity to the class without saying what it is. The other students must guess.

For example:
S1: *Are you ice skating?*
S2: *No, I'm not.*
S1: *Are you rollerblading?*
S2: *Yes, I am.*

Active Grammar: *Wh*- Questions

Ask students to study the grammar chart. Explain that to form a *wh*-question in the present continuous, we put the question word first and then reverse the order of subject and verb. For example: *You are going* becomes *Where are you going?* Ask students to repeat the forms in the box.

🔊 **A** **Listen to each question. Write the name of the correct person.** (CD2 • TR36)

• First, ask students to look at and talk about the picture. They should make present continuous sentences about each of the ten people: *Roberto is talking on his cell phone.*
• Have students listen to the audio while looking at the picture and reading the questions silently.
• Students listen again, this time pausing to write the correct names. Call on individuals for the answers.

👥 **B** **Working Together Ask and answer *wh*- questions about the picture.**

• Ask students to look at the picture again and make *wh*- questions about each person.
• Ask students to answer the questions in writing. Move among them, checking their answers.

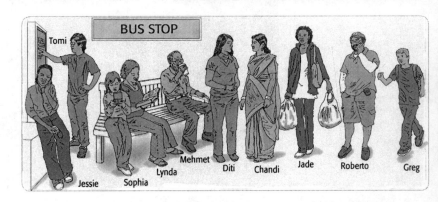

Where	am	I	going?	You're going to the bank.
What	are	you	doing?	I'm reading.
Where	is	he	standing?	He's standing at the bus stop.
What	are	they	carrying?	They are carrying their books.

🔊 **A** **Listen to each question.** Write the name of the correct person.
CD2·TR36

1.	Tomi	4.	Chandi / Diti	7.	Roberto
2.	Jessie	5.	Greg	8.	Sophia
3.	Greg	6.	Lynda	9.	Jade

👥 **B** **Working Together** **Ask and answer *wh*- questions about the picture.**

> What is Roberto doing?

> He's talking on the phone.

Teaching Tip

Point out that in casual speech we sometimes run words together and drop endings. For example: *Where are you going?* sounds like *Where 'er you goin?*

C **Complete the questions with *Who, Where, What, Why.***

1. __Where__ is everyone standing?   At the bus stop.
2. __Who__ is Roberto talking to?   His boss.
3. __Where__ is Jade standing?   Next to Roberto.
4. __What__ is Lynda doing?   She's reading.
5. __Where__ is Sophia standing?   Next to her mother.
6. __What__ is Tomi looking at?   A bus schedule.
7. __Why__ is Greg running?   Because the bus is coming.

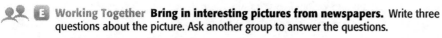

D **Write questions and answers about the picture.**

1. Where / Roberto / stand?   Where is Roberto standing?
He's standing at the bus stop.

2. What / Jade / carry?   What is Jade carrying?
She's carrying two shopping bags.

3. What / Lynda / do?   What is Lynda doing?
She's reading.

4. Who / Chandi / talk to?   Who is Chandi talking to?
She's talking to Diti.

5. Where / Mehmet / sit?   Where is Mehmet sitting?
He's sitting on the bench.

E **Working Together** **Bring in interesting pictures from newspapers.** Write three questions about the picture. Ask another group to answer the questions.

1. (Answers will vary.)
2. _____
3. _____

C **Complete the questions with *Who, Where, What, Why.***

• Warm up for this exercise by giving answers to students and asking them to come up with the correct questions.
For example:
T: *He's going to the movies.*
S: *Where is he going?*

T: *They're eating pizza.*
S: *What are they eating?*

• Ask students to match the questions and answers. Call on individuals for the correct matches.

D **Write questions and answers about the picture.**

• Create more cues for sentences using the other people in the picture: *What / Jessie / listen?*
• Ask students to come to the board and write the questions and answers. Students can correct each other.

E **Working Together Bring in interesting pictures from newspapers. Write three questions about the picture. Ask another group to answer the questions.**

Have students bring in their own photographs or use the same photographs you brought to class for the **More Action!** activity on page 117.

The Big Picture: The Train Station

Ask students to look carefully at the picture and to talk about it, making *wh-* questions and answering them. For example:

S1: *What is the ticket agent doing?*
S2: *She's selling tickets.*
S1: *Who is buying a ticket?*
S2: *Ali is buying a ticket.*

Ⓐ Circle the things that people are carrying or holding.

Ask students to take one item from the box at a time and search the picture to see if they can find it. If they can, they should circle the word in the box.

Ⓑ Listen and write each *Who* question. Then, write the answer.

(CD2 • TR37)

• Have students listen to the audio while closely at the picture for the answers.
• Students listen again, pausing to write the questions and answers. Call on individuals for the correct answers.

Ⓐ Circle the things that people are carrying or holding.

- a ticket
- a pocketbook
- an umbrella
- a briefcase
- a cup of coffee
- a cell phone
- money
- a newspaper
- a computer
- a camera
- a backpack
- a shopping bag

Ⓑ Listen and write each *Who* question. Then, write the answer.

CD2 • TR37

1. Who is running for the train?   Jason is.
2. Who is carrying a briefcase?   Fabio is.
3. Who is reading a newspaper?   Kelly is.
4. Who is talking on a cell phone?   Paul is.
5. Who is looking at the clock?   Lee is.
6. Who is drinking a cup of coffee?   Kalee and Alissa are.
7. Who is buying a ticket?   Ali is.

122 • Unit 9

Teaching Tip

Note that the question *Who is running for the train?* sounds very similar to the question *Who's running for the train?* It's okay if students use the short (contracted) form as long as they understand the difference between the two forms.

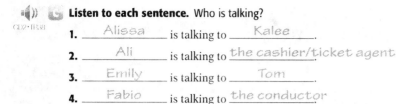 **Listen to each sentence.** Who is talking?

1. _____Alissa_____ is talking to _____Kalee_____.
2. _____Ali_____ is talking to _the cashier/ticket agent_
3. _____Emily_____ is talking to _____Tom_____.
4. _____Fabio_____ is talking to _the conductor_
5. _____Paul_____ is talking to _his wife / friend_

Ask and answer *yes/no* **questions about the picture.**

> Is Lee looking at the train?
>
> No, he isn't.

1. Lee / look at / the train?
2. Kalee and Alissa / drink coffee? Yes, they are.
3. Kalee and Alissa / sit on the bench? No, they aren't.
4. the conductor / stand on the train? No, he isn't.
5. Fabio / talk to the conductor? Yes, he is.
6. Paul / listen to music? No, he isn't.
7. Emily / get on the train? No, she isn't.
8. Paul and Kelly / talk to each other? No, they aren't.
9. Kelly / read the newspaper? Yes, she is.
10. Jason / run for the train? Yes, he is.

Listen to the story and complete the questions.

1. Where ___is Emily standing___? Next to the train.
2. What ___is Emily / she doing___? She's crying.
3. Why ___is Emily / she crying___? Because Tom is leaving.
4. Where ___is Tom / he going___? He's going to New York.
5. What ___is Tom / he saying___? "Don't cry."

Transportation · **123**

• Tell students to look at the picture again. There are several pairs of people who are talking in the picture. Ask them to find these pairs: Alissa and Kalee, the agent and Ali, etc.
• Students listen again, writing the names.

Ask and answer *yes/no* **questions about the picture.**

One student joins the words to make the question and the other student looks at the picture to find the correct answer. Do the exercise orally.

Listen to the story and complete the questions. (CD2 • TR39)

• Have students listen to the audio while looking at the picture.
• Students listen again, pausing to repeat parts of the audio in chunks: *is standing, saying goodbye, is leaving, she's a senior, he is going into, he's excited, I'll call you, I'll see you.*
• Students complete the questions in writing and then listen to the audio a third time to check their answers.

Reading: Bicycles

A Discuss. Then read.

- Point out that the words *bike* and *bicycle* mean the same thing. Ask students to compare bicycle use here and in their native countries. What percentage of the population rides bicycles? Do adults ride or only children?
- Tell students to read the passage silently, circling words they don't understand, such as *healthy, cheap, gas, bike-friendly, environment,* etc. Help them to figure out the meaning from the context.
- Call on individuals to read single paragraphs of the story. After each paragraph, ask students to ask and answer *wh-* comprehension questions. For example:
  What is good for the environment?
  Where is the bike capital of the world?

B Circle a good title for this story.

Explain that in choosing a title, it's best to look for a general theme throughout the piece of writing, not just a fact or idea that appears in only one or two sentences.

C Write the name of the city or cities.

- Tell students to look back at the reading and to underline the sentence that contains the correct answer for each question.
- Students can write the names of the cities in the blanks.

124 • Unit 9

A Discuss. Then read.

1. Do you own a bicycle? Do you ride it to school or to work?
2. What is a bike path? Are there bike paths in your city?

Travel by bicycle is healthy. It is cheap, it saves gas, and it is good for the environment. What are the most bike-friendly cities in the world?

Amsterdam, Netherlands, is the bike capital of the world. Forty percent of the people ride a bicycle to work. Amsterdam is building a parking garage for 10,000 bicycles at the train station.

In Bogotá, Colombia, people enjoy *Ciclovía*. On Sundays, people cannot ride their cars on many city streets. More than a million people bike, walk, run, and exercise on the city streets.

In the United States, Portland, Oregon, has more than 65 miles (100 km) of bike paths. These are small roads only for bicycles. It is easy to travel by bike. At school, children learn about bicycle safety. If you do not have enough money to buy a bicycle, the city will give you a bike, a helmet, and a lock.

B Circle a good title for this story.

1. Bicycles and Health   **2.** Biking in Amsterdam   **(3.** Bike-Friendly Cities**)**

C Write the name of the city or cities.

1. City streets are closed on Sundays.   *Bogotá*
2. This city teaches children about bicycle safety.   *Portland*
3. This city gives free bicycles to people.   *Portland*
4. Forty percent of the people bike to work.   *Amsterdam*
5. There are many bike paths in this city.   *Portland*
6. This city has a parking garage for bicycles.   *Amsterdam*

124 • Unit 9

A Read.

> I live in Portland, Oregon. I don't have a car.
> A car is expensive, gas is expensive, and insurance
> is expensive.
>   I go to school, and I work. I live close to school,
> so I walk to school. I live six miles from work. When
> the weather is clear, I ride my bike to work. It is easy
> and safe. It only takes me 30 minutes. My company
> has a place to park bicycles. It rains a lot in the winter.
> When it rains, I take the bus to work.
>   One problem is food shopping. I go to the supermarket
> once a week, and I have four or five bags of food. I call
> a taxi to take me home.

B Complete the sentences. (Answers will vary.)

1. I live in _____.
2. I **do / don't** have a car.
3. I live _____ miles/km from school.
4. I _____ to school.
5. I live _____ miles/km from work.
6. I _____ to work.

C Write about your daily transportation. (Answers will vary.)

D Sharing Our Stories Read your partner's story and discuss.

1. Who lives closer to school?
2. Who walks to work or to school?
3. What problem does your partner have with transportation?

WRITING NOTE
Before you hand your paper to your teacher, check the spelling. If you write on a computer, use the "Spell Check" function.

Transportation · 125

More Action!

Internet Option: Ask students to find out the most common ways Americans travel to and from work. They can enter search words, such as *commute* or *commuting*. Have students report their findings to the class.

Writing Our Stories: Getting Around

A Read.

- Ask students to scan the reading for details. Each paragraph has several details for the students to find. What are they?
- Read the passage to the students, pausing to explain any new vocabulary and to ask comprehension questions.

B Complete the sentences.

Discuss with students their situations concerning transportation to and from school and work. Then, have them answer the questions.

C Write about your daily transportation.

Show students how to turn their answers to the questions in Exercise B into a paragraph. Remind them that they should establish their main idea in the first sentence and then give details which support the main idea in the following sentences.

D Sharing Our Stories Read your partner's story and discuss.

Students should exchange papers and then ask and answer each other's questions about the paragraphs.

English in Action: At the Bus Stop

 A **Read and practice the conversations.**

- Ask students to look at the bus information on the sign. Do students have similar public transportation signs in their area? Where do the buses go?
- Ask pairs of students to read the three dialogues. Then, ask other pairs to role-play the dialogues using other bus stops listed on the sign.

 B **Working Together**
You are at the bus stop. Write a conversation. Act it out.

Have two students come to the board to write alternating lines of the dialogue. Suggest that Student A does not know how to get to the beach or train station. Student B must direct him. Use different destinations with other pairs of students.

 A **Read and practice the conversations.**

1. A: I'm going to Clinton. Which bus do I take?

   B: You want the M7.

2. A: Is this the bus to the mall?

   B: No, you want the M12.

3. A: Is this the bus to Paterson?

   B: Yes.

   A: When is the next bus?

   B: In about ten minutes.

 B Working Together **You are at the bus stop.** Write a conversation. Act it out.

A: (Answers will vary.) _____

B: _____

A: _____

B: _____

126 · Unit 9

More Action!

Explain that when taking a taxi, you should have a specific destination in mind. It is common for customers to tip their taxi driver 10 to 15% of the amount on the meter. Write the dialogue below on the board and have students role-play, substituting other routes.

A: *Excuse me, are you free?*
B: *Sure. Hop in. Where to?*
A: *1057 Charles Street. Please take College Avenue and turn left on Main Street. Charles is the next right.*
B: *You got it!*

Look at the bus schedule and complete the information.

Bus 12 Newton to Bayside	Broad St. & 2nd Street	Broad Street & 25th Street	Davis Mall	Canal Street & Pine Ave.	Bayside Hospital
	7:00	7:11	7:19	7:25	7:40
	7:30	7:41	7:49	7:55	8:08
	8:00	8:11	8:19	8:25	8:40
	8:30	8:41	8:49	8:55	9:08
	9:00	9:11	9:19	9:25	9:40
	10:00	10:11	10:19	10:25	10:48
	11:00	11:11	11:19	11:25	11:48
	12:00	12:11	12:19	12:25	12:48
	1:00	1:11	1:19	1:25	1:48
	2:00	2:11	2:19	2:25	2:48
	3:00	3:11	3:19	3:25	3:48
	3:34	3:45	3:53	3:59	4:12
	5:15	5:26	5:36	5:42	5:55
	5:30	5:41	5:51	5:57	6:10
	6:00	6:11	6:19	6:25	6:40
	7:00	7:11	7:19	7:25	7:40
	9:00	9:11	9:19	9:25	9:40

1. The first bus at Broad Street and 2nd Street is at _7:00 A.M._

2. The 7:00 A.M. bus from Broad Street and 2nd Street arrives at Bayside Hospital at _7:40 A.M._.

3. It takes ___19___ minutes to go from Broad Street and 2nd Street to the Davis Mall.

4. It's 7:20 A.M. You are at Broad and 2nd Street. The next bus is at _7:30 A.M._

5. It's 9:00 A.M. You are at the Davis Mall. The next bus is at _9:19 A.M._

6. Brian lives in Newton near 2nd Street and he works at the Davis Mall. Work begins at 9:00 A.M. He gets the bus at _8:30 A.M._

7. Nellie lives near Canal Street. Her mother is in Bayside Hospital. She wants to visit her at 4:00 P.M. She is going to take the bus at _3:25 P.M._

8. The last bus from the Davis Mall is at _9:19 P.M._

Working Together With a partner, write two sentences about the bus schedule. Use the same format as Exercise C. One piece of information is missing. Then, ask another group to complete your sentences.
(Answers will vary.)

 Look at the bus schedule and complete the information.

- Ask students to study the bus schedule. Point out that the times listed are A.M. and P.M.
- Do a warm up to the exercise by asking questions, such as: *I'm at Pine Avenue, and I want to get to Bayside Hospital by 9 P.M. What time should I catch the bus?*
- Ask students to write the answers to the exercise and then to read them aloud and correct each other.

Working Together With a partner, write two sentences about the bus schedule. Use the same format as Exercise C. One piece of information is missing. Then, ask another group to complete your sentences.

First, form the class into even-numbered groups. Move among the various groups as pairs of students write the two statements. When they're ready, say: *Change groups.* Check answers in the new groups and then repeat the exercise with other pairs.

More Action!

Ask students to bring real bus or subway schedules from their areas to class. Ask pairs of students to come to the front of the room. Role-play this dialogue, adapting it as necessary.

S1: *Excuse me. Do you have a schedule? I don't know what bus/train to take from _____ to _____.*

S2: *Hmm, let's see. Take the _____ bus/train at _____ A.M/PM.*

Clothing and Weather

Dictionary: Clothing and Colors

Ask students to look at the pictures of clothing. Are the styles similar to what they like to wear? Why or why not? Are there other items not pictured here that they or members of their families often wear? What are they?

 A **Listen and repeat.**
(CD2 • TR40)

• Have students look at the pictures and listen to the audio for items 1-18 on page 128.
• Students listen again, this time repeating the words for clothing.
• Ask students to close their books. Point to a student's (or your own) visible article of clothing and ask a student to identify the item, such as *jacket*. Continue this with the other items.

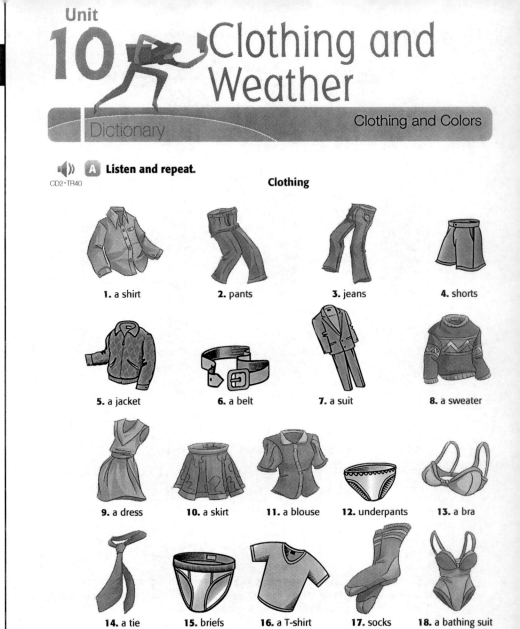

Unit

10 Clothing and Weather

Dictionary   Clothing and Colors

 A Listen and repeat.
CD2 • TR40

Clothing

1. a shirt   2. pants   3. jeans   4. shorts

5. a jacket   6. a belt   7. a suit   8. a sweater

9. a dress   10. a skirt   11. a blouse   12. underpants   13. a bra

14. a tie   15. briefs   16. a T-shirt   17. socks   18. a bathing suit

128 • Unit 10

Teaching Tips

• Ask students to categorize the articles of clothing. Which can be worn by men and which by women? By both?
• Ask students to memorize the spelling of the items for a spelling bee later in the unit.

19. sneakers   **20.** sandals   **21.** shoes   **22.** boots

23. a coat   **24.** a hat   **25.** a cap   **26.** gloves

Colors

1. a red cap   **2.** an orange cap   **3.** a blue cap   **4.** a white cap   **5.** a green cap

6. a black cap   **7.** a purple cap   **8.** a brown cap   **9.** a yellow cap   **10.** a beige cap

Sizes

1. extra small (XS)   **2.** small (S)   **3.** medium (M)   **4.** large (L)   **5.** extra large (XL)

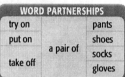

WORD PARTNERSHIPS		
try on		pants
put on	a pair of	shoes
		socks
take off		gloves

Clothing and Weather • **129**

- Have students listen to the audio for the items on 129.
- Students listen again, this time repeating the words for clothing.
- Ask students to close their books. Point to a student's (or your own) article of clothing and ask a student to identify the item, such as *shoes*. Continue this with the other items.

Colors

- Have students listen to and repeat after the audio.
- Point out an article of clothing and ask students to say both color and name:
  T: *#20*
  S: *brown sandals*

Sizes

- Have students listen to and repeat after the audio.
- Call out the number of a T-shirt and ask the students to tell the size.

Word Partnerships

Ask students to take the two-word verbs in the box and make sentences with them using the items of clothing on pages 128 and 129.

More Action!

Have students work in pairs. Student A should choose an item from pages 128 or 129. Encourage students to vary the size and color of the item they select.
Student B must guess what item of clothing Student A has in his or her mind, along with its color and size.
Student B can ask a variety of *yes/no* questions, such as:

    Is it for a woman?
    Is it in a pair?
    Is it blue?
    Is it medium?

Through elimination, Student B can arrive at the correct article of clothing. Then, have students switch roles and repeat the activity.

Word Builder

Word Builder

Complete.

- Discuss with students what kinds of clothing they wear in summer versus winter or in the in-between seasons of spring and fall.
- Ask them to do the exercise, organizing the clothing on pages 128 and 129 into seasonal groups.

Cross out the word that doesn't belong.

Before doing the exercise, make sure that students understand that the idea is to work out what three of the items have in common and then eliminate the one that doesn't belong. For example: *Pants, jeans,* and *shorts* are items that are worn below the waist. *T-shirt* doesn't belong.

Look at your classmates. Ask and answer the questions.

- Encourage students to talk about the clothes their classmates are wearing. Depending on the time of year, you may need to teach additional vocabulary.
- Ask students to do the exercise orally.

Discuss.

Move among the students as they talk about their clothing preferences. Answer the questions about your own preferences.

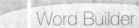

Word Builder

A **Complete.** (Answers may vary.)

Clothes for hot weather		Clothes for cold weather	
shorts	sandals	boots	jacket
T-shirts	sneakers	pants	sweater
bathing suit	cap	jeans	coat

B **Cross out the word that doesn't belong.**

1. pants, jeans, shorts, ~~T-shirt~~
2. shirt, blouse, T-shirt, ~~sandals~~
3. sneakers, sandals, ~~hat~~, shoes
4. coat, hat, gloves, ~~bathing suit~~

5. blouse, ~~tie~~, skirt, dress
6. ~~sweater~~, briefs, underpants, bra
7. jacket, sweater, coat, ~~shorts~~

> Who is wearing glasses?
> Marc is.
> No one is.

C **Look at your classmates.** Ask and answer the questions.

1. Who is wearing sneakers?
2. Who is wearing a sweater?
3. Who is wearing a dress?
4. Who is wearing a white shirt?

5. Who is wearing a tie?
6. Who is wearing sandals?
7. Who is wearing black pants?
8. Who is wearing jeans?

D **Discuss.** (Answers will vary.)

1. How many pairs of shoes do you have?
2. How many pairs of jeans do you have?
3. What's your favorite color for clothes?
4. What do you usually wear to school?
5. What do you usually wear to work?
6. Do you wear a uniform at work?
7. What are you wearing now?

a uniform

Teaching Tip

Explain that some places, such as restaurants or offices, have guidelines (or dress codes) for what employees can wear. Give some examples of accepted or prohibited clothing. Can the class think of others?

Active Grammar

A What is Amy wearing?

A   B   C

> I'm **wearing** a sweater.
> She's **wearing** jeans.
> They're **wearing** hats.

B Listen. What is Amy wearing? Write the letter of the correct picture.

CD2·TR41

1. B   3. C   5. A   7. A   9. B
2. A   4. B   6. C   8. C   10. B

C Pronunciation: Stress Listen for the stress. Put an accent mark over the stressed words.

CD2·TR42

1. Is Amy wearing white pants?   No, she's wearing black pants.
2. Is Amy wearing a blue jacket?   No, she's wearing a green jacket.
3. Is Amy wearing a red dress?   No, she's wearing a blue dress.
4. Is Amy wearing a blue belt?   No, she's wearing a white belt.
5. Is Amy wearing brown sandals?   No, she's wearing white sandals.
6. Is Amy wearing black shorts?   No, she's wearing beige shorts.

D Working Together Ask and answer questions about your classmates' clothes.

> Is Carlos wearing a green shirt?

> No, he's wearing a <u>blue</u> shirt.

(Answers will vary.)

Clothing and Weather · **131**

Active Grammar: Present Continuous Tense Review

A What is Amy wearing?

Ask students to look at the three pictures of Amy. Have pairs of students ask and answer *yes/no* questions about what she's wearing. For example:
S1: *In picture A, is she wearing a bathing suit?*
S2: *No, she isn't.*

B Listen. What is Amy wearing? Write the letter of the correct picture. (CD2 • TR41)

• Have students listen to the audio while looking at the three pictures.
• Students listen again, pausing to write the correct letters. Call on individuals for the answers.

C Pronunciation: Stress Listen for the stress. Put an accent mark over the stressed words. (CD2 • TR42)

• Explain that stress on a word means that we are emphasizing it or giving it extra attention. Give some examples.
• Ask students to put in the accent marks. Then, ask them to read their answers with correct stress.

D Working Together Ask and answer the questions about your classmates' clothes.

Ask students to look at the dialogue in the speech balloons and use it as a model.

Dictionary: The Weather

🔊 **A** **Listen and repeat.**
(CD2 • TR43)

• Have students listen to the audio while they look at the pictures.
• Students listen again, repeating the descriptions of weather.

Seasons

• Students listen to the audio for the four seasons, pointing to each of the pictures.
• Students listen again, repeating the words.

🔊 **A** **Listen and repeat.**
CD2•TR43

Weather

1. It's sunny.

2. It's cloudy.

3. It's windy.

4. It's raining.

5. It's snowing.

6. It's foggy.

7. It's hot.

8. It's warm.

9. It's cool.

10. It's cold.

Seasons

11. spring

12. summer

13. fall

14. winter

More Action!

Have a spelling bee. Divide the class into two teams. Using words from pages 128, 129, and 132, give a student from Team A a word to spell. If he or she spells it correctly, move on and give a new word to a student from Team B. When a student from either team misspells a word, he or she is out and the word passes to the other team. The team with the most players still standing at the end of the game wins.

More Action!

Bring to class a recording of Vivaldi's *The Four Seasons*. Ask students to guess the season from the mood of the music.

A Listen to the weather. Find the city and write the temperature on the map.

CD2·TR44

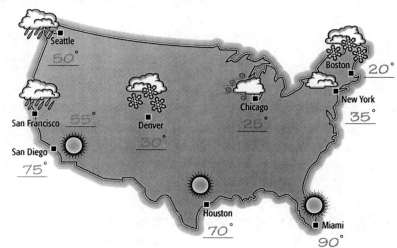

B Write about the weather in each city. Use words from the box.

| cold | cloudy | cool | hot | raining | snowing | sunny | warm | windy |

1. It's ___cold___ and ___snowing___ in Boston.
2. It's ___cloudy___ and ___cold___ in New York.
3. It's ___sunny___ and ___hot___ in Miami.
4. It's ___sunny___ and ___warm___ in Houston.
5. It's ___warm___ and ___sunny___ in San Diego.
6. It's ___raining___ and ___cool___ in San Francisco.
7. It's ___raining___ in Seattle.
8. It's ___snowing___ in Denver.
9. It's ___cloudy___, ___cold___, and ___windy___ in Chicago.

C What is the weather in your area today? (Answers will vary.)

Clothing and Weather · **133**

Word Builder

A Listen to the weather. Find the city and write the temperature on the map. (CD2•TR44)

• Ask students to look at the map and talk about the weather symbols. What does each one mean?

• Students listen to the audio, pointing to the cities as they are mentioned.

• Students listen again, pausing to write the temperatures on the map.

B Write about the weather in each city. Use words from the box.

• Ask students to look again at the symbols on the weather map.

• Ask them to write the weather in the exercise. Call on individuals for the correct answers.

C What is the weather in your area today?

Ask students to talk about the weather today including the temperature, precipitation (if any), wind, and clouds. Is the weather good? Can they forecast what the weather will be tomorrow?

More Action!

Point out the drawing of the Fahrenheit and Celsius thermometer. Remind students that 32 degrees Fahrenheit is 0 degrees Celsius. Ask: *What's a good temperature for a hot bath? For beach weather? For room temperature?*

Clothing for Different Seasons

A **Complete the sentences with *a, an,* or *X* (for no article).**

- Point out that the word *pair* is singular so it takes the article *a. An* is used before an adjective or before a noun that begins with a vowel (*a, e, i, o, u,* or sometimes *y*).
- Ask students to do the exercise. Have students aloud their answers.

B **Work with a partner. Answer the questions.**

Ask students to look at and talk about the two photos. Then, they can answer the questions.

C **Working Together Write a description of a classmate's clothes. Read the description to the class. The other students will guess the correct student.**

Pairs of students must quietly select the student they intend to write about. They should write only about types of clothing and colors, not about size. Then, they can read their descriptions to the class.

A **Complete the sentences with *a, an,* or *X* (for no article).**

1. He's wearing <u>a</u> pair of jeans.
2. He's wearing <u>an</u> orange T-shirt.
3. He's wearing <u>X</u> sneakers.
4. He's wearing <u>a</u> belt.
5. He's wearing <u>X</u> briefs.
6. She's buying <u>a</u> dress.
7. She's buying <u>X</u> gloves.
8. She's buying <u>a</u> pair of sandals.
9. She's buying <u>an</u> extra large sweater.
10. She's buying <u>a</u> coat.

> a shirt
> a pair of shorts
> an old belt
> jeans

B **Work with a partner.** Look at the pictures. Answer the questions.

(Answers may vary)

1. What season is it?
   It's <u>spring or summer</u>.
2. What's the weather?
   It's <u>sunny</u>.
3. What is she wearing? <u>She's wearing a shirt, gloves, and a hat</u>.

4. What season is it?
   It's <u>fall or winter</u>.
5. What's the weather?
   It's <u>raining</u>.
6. What is he wearing? <u>He's wearing a shirt, a suit, and a tie</u>.

C Working Together **Write a description of a classmate's clothes.** Read the description to the class. The other students will guess the correct student.

134 · Unit 10

Teaching Tip

When doing pair work, it's sometimes useful to pair a more fluent student with a less fluent student. The stronger student can help the weaker student and help give him or her a sense of confidence. This can also give the stronger student the chance to explain and clarify something that he or she has learned. In this way, both partners benefit.

 Josh needs a new pair of shoes. Listen to the story and number the pictures from 1 to 8.

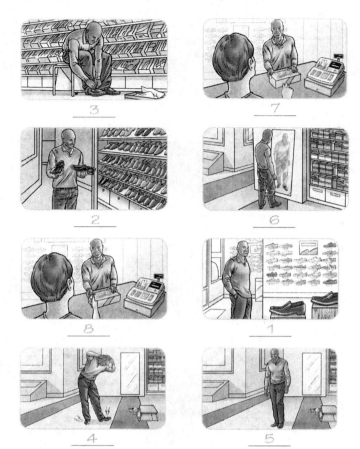

B Working Together **Retell the story in your own words.** What is happening in each picture?
(Answers will vary.)

Josh is walking into a shoe store.

C Working Together **One student will act out the story of Josh buying a new pair of shoes.** Another student will describe the actions.
(Answers will vary.)

Clothing and Weather · **135**

New Shoes

A **Josh needs a new pair of shoes. Listen to the story and number the pictures from 1 to 8.**
(CD2 · TR45)

• Ask students to listen to the audio without looking at the pictures in their books. Ask them to retell the story as they remember it.

• Have students listen again, this time looking at the pictures in their books and numbering them in the correct order.

• Students listen one last time, checking the order of the pictures.

B **Working Together Retell the story in your own words. What is happening in each picture?**

Group students in pairs. One of the students tells the story and the other makes corrections or suggestions. Then, the student retells the story to the class.

C **Working Together One student will act out the story of Josh buying a new pair of shoes. Another student will describe the actions.**

Have students work with their partner from the previous exercise (Exercise B). One student can act out the story while the other student narrates it.

Active Grammar:
How much Questions

Point out the grammar note and explain that we use *how much* to ask the price of something. Also remind students that *this* refers to a single item and *these* refers to more than one.

Ⓐ Complete.

• Ask students to write the answers to the exercise, choosing *is* or *are*, *this* or *these*, and *it's* or *they're*.
• Have students exchange papers with a partner and correct each other's answers.

👥 Ⓑ Working Together
Work with a partner. Put a price on each tag. Then, ask and answer questions about the prices.

• Ask students to look at the advertisement. How much should the advertised items cost? They should discuss the average price for a new pair of jeans, a belt, etc. Once they've decided, they should write the prices on the tags.
• Pairs of students should role-play the clerk/customer conversation from the speech bubbles for each item.

| How much **is** this hat? | **It's** $12.00. |
| How much **are** these socks? | **They're** $5.00. |

Ⓐ Complete.

1. How much __is__ __this__ hat? __It's__ $15.
2. How much __are__ __these__ sandals? __They're__ $20.
3. How much __is__ __this__ skirt? __It's__ $28.
4. How much __are__ __these__ gloves? __They're__ $17.
5. How much __are__ __these__ briefs? __They're__ $7.
6. How much __is__ __this__ sweater? __It's__ $30.
7. How much __is__ __this__ tie? __It's__ $17.
8. How much __are__ __these__ shorts? __They're__ $22.

 Ⓑ **Working Together** **Work with a partner.** Put a price on each tag. Then, ask and answer questions about the prices. *(Answers will vary.)*

| How much is this belt? | $16.00. | How much are these shoes? | They're $37.00. |

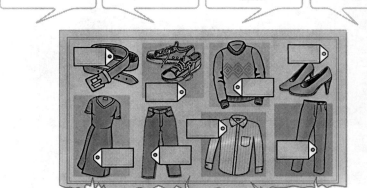

136 · Unit 10

More Action!

Ask students to bring clothing ads from newspapers or magazines to class. Each student should choose one item but not tell the class how much it costs. The other students must take turns guessing the prices. Round off prices to the nearest dollar. The correct answer is the one that comes closest to the price without going above it.

A Listen and complete the conversation.

CD2·TR46

Clerk: Hello. Can I help you?

Customer: Yes. I'm looking for a shirt .

Clerk: What size?

Customer: Medium .

Clerk: The shirts are here.

Customer: I like this shirt . How much is it ?

Clerk: It's $50. But today it's on sale for $25.

Customer: Great. I'll take it.

B Listen and complete the conversation.

CD2·TR47

Clerk: Hello. Can I help you?

Customer: Yes. I'm looking for a pair of gloves .

Clerk: What size?

Customer: Extra large .

Clerk: Here they are.

Customer: I like these gloves . How much are they ?

Clerk: They're usually $30. But today they're on sale for $19.

Customer: Great. I'll take them.

C Working Together Write a conversation between a clerk and a customer. Then, act it out. (Answers will vary.)

Clothing and Weather · 137

The Clothing Store

A Listen and complete the conversation.

(CD2 • TR46)

- Students should listen to the conversation while looking at their books.
- They should listen a second time, pausing to fill in the blanks.
- Students listen a third time, checking their answers.

B Listen and complete the conversation.

(CD2 • TR47)

- Students should listen to the conversation while looking at their books.
- They should listen a second time, pausing to fill in the blanks.
- Students listen a third time, checking their answers.

C Working Together Write a conversation between a clerk and a customer. Then, act it out.

Group students into pairs. One student should be the clerk and the other should be the customer. They should choose an item of clothing from the ad on page 136. In addition to the listed price, they should make up a sale price. They should also choose the customer's way of paying: cash, check, or credit card. Each pair can rehearse the conversation quietly to themselves before acting it out in front of the class.

The Big Picture: The Clothing Store

Ask students to look at the picture and discuss it. Ask:
Who are these people?
Where are they?
What are they doing?
What season is it?
What is she trying on?
What are they saying to each other?

  Listen. Circle the clothes that Monica is going to buy. (CD2•TR48)

• Have students listen while looking at the picture and the words in the box.
• Students listen again, this time pausing to circle the words for clothing Monica is going to buy.
• Students listen a third time, checking their answers.

 Listen again and circle *True* or *False*. (CD2•TR48)

• Ask students to read the statements silently. They may want to hear the audio again before choosing *True* or *False*.
• Ask them to circle the answers. Call on individuals for answers and make corrections.

The Big Picture

 Listen. Circle the clothes that Monica is going to buy.
CD2•TR48

coat	gloves	sneakers	hat
dress	skirt	sweater	socks

 Listen again and circle *True* or *False*.
CD2•TR48

1. Monica is in the shoe store.   True   (False)
2. Monica is shopping with her mother.   True   (False)
3. It's cold now.   (True)   False
4. Monica likes the coat she is trying on.   True   (False)
5. Monica is going to spend a lot of money today.   (True)   False
6. Monica needs winter clothing.   (True)   False
7. Monica was in the United States last winter.   True   (False)
8. It's hot all year in Boston.   True   (False)

138 · Unit 10

More Action!

Ask students to visit a clothing store in the area and report back to the class on prices, styles, and colors of items they tried on. (They don't need to buy anything.)

Teaching Tip

Explain that although it's all right for a clothing store clerk to ask what size clothing you wear, it's not polite to ask someone else unless you know the person well.

Complete the sentences.

Boston	cold	clothing store	May	~~Cuba~~
winter	snow	temperature	summer	hot

1. Monica is from _____ Cuba _____.

2. She came to the United States in _____ May _____.

3. She lives in _____ Boston _____.

4. In Boston, it is hot in the _____ summer _____.

5. In Boston, it is cold in the _____ winter _____.

6. In January, it is going to _____ snow _____.

7. In Cuba, the weather is _____ hot _____ all year.

8. Right now, Monica is in a _____ clothing store _____.

9. The _____ temperature _____ is 30°.

10. It's very _____ cold _____ outside now.

 Listen and complete the conversations.

1. **Monica:** I don't like this _____ weather _____. It's _____ too _____ cold.

   Lydia: It's only December. It _____ isn't _____ cold yet. Wait until January!

2. **Lydia:** Here's a nice coat. _____ Try it on _____.

   Monica: I _____ don't like _____ the color. Do they have a _____ red coat _____ or a _____ blue _____ coat?

3. **Monica:** Gloves? _____ Why _____ do I need gloves?

   Lydia: _____ Try on _____ these gloves. Believe me. You need gloves.

4. **Monica:** How do you like _____ this coat _____?

   Lydia: It doesn't fit you. It's _____ too big _____.

5. **Monica:** Do you like _____ this sweater _____?

   Lydia: Yes, it looks _____ good _____ on you.

Working Together **Write a conversation between Monica and her sister in the clothing store.** Act out your conversation.
(Answers will vary.)

Clothing and Weather • 139

Teaching Tip

Remind students again that in a dictation, it's helpful to repeat the dictated word or words silently before writing them.

Complete the sentences.

• Do the exercise orally first, reviewing the facts of the situation: where Monica is from, where she's living now, etc.

• Ask students to write in the answers, exchange papers with a partner, and check each other's answers.

Listen and complete the conversations.
(CD2 • TR49)

• Have students listen to the audio while looking at the incomplete conversation in their books.

• Students listen again, this time pausing to write in the answers.

• They listen a third time, checking their answers against the audio.

Working Together
Write a conversation between Monica and her sister in the clothing store. Act out your conversations.

To help students organize their ideas in a logical sequence, suggest that they write several sentences on a scrap of paper and then place the ideas in an order that makes sense to them. The simplest way to do this is to organize according to time: *What happened first? What happened second? What happened third?*

Reading:
The Clothing Catalog

A Discuss.

Talk about clothing catalogs that come in the mail (or that you can find online). How many times a year are they mailed out? Is there one for every season? More than one? Do you like or dislike getting them?

B Read these ads from a catalog.

Ask students to look at the ads. Can they guess the meaning of new vocabulary from the context?

C Complete the information.

• Ask students to underline the words in the ads that will help them complete the information.
• Ask them to complete the information and call on individuals for the correct answers.

 Reading

A Discuss.

1. Which clothing catalogs do you receive in the mail?

2. Did you ever order anything from a catalog? Did you like the item?

B Read these ads from a catalog.

C Complete the information.

1. The raincoat is $ _69.00_ .

2. The raincoat comes in two colors, beige and _black_ .

3. You **can** / can't wash the jeans.

4. The sweater is **cotton** / **wool** .

5. You can order the sweater in four sizes: _S_ , _M_ , _L_ , and _XL_ .

6. The sweater is $ _45.00_

7. The order number for the jeans is _7701-6232_ .

8. The jeans have _two_ pockets.

9. The jeans are $ _39.00_ .

10. If you want to order something from this catalog, call _800-555-5555_ .

140 · Unit 10

More Action!

Tell students to bring to class copies of clothing catalogs they've received in the mail. (Or use the catalog page on 140.) Each student should pick several items of clothing he or she wants to buy. Provide help for any new vocabulary. Have students work with a partner and role-play placing an order by phone. Use this conversation as a model:

S1: *How may I help you?*
S2: *I want to place an order.*
S1: *What's the number of the first item?*
S2: *G596742.*
S1: *That's the winter jacket, right? What size and color?*
S2: *Medium and brown, please.*
S1: *Will there be anything else?*
S2: *No, thank you.*

A Read.

Spring in Virginia

I live in Virginia. We have four seasons.
The summer is long and hot, and the
winter is mild. It doesn't snow very often.
Right now, it is spring, my favorite season. The days are warm,
and the nights are cool. I usually wear jeans and a shirt.
I am from Puerto Rico. The climate is hot and
tropical. It is sunny and hot almost every
day. The fall is hurricane season, and we
sometimes have bad storms with heavy
wind and rain. But most of the time, the
weather is beautiful.

Virginia *Atlantic Ocean*
Puerto Rico

B Complete the sentences. (Answers will vary.)

I live in _____. We have _____ seasons.

My favorite season is _____ because _____.

I am from _____. We have _____ seasons.

The weather is _____.

C Write about the weather in your area. What is your favorite season? Why? How is the weather in your country? (Answers will vary.)

D Sharing Our Stories Read your partner's story and complete the sentences.

1. My partner is from _____.

2. My partner's country has _____ seasons.

3. My partner's favorite season is _____.

4. She / He **likes / doesn't like** the weather in this country.

> **WRITING NOTE**
> The names of states and countries begin with a capital letter.
> Example: Virginia

Clothing and Weather • 141

Writing Our Stories: Weather

A Read.

- Ask students to scan the reading for factual information. *Where does he live? What's the weather like? What does he wear? Where's he from?*
- Now ask students to read the passage to themselves, underlining anything they don't understand.
- Ask students to work in pairs, asking and answering questions about the reading.

B Complete the sentences.

Have students complete the sentences using information about themselves, where they live now, and where they are from.

C Write about the weather in your area. What is your favorite season? Why? How is the weather in your country?

Tell students to use the reading as a model for their compositions. They can adapt sentences, substituting their own information.

D Sharing Our Stories Read your partner's story and complete the sentences.

After pairs of students have exchanged papers and read each other's stories, students should come to the front of the room one by one and tell the class about their partner.

Teaching Tip

Try to make students feel comfortable in front of the class. Allow them to use notes, if they wish.

English in Action: Returning an Item to the Store

A **Discuss the store signs.**

Ask students if they've ever seen these signs before. What do they mean? Have they ever returned anything to a store? Did they have a receipt? Did the store refund their money or exchange the item(s)?

B **Listen. Then, act out the conversations with a partner.** (CD2 • TR50)

• Ask students to look at the receipt. What was purchased? How much did it cost? How much was the tax? What was the total?
• Students listen to **Conversation 1** while looking at it in their books.
• Students listen again, pausing to repeat each line.
• They listen a third time but this time, call on individuals to provide the correct line before he/she hears it. Then, play the actual line.
• Ask pairs of students to role-play the conversation from memory.
• Follow the same process with **Conversation 2.**

C **Working Together**
Act out a conversation between a clerk and a customer. The customer wants to return a pair of jeans to the store.

A **Discuss the store signs.**

| No returns without store receipt. | No returns. Exchanges only. |

 B **Listen.** Then, act out the conversations with a partner.
(CD2 • TR50)

Conversation 1

Clerk: Can I help you?

Customer: Yes, I want to return this sweater.

Clerk: Do you have the receipt?

Customer: Yes, here it is.

Clerk: Let's see. The sweater was $29.

Customer: With tax, it was $30.45.

Clerk: Do you want to exchange the sweater?

Customer: No, I'd like a refund.

Clerk: Okay. No problem.

Conversation 2

Clerk: Can I help you?

Customer: Yes, I want to return this sweater.

Clerk: Do you have the receipt?

Customer: No, I don't.

Clerk: Sorry. There are no returns without the store receipt.

PATEL'S CLOTHING STORE	
Wool Sweater	$29.00
State Sales Tax	$1.45
TOTAL	$30.45

Don't throw away your receipts. Keep your receipts in a small box or an envelope.

Working Together **Act out a conversation between a clerk and a customer.**
The customer wants to return a pair of jeans to the store. *(Answers will vary.)*

142 • Unit 10

Teaching Tip

Have students bring props to use during conversations, such as a pair of jeans. Make a receipt for the students to use in the conversation in Exercise C.

Working Together **Answer the questions.**

1. Monica is buying a blue coat for $75. Her hat is $15, and her gloves are $20. What is the total? $110

2. Monica is buying a hat for her sister. It's $17. Monica is giving the clerk $20. How much is her change? $3

3. Monica is buying a pair of gloves. They are $23. She is giving the clerk $50. How much is her change? $27

4. Monica likes a blue sweater. It is $60, but it's on sale for 50% off. How much is the sweater? $30

5. Monica is trying on a red dress. It's $40. All the dresses in the store are 10% off today. How much is the dress? $36

Every item in the store is 50% off today. Write the new price.

$15

$32.50

$30

$22.50

$40

$7.50

Clothing and Weather · 143

Working Together Answer the questions.

Ask students to do the problems at the board. They should figure the math aloud. For example (#1): *Five and five and zero make ten. Write the zero and carry the one. Seven and one make eight and one and two make eleven. So the total is $110.*

Every item in the store is 50% off today. Write the new price.

Ask students how to find a percentage of a number. Have a volunteer demonstrate on the board. Make sure they understand that they must *multiply* the old price by the percentage with a *decimal point*. Then, they must *subtract* the amount from the old price and that's the sale price. Since all these prices are 50% off, they'll get the right answer even if they skip the last step. Call on individuals to say the new sales prices.

More Action!

Internet Option: Tell students they have $1,000 to spend on new clothing. Ask them to make a plan for spending the money. They do not have to spend every penny, but they must buy at least seven items. One or more items should be on sale. They can search online catalogs and choose the clothing they want. They should estimate the sales tax for each item. They should also record the color of each item and the size (if they are comfortable doing so). When they've completed their plans, they can tell the class about their choices.

Dictionary:
Everyday Activities

  A **Listen and repeat.**

(CD3 • TR1)

- Have students listen to the audio while looking at the corresponding pictures.
- Students listen again, pausing to repeat the phrases.
- Call out a number and have students say the correct phrases.
- Students point to the appropriate pictures as you say the phrases.

Unit 11 Daily Life

Dictionary

Everyday Activities

  A **Listen and repeat.**

CD3·TR1

1. get up

2. take a shower

3. get dressed

4. eat breakfast

5. leave the house

6. work

7. go to school

8. get home

9. cook dinner

10. watch TV

11. check e-mail

12. go to bed

144 • Unit 11

More Action!

Ask students to mime actions taken from the pictures on this page. The other students can try to guess the action. A student who guesses correctly takes the place of the previous student and mimes a new action.

Teaching Tip

To introduce this unit, talk about a typical day for you. What do you usually do in the morning, afternoon, and evening? What do you like to do? What don't you like to do?

A **Look at the dictionary pictures and number the sentences in order.**

_____5_____ **a.** Eric leaves the house at 8:00.

_____1_____ **b.** Eric gets up at 7:00.

_____3_____ **c.** After he takes a shower, he gets dressed.

_____2_____ **d.** First, he takes a shower.

_____6_____ **e.** Eric walks to work.

_____4_____ **f.** Eric eats breakfast at 7:30.

B (Circle) *True* or *False* about *your* schedule. (Answers will vary.)

1. I get up very early.	True	False	
2. I take a shower in the morning.	True	False	
3. I eat breakfast every day.	True	False	
4. I work full time.	True	False	
5. I eat lunch at home.	True	False	
6. I study for two hours every day.	True	False	
7. I cook dinner.	True	False	
8. I eat dinner with my family.	True	False	
9. I watch TV in the evening.	True	False	
10. I go to bed early.	True	False	

> **WORD PARTNERSHIPS**
>
> take — a break / a shower / a walk / a nap

C **Working Together** **What is your routine?** Number the activities below. Then, tell your partner about your day. Use the words *first, then,* and *after that.*

_____ eat breakfast
_____ go to bed
_____ do my homework

_____ eat dinner
_____ take a shower
_____ get up
_____ get dressed

_____ go to work
_____ watch TV
_____ go to school
_____ eat lunch

(Answers will vary.)

Word Builder

A **Look at the dictionary pictures and number the sentences in order.**

• Ask students to study the pictures on page 144 in order.

• Do the exercise orally, asking students to re-order the sentences in relation to the pictures.

B **Circle *True* or *False* about *your* schedule.**

• Ask students to talk about their daily schedules.

• Tell them to do the exercise and then to tell the class which statements are true and false for themselves.

Word Partnerships

Point out the phrases in the box and ask students to repeat them after you. Then, ask students to work in pairs, asking and answering questions with the phrases. For example: *When do you take a break?*

C **Working Together What is your routine? Number the activities below. Then, tell your partner about your day. Use the words *first, then,* and *after that.***

After students have completed the exercise, ask them to go back and complete the exercise as if they were another member of their family.

Dictionary: Time

  Listen and repeat.

(CD3 • TR2)

• Have students listen to the audio while looking at the corresponding clocks.

• Students listen again, repeating each time.

• Ask students to cover the written times. Point to individual clocks. Call on students for the correct times.

 Write the correct time.

Do the exercise orally. Once students have completed it, point out that *nine fifteen* can also be *quarter past nine. Six thirty* can also be *half past six. Seven forty-five* can be *quarter to eight.*

 Listen and show the time on the clocks.

(CD3 • TR3)

• Have students listen to the audio and repeat the times they hear.

• Have them listen a second time, drawing the hands on the clocks.

   **Listen and repeat.**

CD3 • TR2

a. two o'clock
2:00

b. two oh-five
2:05

c. two ten
2:10

d. two fifteen
2:15

e. two thirty
2:30

f. two forty
2:40

g. two forty-five
2:45

h. two fifty
2:50

i. two fifty-five
2:55

j. three o'clock
3:00

 Write the correct time.

a. _six thirty_   **b.** _nine fifteen_   **c.** _twelve forty_   **d.** _seven forty-five_

 Listen and show the time on the clocks.

CD3 • TR3

a.   **b.**   **c.**   **d.**

e.   **f.**   **g.**   **h.**

146 • Unit 11

More Action!

In some cultures, the beginning times of *morning, afternoon, evening,* and *night* differ from here. For example: 5 P.M. may be considered *afternoon.* Ask students to discuss and compare.

Teaching Tip

Explain that we often omit *o'clock* when telling time, and we never use it with half or quarter hours. For example, we never say *two thirty o'clock.*

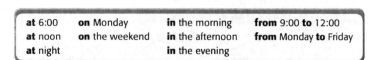
at 6:00	**on** Monday	**in** the morning	**from** 9:00 **to** 12:00
at noon	**on** the weekend	**in** the afternoon	**from** Monday **to** Friday
at night		**in** the evening	

A **Complete the sentences with the correct preposition.**

1. Henry gets up ___*at*___ 6:00.

2. Laura takes a shower ___*in*___ the evening.

3. Clara works ___*from*___ 9:00 ___*to*___ 5:00.

4. Allan goes to the supermarket ___*on*___ Friday.

5. We eat dinner ___*at*___ 7:00.

6. I take a break ___*in*___ the morning and ___*in*___ the afternoon.

7. I watch TV ___*at*___ night.

8. The baby takes a nap ___*in*___ the afternoon.

9. Edwin plays soccer ___*on*___ the weekend.

10. The children eat breakfast ___*at*___ 7:00.

11. The school bus comes ___*at*___ 7:30.

12. Daisy studies ___*from*___ 8:00 ___*to*___ 10:00.

B **Ask and answer these questions.** Use the correct preposition of time.

What time do you get up?	I get up at 7 o'clock.	*(Answers will vary.)*

1. What time do you get up?

2. When do you eat breakfast?

3. When do you leave your house?

4. What hours do you work?

5. When do you do your homework?

6. When do you go to the supermarket?

7. When do you do the laundry?

8. When do you watch TV?

9. When do you eat out?

10. What day do you relax?

Daily Life · **147**

Active Grammar: Prepositions of Time

- Ask students to look at the grammar chart. Explain that we use *at* with specific times, *on* with days of the week, *in* with parts of the day, and *from/to* to show the starting and ending points of amounts of time.
- Encourage students to create example sentences illustrating the prepositional/time phrases in the chart.

A **Complete the sentences with the correct preposition.**

Ask students to do the exercise orally first and then to write the answers.

B **Ask and answer these questions. Use the correct preposition of time.**

Encourage students to answer with complete sentences. For example: *I get up at 6:30 in the morning.*

More Action!

Take a poll, having students ask each other what time they regularly get up and go to bed. One student keeps track on the board of how many get up between 5 and 7 A.M. (early birds) and how many go to bed after 11 P.M. (night owls). Make pie charts showing the percentage of early birds, night owls, and those who have other schedules. Which is the largest group in the class?

Teaching Tip

Point out that while we use *in* with a part of the day (*in the afternoon*), we use *on* if there's a day of the week before it (*on Monday afternoon*).

Daily Life · **147**

Active Grammar: Simple Present Tense

Ask students to look at the grammar chart. Call on individuals to explain other activities they do every day. Then, ask students to find out what those seated near them do every day.

A **Circle the correct form of the verb.**

• Point out that the third person singular verb for *he/she/it* is usually formed by adding *s* at the end. If the word ends in *y*, we change the *y* to *i* and add *es*. For example: *study/studies*.

• Ask students to do the exercise and then to exchange papers to correct answers.

◀)) **B** **Pronunciation: Final *s* Listen and repeat.** (CD3 • TR4)

• Have students listen to the audio while looking at the words.

• Students listen again, repeating the words and paying attention to the ending sounds.

◀)) **C** **Listen. Which sound do you hear at the end of each verb: /s/, /z/, or /əz/? Listen again and repeat.** (CD3 • TR5)

• Students listen to the audio for the sounds at the ends of words.

• Students listen again, this time repeating the word and writing the correct sound.

Active Grammar

A Circle the correct form of the verb.

I You We They	**work**	every day.
He She	**works**	

1. Eric get up /(gets up) at 7:00 in the morning.
2. I (get up)/ gets up early.
3. I (eat)/ eats breakfast.
4. My parents (eat)/ eats breakfast.
5. I (leave)/ leaves the house at 8:00.
6. I (go)/ goes to school. I (take)/ takes the bus.
7. Eric go /(goes) to work. He drive /(drives.)
8. My parents (work)/ works full time. I (work)/ works part time.
9. I (study)/ studies English from 9:00 to 12:00.
10. The students (have)/ has a lot of homework.

◀)) CD3 • TR4 **B** **Pronunciation: Final *s* Listen and repeat.**

/s/	/z/	/əz/
get–gets	drive–drives	watch–watches
work–works	go–goes	wash–washes
take–takes	study–studies	
	have–has	

◀)) CD3 • TR5 **C** **Listen.** Which sound do you hear at the end of each verb: /s/, /z/, or /əz/? Listen again and repeat.

1. leaves ___z___
2. plays ___z___
3. relaxes ___əz___
4. writes ___s___
5. eats ___s___
6. does ___z___

7. makes ___s___
8. watches ___əz___
9. takes ___s___
10. reads ___z___
11. lives ___z___
12. drinks ___s___

Teaching Tip

Ask students to hold up one hand if they hear a final *s* sound and two hands for a *z* sound. Say these words: *this, he's, thanks, yes, is, she's, Ms., Miss, please.*

A **Work with a partner.** Number the pictures from 1 to 10. *(Answers may vary.)*

B **Work with a partner.** Write a story about Laura's day. Use your imagination!

(Answers will vary.)   Laura has a busy day.

_____

_____

_____

_____

_____

_____

_____

_____

Daily Life • **149**

Laura's Day

A **Work with a partner. Number the pictures from 1 to 10.**

• Ask students to look at the pictures of Laura's day. Can they describe each one? Is there vocabulary they need help with?

• Explain that the pictures are not in the right order. Ask students to number them, beginning with the first thing Laura does in the morning and on to the last thing she does at night.

• Call on individuals to explain the order they chose.

B **Work with a partner. Write a story about Laura's day. Use your imagination!**

Tell students to feel free to add other actions to Laura's day that are not in the pictures. They should write in paragraph form, not just a list of actions.

More Action!

Tell students that Eleanor Roosevelt (the wife of former United States President Franklin D. Roosevelt) used to write a newspaper column called *My Day.* She wrote about things she did every day. Ask students to write a column called *My Day.* What do they do in the morning, afternoon, and evening? Who do they talk to? What do they see? What do they think about? Is their day a good or bad day? Why?

Teaching Tip

The ordering of Laura's day may differ from student to student. She could study English or read the paper in either the morning or at night.

Active Grammar: Simple Present Tense: Negative Statements

Ask students to look at the grammar chart. Point out that *do not = don't* and *does not = doesn't*. In casual speech, we usually use the contracted (short) forms.

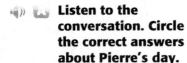 **Listen to the conversation. Circle the correct answers about Pierre's day.** (CD3 • TR6)

• Have students listen to the conversation, paying attention to the details of his day.
• Students listen again, pausing to circle the correct answer. Ask them to listen once more and correct their answers.

 Listen to the conversation. Talk about Maria's day. Some of the sentences are negative. (CD3 • TR7)

• Have students listen to the conversation. Ask them what they remember from it. Use comprehension questions, such as: *Does she have a lot of homework?*
• Have students listen to the conversation again. Then, call on individuals to narrate the story of the student's day. Tell them to correct each other, if necessary.

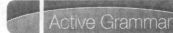

 Active Grammar

I			
You	**do not**		
We	**don't**		
They		**work**	every day.
He	**does not**		
She	**doesn't**		

 A Listen to the conversation. (Circle) the correct answers about Pierre's day.
CD3 • TR6

1. Pierre (goes) / doesn't go to Bayside College.
2. He **has** / (doesn't have) school on Friday.
3. He goes / (doesn't go) to school at night.
4. He (has) / doesn't have a lot of homework.
5. He (eats) / doesn't eat lunch with his friends.
6. He (studies) / doesn't study in the library.
7. He works / (doesn't work) during the week.
8. He (works) / doesn't work in a restaurant.

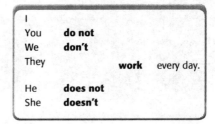

B Listen to the conversation. Talk about Maria's day. Some of the sentences are negative.
CD3 • TR7

> She goes to South Street Adult School.

1. she / go / South Street Adult School
2. she / go to school / four days a week
   She doesn't go to school four days a week.
3. she / go to school / in the morning
   She doesn't go to school in the morning.
4. she / have / a lot of homework
   She has a lot of homework.
5. she / have / time to study
   She doesn't have time to study.
6. she / work
   She works.
7. she / four children
   She doesn't have four children.
8. she / be tired at night
   She is tired at night.

150 • Unit 11

More Action!

Ask students to explain the steps of simple things they often do: *make a cup of coffee, set an alarm clock, sew on a button, make a sandwich, set a table, get ready for class,* etc.

  Working Together **Read the conversation between Rosa and her teacher.** Then, act out the conversation with a partner.

Rosa: I'm sorry, Ms. Jackson. I don't have my homework.

Teacher: Again?

Rosa: I don't have time to do my homework.

Teacher: Do you study in the morning?

Rosa: I don't. I have two children. I make breakfast. I drive the kids to school.

Teacher: Do you study during the day?

Rosa: No, I don't. I work full time.

Teacher: Do you study at night?

Rosa: No, I don't. I cook dinner. I take care of the children. And I want to relax.

Teacher: Do you study on the weekend?

Rosa: No, I don't. But that's a good idea.

Working Together **Work with a partner.** Write a conversation between a teacher and a student. Talk about study time. (Answers will vary.)

Work with a partner. Ask these questions. Circle your partner's answers.
(Answers will vary.)

1. Do you have a lot of homework?	Yes, I do.	No, I don't.
2. Do you study at the library?	Yes, I do.	No, I don't.
3. Do you study with a partner?	Yes, I do.	No, I don't.
4. Do you speak English with your friends?	Yes, I do.	No, I don't.
5. Do you watch TV in English?	Yes, I do.	No, I don't.
6. Do you study English on the computer?	Yes, I do.	No, I don't.
7. Do you use English at work?	Yes, I do.	No, I don't.
8. Do you read the newspaper in English?	Yes, I do.	No, I don't.

Write four sentences about how your partner studies English.
(Answers will vary.)

More Action!

What makes you crabby? Ask students to interview each other about what they **don't** like to do. For example: *take out the garbage, cut the grass, do the laundry, scrub the bathroom, wash the dishes, clean up after your dog on the sidewalk,* or *pay monthly bills.* Then, each student should tell the class what his or her partner does not like to do: *She doesn't like to take out the garbage every night.* How many students dislike the same things? Keep track on the board.

No Time to Study

 Working Together Read the conversation between Rosa and her teacher. Then, act out the conversation with a partner.

• Ask students to take roles and act out the conversation. Ask students to circle the negative present tense verbs.
• Call on individuals to make the statements into questions.
For example: *Why doesn't Rosa have her homework?* Call on other students to answer.

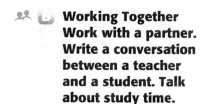 **Working Together Work with a partner. Write a conversation between a teacher and a student. Talk about study time.**

• Write some cues on the board, such as *job, office, children, housework, meals, spouse, free time, television.* Tell students they can use these words in their dialogue.
• Have pairs act out the dialogues for the class.

 Work with a partner. Ask these questions. Circle your partner's answers.

Write four sentences about how your partner studies English.

Ask students to read their sentences to the class.

Daily Life · **151**

The Big Picture: Trouble with Math

🔊 **A** **Listen to Emily's day. Write the correct time under each picture.**
(CD3 • TR8)

• Have students listen to the audio of the first half of the passage. Help them with vocabulary, such as *sophomore*, *alarm*, and *rings*.

• Repeat this process with the second half. Ask comprehension questions about Emily: *Why does she have two alarm clocks?*

• Students listen to the whole passage, pausing to write the correct times under the pictures. Call on individuals for answers.

B **Number the sentences in the correct order.**

• First, ask students to summarize Emily's day orally. Have the other students correct any mistakes of sequence.

• Then, ask them to number the sentences in the correct order. You may want to play the audio again at this point.

🔊 **A** **Listen to Emily's day.** Write the correct time under each picture.
CD3 • TR8

1. ___6:05___   2. ___7:30-2:00___

3. ___2:00___   4. ___7:00-8:00___

5. ___8:00___   6. ___11:00___

B **Number the sentences in the correct order.**

___4___ She plays baseball after school.   ___7___ Then, she watches TV.

___3___ She goes to school.   ___2___ After that, she gets up.

___5___ She takes a shower.   ___8___ She sets her alarm clocks.

___1___ Emily turns off her alarm clock.   ___9___ Then, she goes to bed.

___6___ She does her homework.

152 • Unit 11

Listen again and (circle) True or False.

1. Emily gets up early.   (True)   False
2. She takes a shower in the morning.   True   (False)
3. Then, she eats breakfast.   (True)   False
4. After that, she takes the bus to school.   (True)   False
5. Emily likes math.   True   (False)
6. Her father watches her play baseball every day.   True   (False)
7. She eats dinner with her family.   (True)   False
8. She studies for three hours every night.   True   (False)
9. At midnight, she goes to bed.   True   (False)

Listen and write each sentence you hear.

1. *Emily goes to high school.*
2. *She feels tired in the morning.*
3. *She doesn't like math.*
4. *Emily doesn't play tennis.*
5. *She doesn't have a lot of homework.*
6. *She goes to bed at 11:00.*

Listen to the conversation between Emily and her mother. Complete the sentences.

1. Emily is having trouble in _____ *math* _____
2. Emily studies for _____ *one* _____ hour every night.
3. Emily needs to study for _____ *two* _____ hours every night.
4. She needs to study math from _____ *8:00* _____ to _____ *9:00* _____ .

Daily Life • **153**

◀)) C **Listen again and circle True or False.** (CD3•TR8)

Have students listen to the audio again (if necessary), and then do the exercise. Call on individuals for the correct answers.

◀)) D **Listen and write each sentence you hear.** (CD3•TR9)

Have students listen to the audio without writing. Then, have students listen again, writing the sentences they hear. Move among them, checking answers.

◀)) E **Listen to the conversation between Emily and her mother. Complete the sentences.** (CD3•TR10)

• Have students listen to the conversation and then ask and answer questions about it.
• Students listen a second time, pausing to fill in the blanks.

More Action!

Ask students to make up false statements. For example:
The President of the U.S. lives in Los Angeles.
We're studying French in this class.
Canada is below the United States.
My nose is green.
Our teacher is a famous movie star.
Ask other students to correct the statements, using negatives in the present:
No, the President of the U.S. doesn't live in Los Angeles. He lives in Washington, D.C.

Reading:
Studying English on the Computer

A **Discuss. Then, read.**

• Talk about computer use. What do members of the class use computers for? How many have computers at home? Do they use their computers in English or in their native languages? What Web sites do they visit regularly?

• Ask students to read the first paragraph to themselves. Then, call on individuals to tell you what they remember.

• Ask a student to read aloud the first paragraph. Ask others when the student studies English. What does the student like to use? How does the student use them?

• Ask another student to read the second paragraph aloud. Ask questions about the student's study habits and computer use.

• Which of the two students are most like those in the class?

B **Check the correct answer.**

Do the exercise as a class. Ask students to correct each other.

A **Discuss.** Then, read.

1. Do you have a computer?

2. Did you ever study English on the computer?

Nadia

I like studying on the computer. I don't live in an English-speaking country. I don't know anyone who speaks English. On the computer, I study when I want, in the morning or at night. On the computer, I like to use listening sites. I listen to people speak. Sometimes, I listen to the same conversation four or five times. I repeat the sentences. I like using my computer to learn English.

Kim

I have a computer, but I like my class better. For me, class is more interesting. I live in an English-speaking country. I like to speak to other people and use my English. I like to have a teacher. My teacher explains the grammar, and I can ask questions. Also, a class makes me study. I have to come to class, I have to do my homework, and I have to study for tests.

B **Check (✓) the correct answer.**

	Nadia	Kim
1. She has a computer.	✓	✓
2. She lives in an English-speaking country.		✓
3. She goes to English class.		✓
4. She can study in the morning or at night.	✓	
5. She has homework.		✓
6. She has tests.		✓
7. She likes to listen and repeat.	✓	
8. She likes to study English.	✓	✓

More Action!

Internet Option: Ask students to do internet searches, typing in *ESL listening* or *ESL grammar*. Ask them to look for Web sites which might be useful for learning English. Then, ask them to share the information they've found with the class.

Read.

I am very busy. I don't have much time to
study. I go to school on Monday and Wednesday
night. I study for one hour on Tuesday and
Thursday night.

I study after my children go to sleep. It's quiet.
I study at the kitchen table. I do my homework. Then,
I read some of the conversations in the book and I memorize them.
Sometimes, I listen to the CD. I repeat or I copy some of the sentences.

I also try to use my English. I speak English at the store and
at the bank. At work, some of the workers speak English, so I talk a
little at break time. I am friends with one of the men, and I speak
English with him for a few minutes every day.

Complete. Write or circle words to make sentences about yourself. (Answers will vary.)

1. I study _____ hours a week.

2. I **speak / do not speak** English every day.

3. I like to study **alone / with a partner**.

4. My house is **noisy / quiet**.

5. I study **at home / in the library / in the learning center**.

6. I **use / don't use** a computer to study English.

> **WRITING NOTE**
> Remember to indent
> each paragraph.

Write about how you study and practice English.
(Answers will vary.)

Sharing Our Stories Read your partner's story. Complete the information.

1. My partner studies about _____ hours a week.

2. My partner speaks English with _____.

Daily Life · 155

Writing Our Stories: Studying English

Read.
- Ask students to read the whole passage to themselves, circling words or phrases they don't understand.
- Help them with any new vocabulary, such as *break time*.
- Call on a student to summarize the first paragraph in the third person, starting with *He's busy*.
- Call on others to do the same with the next two paragraphs.

Complete. Write or circle words to make sentences about yourself.

Ask the questions orally at first. Then, have the students write and circle answers.

Write about how you study and practice English.

Ask students to choose a title and organize their thoughts into two or more paragraphs.

Sharing Our Stories Read your partner's story. Complete the information.

Each student should report to the class about his or her partner's story.

Teaching Tip

Before students begin writing, tell them to brainstorm a few things they want to say and to organize similar thoughts in groups or clusters. They can turn these groups into paragraphs. Students can also write rough drafts quickly and then go back and polish what they've written.

English in Action: Studying English

A How do *you* practice English? Read each idea. Circle the ones you like.

Discuss each idea:

1. Have you made flashcards? Should they be only in English or in two languages?

2. What TV programs do you watch in English? How do they help you?

3. What have you memorized from this unit?

4. Do you have co-workers and neighbors who speak English? Can you understand them?

5. Do you know any songs in English? What are they? Do you like to sing?

6. How often do you re-copy written assignments and correct them?

7. Do you have a friend to study with? Do you two speak in your native language or English?

B Working Together Work with a group. Talk about how you study and practice English. Add two more ideas to help you practice your English.

Some possibilities might be using newspapers and magazines, listening to radio programs, and reading advertisements or product information about items that students buy.

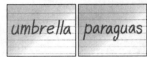

A How do *you* practice English? Read each idea. Circle the ones you like.

(Answers will vary.)

1. Make flash cards. Study them when you have a few minutes.

2. Watch TV in English. Repeat some of the sentences as you listen.

3. Study from your book. Memorize some sentences.

4. Speak English with co-workers and neighbors.

5. Listen to songs in English. Learn the words. .

6. Re-copy compositions and homework. Correct mistakes.

7. Study with another student. Try to speak English!

B Working Together **Work with a group.** Talk about how you study and practice English. Add two more ideas to help you practice your English.

1. (Answers will vary.) _____

2. _____

More Action!

Ask students to bring to class everyday examples of English writing that help them increase their vocabulary. For example: *want ads, political cartoons, directions for use on purchased products, flyers*. Each student should present his or her examples to the class and tell what he or she learned from them.

A **When can you study?** Complete your typical schedule for the week. Show the time you need for work, meals, and school. Then, schedule your study time.

	Monday	Tuesday	Wednesday	Thursday	Friday	Saturday	Sunday
6:00 A.M.							
7:00							
8:00							
9:00							
10:00							
11:00							
12:00 P.M.							
1:00							
2:00							
3:00							
4:00							
5:00							
6:00							
7:00							
8:00							
9:00							
10:00							
11:00							

B **Complete.** (Answers will vary.)

1. I am going to study on _____ from _____ to _____.

2. I am going to study on _____ from _____ to _____.

C **Working Together** **Show your schedule to a partner.** Explain when and where you are going to study. (Answers will vary.)

Daily Life · **157**

English in Action: Scheduling Study Time

A **When can you study? Complete your typical schedule for the week. Show the time you need for work, meals, and school. Then, schedule your study time.**

• Some students' activities will vary from week to week. Show them how to block chunks of time for activities that take up more than one hour.

• When students have completed the schedules, ask them to work out what percentage of each day they use for studying English. What can they change in their schedules to get more study time?

B **Complete.**

Encourage students to change their schedules as needed. Some may wish to revise by making a clean copy.

C **Working Together Show your schedule to a partner. Explain when and where you are going to study.**

Encourage pairs of student to learn from each other. Ask: *Do you like any of your partner's study ideas? Which ones?*

Teaching Tip

Help students with time management. Ask them to make lists of their usual time wasters, such as watching television or talking on their cell phones. Then, help students set goals to improve their use of time.

Unit 12

Food

Dictionary: Snacks, Beverages, and Meals

  Listen and repeat.

(CD3•TR11)

- Have students listen to the audio for breakfast and lunch vocabulary while looking at the pictures.
- Students listen again, repeating the words after the audio. Correct pronunciation.
- Call out the number of an item and ask individuals to tell you what the item is.
- Say the words out of order and ask students to point to the appropriate pictures.

 Listen and repeat.

Breakfast

1. eggs   **2.** cereal   **3.** pancakes   **4.** bacon

5. toast   **6.** a donut   **7.** a bagel

Lunch

1. a hamburger   **2.** French fries   **3.** a salad   **4.** soup

5. a turkey sandwich   **6.** a tuna salad sandwich   **7.** lettuce   **8.** a tomato   **9.** a cucumber

158 · Unit 12

More Action!

Call a volunteer to the front of the class. The student thinks of one of the food items pictured on this page and the other students must guess which item it is by asking questions that can only be answered with *yes* or *no*. Each student gets four questions. The student who guesses correctly then goes to the front of the class and becomes the next student to think of an item.

Teaching Tip

Make sure the stressed syllables in this new vocabulary are clear to the students: *toMAto, TUna SAlad, CUcumber*, etc.

Dinner

1. pasta
2. chicken
3. fish
4. steak
5. rice
6. pizza
7. potatoes
8. green beans
9. corn
10. beans

Beverages

1. coffee
2. tea
3. soda
4. iced tea
5. juice
6. milk

Dessert

1. ice cream
2. cake
3. cookies
4. pie

Fruit

1. bananas
2. apples
3. oranges
4. grapes
5. mangoes

Food · **159**

- Have students listen to the audio for dinner vocabulary while looking at the pictures.
- Students listen again, repeating the words after the audio. Correct pronunciation.
- Call out the number of an item and ask individuals to tell you what it is.
- Say the words out of order and ask students to point to the appropriate pictures.
- Follow the same process for the beverages, dessert, and fruit vocabulary.

More Action!

Have students play a memory game. Students stand in a line. The first student says, *My name is _____ and I like French fries.* The next student says, *His/her name is _____ and he/she likes French fries.* Then, he or she must say her or his own name and a favorite food. *My name is _____ and I like _____.* As the game progresses, each person must name all of the others and their favorite foods before telling his or her own. Anyone who makes a mistake is out of the game and must sit down.

Teaching Tip

Write the food categories (breakfast, lunch, dinner, beverages, dessert, fruit) on the board. Ask students to come to the board and write individual items (as you dictate them) under the correct categories. You can also designate areas of the classroom as categories, give each student a food item, and ask him or her to go to the appropriate area.

Word Builder

Word Builder

A **Write four foods that you like. Write four foods that you don't like.**

Ask students to brainstorm their food likes and dislikes before writing. They can write traditional foods from their own countries (which may not be in the dictionary).

A **Write four foods that you like.** Write four foods that you don't like.

I LIKE . . .	I DON'T LIKE . . .
1. (Answers will vary.)	1. _____
2. _____	2. _____
3. _____	3. _____
4. _____	4. _____

B **Listen and complete.**

Breakfast (CD3•TR12)

• Have students listen to the audio about Mike.
• Then, they listen again and fill in the blank.

Lunch

• Have students listen to the audio about Jenny, repeating all the food items Jenny eats.
• They listen a second time, pausing to fill in the blanks.

Dinner

Follow the same process as for breakfast and lunch above. Ask students to listen to the track again and check their answers for the entire exercise.

Word Partnerships

Encourage students to make sentences with the phrases. Can they think of others? For example: *a sip of soda, a bowl of cereal, a slice of bacon, a glass of milk.*

CD3•TR12 **B** **Listen and complete.**

Breakfast

Mike eats breakfast at ___7:15___.
Mike eats ___cereal___ and ___toast___.
He drinks ___coffee___.

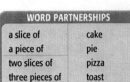

Lunch

Jenny eats lunch from ___1:00___ to ___2:00___.
Jenny eats ___a large salad___ with Italian dressing.
She has ___cucumbers___, ___tomatoes___, carrots
and ___chicken___ or shrimp on her salad.
She drinks ___iced tea___.
For dessert, she has ___a piece of fruit___.

Dinner

Sara and her family eat dinner at ___7:00___.
Sara and her family eat ___chicken___
or ___pasta___.
She likes ___cookies___ for dessert.
She and her brother drink ___milk___
or ___water___.

WORD PARTNERSHIPS	
a slice of	cake
a piece of	pie
two slices of	pizza
three pieces of	toast

CULTURE NOTE
Americans usually eat three meals a day. The big meal is dinner.

160 • Unit 12

Teaching Tip

It's not necessary for students to understand all the words they hear on the audio. They just need to understand enough to fill in the blanks.

C Working Together **What food is typical in your country?** (Circle) and complete.
Then, read your answers to a partner. (Answers will vary.)

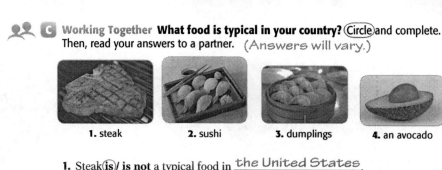

1. steak   2. sushi   3. dumplings   4. an avocado

1. Steak (**is**) / **is not** a typical food in _the United States_.

2. Sushi **is** / **is not** a typical food in _____.
name of country

3. Dumplings **are** / **are not** a typical food in _____.
name of country

4. An avocado **is** / **is not** a typical food in _____.
name of country

D Make a list of popular foods in your country. Talk about your list in a group.

Breakfast	Lunch	Dinner
(Answers will vary.)	_____	_____
_____	_____	_____
_____	_____	_____

Dessert	Fruit	Beverages
_____	_____	_____
_____	_____	_____
_____	_____	_____

E Ask and answer the questions with a partner. (Answers will vary.)

1. What is your favorite food?

2. What is your favorite beverage?

3. What is your favorite dessert?

4. What is your favorite fruit?

Food · **161**

C Working Together
What food is typical in your country? Circle and complete. Then, read your answers to a partner.

• It's possible that none of the foods on this page are typical in the countries of the students in the class. Ask them to mention typical foods before doing the exercise.
• Do the exercise as a class activity, calling on individuals to tell which answer should be circled.

D **Make a list of popular foods in your country. Talk about your list in a group.**

• Ask students to complete the exercise individually and then to compare their lists with those of partners.
• You may want to have students from the same geographical area sit together and share their lists. Then, they can tell the rest of the class about their typical foods. If these are hard to explain in English, encourage students to draw pictures on the board.

E **Ask and answer the questions with a partner.**

After students have done the exercise, call on them to talk about their partner's likes and dislikes: *His/her favorite beverage is soda.*

Teaching Tip

Students can learn words for each other's ethnic dishes in the original languages. They can teach each other these words.

Containers

A Read.

• Call on individuals to read the phrases below the pictures.
• Look back at pages 158 and 159. Which of the foods can be used with these containers?

B Put the items in the correct columns. You may put an item in more than one column.

Put the chart on the board and do this as a class activity. Ask six students to come to the board and assign each one a category. He or she must write all the items for that category. Correct answers as a class.

A Read.

1. a can of soda
2. a glass of milk
3. a cup of coffee
4. a bottle of juice
5. a carton of milk
6. a bowl of soup

B Put the items in the correct columns. You may put an item in more than one column.

soda	hot chocolate	rice	cereal
chocolate milk	orange juice	water	tea
iced coffee	milk	lemonade	
espresso	coffee	iced tea	

a can of	**a bottle of**	**a cup of**
soda	soda	espresso
lemonade	chocolate milk	hot chocolate
iced tea	orange juice	coffee
	milk	tea
	water	
	lemonade	
	iced tea	

a glass of	**a carton of**	**a bowl of**
soda	orange juice	cereal
chocolate milk	milk	rice
iced coffee	lemonade	
orange juice	iced tea	
milk		
water		
lemonade		
iced tea		

162 • Unit 12

More Action!

Tell students to pretend that they're television chefs on a cooking show. They can bring their favorite recipes from home. (If possible, recipes should include two or more of the foods listed on pages 158 and 159.) At a table in front of the class, they can introduce themselves by saying: *Hello. I'm the Chef of the Day. Guess what we're going to cook today! First, we _____ and then we _____.* Students should explain the ingredients needed and demonstrate the process of cooking. The class must guess what it is they're making. The first one to guess correctly becomes the next Chef of the Day.

Teaching Tip

Teach some basic cooking verbs: *boil, bake, fry, grill, broil, mix, blend, chop, peel, stir,* and *beat.*

> I **like** fruit.
> He **eats** a banana every morning.
> They **eat** meat.
>
> I **don't like** salad.
> He **doesn't eat** cereal.
> They **don't eat** meat.

A **Complete with the correct verb form.**

1. I _____cook_____ (cook) dinner every night.

2. My children _____like_____ (like) pizza.

3. My family _____eats_____ (eat) dinner together every Sunday.

4. I _____like_____ (like) to cook outside on the grill.

5. Every summer, my neighbor _____catches_____ (catch) fresh fish.

6. My mother _____shops_____ (shop) at a local supermarket.

7. My children _____eat_____ (eat) cereal for breakfast.

8. Mrs. Jones _____bakes_____ (bake) excellent cakes.

B **Listen and complete.**

> A fussy eater doesn't like many kinds of food.

cheese	tomato
fruit	vegetables
hamburgers	white bread
peanut butter	milk

1. Christopher doesn't like _____vegetables_____.

2. Christopher doesn't like _____tomato_____ sauce.

3. He doesn't like _____cheese_____, either.

4. He doesn't like hot dogs or _____hamburgers_____.

5. He doesn't like _____fruit_____.

6. Christopher likes _peanut butter_, _white bread_, and _____milk_____.

More Action!

Have each student tell how he or she makes a favorite sandwich. Then, take a poll to see how many students like each kind of sandwich.

Active Grammar: Simple Present Tense

Ask students to look at the grammar chart. Review the present tense. Tell students your own likes and dislikes about food. Encourage students to tell you theirs.

Complete with the correct verb form.

• Remind students that we usually form the third person singular of the present by adding *s*. If the verb ends with a *ch*, *x*, or *z* sound, we add *es* (*watch/watches*). If the verb ends in *y*, we change the *y* to *i* and add *es* (*study/studies*).
• Ask students to complete the exercise and move among them, checking answers.

 Listen and complete.
(CD3 • TR13)

• Students listen to the audio while looking at the picture. Then, ask them what they remember.
• Students listen again. Ask them comprehension questions: *Why is Stacy unhappy? Why doesn't Christopher like spaghetti? Why doesn't he like pizza? What does he like? How old is he?*
• Students fill in the blanks and then listen one more time to check their answers.

Active Grammar: Present Tense: Negatives

Ask students to look at the grammar chart. Encourage them to talk about likes and dislikes for food.

A **Working Together Work with a partner. Ask questions and check the answers.**

- Have pairs of students read the dialogue in the speech balloons.
- Have them read it again but this time call out *lunch* or *dinner* as substitutions for *breakfast*. Substitute other foods for *chicken*.
- Ask students to fill in the chart and compare answers with the rest of the class.

B **Complete the sentences about you and your partner. Use the information in Exercise A.**

Do the exercise as a class activity, comparing likes and dislikes.

 A **Working Together** **Work with a partner.** Ask questions and check (✔) the answers.

> Do you eat breakfast? — Yes, I do.

> Do you like chicken? — No, I don't.

I **don't like** cereal.
We **do not eat** pork.
He **doesn't like** fish.
She **doesn't drink** tea.

do not = don't
does not = doesn't

	Yes	No
1. Do you eat breakfast?		
2. Do you eat pork?		
3. Do you like fish?		
4. Do you like vegetables?		
5. Do you cook at home?		
6. Do you eat with your family?		
7. Do you drink coffee?		

(Answers will vary.)

 B **Complete the sentences about you and your partner.** Use the information in Exercise A. (Answers will vary.)

1. I _____ (eat) breakfast.
2. My partner _____ (eat) breakfast.
3. My partner _____ (eat) pork.
4. My partner _____ (like) fish.
5. I _____ (like) vegetables.
6. My partner _____ (cook) at home.
7. My partner _____ (eat) with his/her family.
8. I _____ (drink) coffee.
9. My partner _____ (drink) coffee.

164 • Unit 12

More Action!

Plan a class dinner. Ask students to brainstorm a menu that includes appetizers, salad, entrées, vegetable(s), beverages, and dessert. Remind them to take into account any class members who have dietary preferences or restrictions. Then, they can make a list of all the ingredients necessary to prepare the items on the menu. How much will they need of each one and approximately how much will each ingredient cost? They can make a budget based on their estimates.

> Always = 100%
> Sometimes = 50%
> Never = 0%

> Place adverbs of frequency **before** the main verb.
> I **always** drink water on hot days.
> I **sometimes** drink coffee in the morning.
> I **never** drink coffee at night.

A **Make sentences about you and your family.** Use *always, sometimes,* or *never.* Compare your sentences with a partner's. (Answers will vary.)

1. I _____ eat breakfast.

2. I _____ drink juice at breakfast.

3. I _____ drink coffee in the morning.

4. I _____ eat dinner with my family.

5. I _____ prepare my own meals.

steak on a grill

6. My family _____ eats at fast-food restaurants.

7. My family _____ cooks food outside on a grill.

B **Put the words in the correct order.**

1. always / eats / dinner / my family / together
   My family always eats dinner together.

2. drink / I / at night / coffee / never
   I never drink coffee at night.

3. my coworker / for lunch / eat / sometimes / and I / salads
   My coworker and I sometimes eat salads for lunch.

4. desserts / always / my grandmother / delicious / makes
   My grandmother always makes delicious desserts.

5. like / fish / or / chicken / for dinner / I
   I like fish or chicken for dinner.

Food · **165**

More Action!

Have a class debate. Choose teams to argue for and against the following statement: *Fast food is healthy and fun.* The team *for* the statement should list and present its reasons and then the team *against* it does the same. Then, each team disproves the other's reasons. The winner is the team that presents the better case.

Active Grammar: Adverbs of Frequency

Ask students to look at the grammar box. Point out that *frequency* means how often something happens.

A **Make sentences about you and your family. Use *always, sometimes* or *never.* Compare your sentences with a partner's.**

- Talk about your own family activities. What do you *always/sometimes/never* do together? Encourage students to talk about their family activities.
- Ask students to fill in the answers in the exercise. Have students share their answers with the class

B **Put the words in the correct order.**

- Remind students that the best way to do this kind of exercise is to look for the subject and the verb first. Remind students to put the adverb in front of the verb.
- Call on individuals to unscramble the sentences.

The Big Picture: At Mario's Italian Restaurant

  Working Together Work with a group. Discuss the picture.

- Ask students to describe the picture. You might want to use questions like these to get started: *Where are these people? What are they doing? Where are they sitting? What are they eating?*
- Review present continuous tense by having pairs of students ask and answer questions:

  S1: *Is Troy standing up?*
  S2: *No, he isn't.*
  S1: *Oh, I see, he's sitting down.*

  Have students make questions and answers about all the people in the picture.
- Review prepositions. Have pairs of students ask and answer questions:

  S1: *Are the flowers under the table?*
  S2: *No, they're not. They're on the table.*

  Listen and write the orders. (CD3 • TR14)

Ask students to listen for the food and drink items and then to listen a second time before writing.

 **Working Together Work with a group.** Discuss the picture.

 Listen and write the orders.

Emma: Emma will have an iced tea, a green salad, and the pasta.

Troy: Troy will have a soda, a green salad, and the chicken.

166 · Unit 12

More Action!

What's your favorite restaurant? Ask each student to describe a favorite restaurant either here or any other place where he or she has lived. What are the specialities of the restaurant? Which dish is the most delicious? What kind of atmosphere does the restaurant have? Is the service good? What about the prices?

Teaching Tip

Some students may be embarrassed to speak in front of the class. Don't force them. They may be more comfortable writing a paragraph or two about this topic.

Listen and look at the picture. Then, read and (circle.)

1. It's Saturday night.   True   (False)
2. Troy and Emma like to sit by the door.   True   (False)
3. Faye always works on Fridays.   (True)   False
4. Faye is their favorite waitress.   (True)   False
5. Emma is having a soda.   True   (False)
6. Troy and Emma are ordering salads.   (True)   False
7. Troy is having pasta.   True   (False)

Listen and look at the picture. Then, read and (circle.)

1. What kind of pizza is the family having?

     a. cheese   **b.** cheese and peppers   (**c.** cheese and pepperoni)

2. What are the children drinking?

     (**a.** soda)   **b.** juice   **c.** milk

3. When do Bob and Ann like to eat out?

     (**a.** On Fridays.)   **b.** Every weekend.   **c.** Every night.

4. Why are Bob and Ann eating out tonight?

     a. Because they're hungry.   (**b.** Because they're tired.)

Complete the sentences.

is ordering   is eating   are drinking   is looking

are sitting   ~~are eating~~   is taking

1. Troy and Emma ___*are eating*___ at Mario's.
2. They ___*are sitting*___ at Faye's table.
3. Emma ___*is looking*___ at the menu.
4. Troy ___*is ordering*___ a salad and chicken.
5. Faye ___*is taking*___ Troy's and Emma's orders.
6. Bob's family ___*is eating*___ pizza.
7. They ___*are drinking*___ soda.

Food · 167

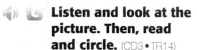

Listen and look at the picture. Then, read and circle. (CD3 • TR14)

• Tell students that the first conversation they'll hear is from the older couple by the window.
• Have students listen to the audio while looking at the picture. Then, ask them what they remember.
• Students listen again and then ask each other comprehension questions: *How often do Emma and Troy eat at Mario's? Who's their favorite waitress?*
• Ask them to do the exercise. Call on individuals for answers.

Listen and look at the picture. Then, read and circle. (CD3 • TR15)

• Tell students that now they'll hear a conversation from the family in the picture.
• Have students listen to the conversation. Then, ask them what they remember.
• Students listen again and then ask and answer comprehension questions: *What kind of pizza does Lori like?*
• Ask students to do the exercise and then listen to the audio again to check answers.

Complete the sentences.

Do the exercise orally, calling on individuals for answers.

Teaching Tip

Remind students again that it isn't necessary for them to understand everything on the audio. They just need to focus on key information.

Reading: Pizza Delivery

A Discuss. Then, read.

• Tell students to look at the pictures of labeled food at the top of the page. Which ones would they like on their pizza? How about pineapple pizza or fish pizza?

• Choose two students to read the roles of clerk and customer.

• Encourage students to figure out new vocabulary from context: *green pepper* and *pepperoni* are clues to the word *toppings*.

• Ask another pair of students to role-play the dialogue. Then, ask students to ask and answer comprehension questions about it: *What's the customer's address? How long will it take for the pizza to arrive?*

B Answer the questions.

• Ask students to underline the parts of the dialogue that help them answer the questions.

• Call on students to come to the board and write the correct answers.

pepperoni — fish
— green pepper
— onion
tomatoes —
— broccoli
pineapple — — mushrooms

A Discuss. Then, read.

1. Do you like pizza?
2. Where do you eat pizza?
3. What toppings do you like on your pizza?

Clerk:	Hello, Buona Pizza. May I take your order?
Customer:	Hello, I'd like to order a large pizza.
Clerk:	What toppings do you want on it?
Customer:	Pepperoni and green peppers.
Clerk:	OK. A large pizza with pepperoni and green peppers. That's $8.50. What's your address?
Customer:	1516 Central Avenue.
Clerk:	What's your phone number?
Customer:	555-6644.
Clerk:	OK. Thank you.
Customer:	How long will it take?
Clerk:	Thirty minutes. It's Friday, and we're always busy on Fridays.
Customer:	OK. Thank you. Good-bye.
Clerk:	Thank you for calling Buona Pizza.

B Answer the questions.

1. What size pizza did the customer order? ___ *large* ___
2. How many toppings did the customer order? ___ *two* ___
3. What toppings did the customer order? *pepperoni and green peppers*
4. It's 7:00. What time will the pizza arrive? ___ *7:30* ___

168 · Unit 12

More Action!

Ask students to study the spelling of the food vocabulary in this unit. Then, they can give each other quizzes, dictating five words each. After the first quiz, they should reverse roles. Move among them, correcting any spelling mistakes.

Teaching Tip

While spelling is important, spelling activities at this level should be optional. Speaking and listening comprehension should take precedence.

A   Read.

> My favorite holiday is July 4th,
> Independence Day. My family, my friends,
> and I always have a barbecue in our
> backyard. My grandfather cooks the meat.
> We have steak, chicken, hamburgers, and ribs. My mother and my
> aunts make other food, such as potato salad, green salad, and
> beans. We drink cold drinks, such as iced tea, soda, or water. For
> dessert, we always have watermelon and ice cream. Everyone sits
> in the backyard, and we have a great time.

B   Complete the sentences. (Answers will vary.)

1. My favorite holiday is _____.

2. On this holiday, we eat **at / in** _____.

3. _____ cooks the meal.

4. We have _____, _____,

    _____, and _____.

5. We drink _____ or _____.

6. For dessert, we have _____.

C   Write about a special holiday and the food you eat on that day.   (Answers will vary.)

WRITING NOTE

Use commas in a list of three or more people, places, or things: cheese, pasta, and meat.

D   Sharing Our Stories   Exchange papers with a partner. Check the commas in your partner's writing.

Food · **169**

Writing Our Stories: Holidays and Food

A   Read.

- As a pre-reading exercise, encourage students to talk about holidays either here in the U.S. or in their own countries. Which ones do they like the most? Have they heard of holidays like Thanksgiving and July 4th? Explain about these holidays to the class.
- Ask students to read the passage to themselves.
- Ask them what they remember and help them with vocabulary, such as *barbecue, backyard, watermelon,* etc.
- Call on individuals to read sentences from the passage aloud. Correct pronunciation.

B   Complete the sentences.

C   Write about a special holiday and the food you eat on that day.

D   Sharing Our Stories Exchange papers with a partner. Check the commas in your partner's writing.

After students have read each other's papers, they can report to the rest of the class about their partner's favorite holiday.

Teaching Tip

Encourage students to choose a title for their composition. Students can brainstorm ideas and these ideas can be formed into paragraphs. Tell them to indent paragraphs.

English in Action: Reading a Menu

Read the menu.

• Ask various students to read items and prices from the menu. Correct pronunciation of the food items. Discuss any new vocabulary, such as *soup of the day.*

• Ask students to make sentences about each item in the menu: *The spaghetti with meat sauce costs eight dollars. The onion soup costs two dollars and ninety-nine cents.*

Pronunciation: I'll Listen and write.

(CD3•TR16)

Ask students to listen to the audio while looking at the sentences. Then, ask them to listen a second time and write the answers.

Listen and practice the conversation with two classmates.

(CD3•TR17)

• Students listen to the conversation while looking at the dialogue in their books.

• Play the audio again, pausing after every other line and asking the students to predict the next line.

• Ask pairs of students to role-play the dialogue, substituting other items from the menu as appropriate.

English in Action

A Read the menu.

The APPLE Diner

PASTA	
Spaghetti with meat sauce	$8.00
Pasta with vegetables	$8.50

MEAT, FISH, and CHICKEN	
Hamburger/Cheeseburger *Special*	$8.99
Chicken and rice	$7.99
7 oz. Steak	$12.99
12 oz. Steak	$15.99
Fish	$14.99

SALADS	
Small green salad	$2.99
Large green salad	$3.99

SOUPS	
Onion Soup	$2.99
Soup of the day	$2.99

BEVERAGES	
Coffee, tea	$1.50
Soda	$1.75
Milk	$1.00

DESSERTS	
Ice cream	$1.99
Apple pie	$2.99

oz. = ounce

 B Pronunciation: I'll Listen and write.

CD3•TR16

1. ___I'll have___ a hamburger.
2. ___He'll have___ the steak.
3. ___She'll have___ a salad.
4. ___I'll have___ the pasta.
5. ___She'll have___ a soda.
6. ___He'll have___ ice cream.

 C Listen and practice the conversation with two classmates.

CD3•TR17

Waiter: Are you ready to order?

Customer 1: Yes, we are.

Waiter: What'll you have?

Customer 1: I'll have onion soup and spaghetti with meat sauce.

Waiter: Anything to drink?

Customer 1: I'll have coffee.

Waiter: And you? What'll you have?

Customer 2: I'll have the cheeseburger special.

Waiter: Would you like a salad?

Customer 2: No, thank you.

Waiter: Anything to drink?

Customer 2: I'll have a soda, please.

Complete the conversation. Then, a few groups of students will act out their conversation for the class. (Answers will vary.)

Waiter: Are you ready to order?

Customer 1: Yes, we are.

Waiter: What'll you have?

Customer 1: I'll have _____.

Waiter: Anything to drink?

Customer 1: I'll have _____.

Waiter: And you? What'll you have?

Customer 2: I'll have _____.

Waiter: Anything to drink?

Customer 2: I'll have _____.

Waiter: _____

CULTURE NOTE

In the United States, Americans leave a tip for the waiter or waitress. Waiters and waitresses do not receive large salaries, so tips are important. People usually leave 15%–20% of the check total.

 What is the total for each bill? How much tip will you leave?

HILL'S DINER

Scrambled Eggs	$3.00
Juice	.75
Coffee	.75
Total	

Total Bill: $4.50
Tip 15%: $.68
Tip 20%: $.90

 **Mario's Italian Restaurant**

2 Salads	$8.00
Spaghetti	$9.50
Chicken	$12.50
2 Coffees	$2.50
Total	

Total Bill: $32.50
Tip 15%: $4.88
Tip 20%: $6.50

Food · **171**

 Complete the conversation. Then, a few groups of students will act out their conversation for the class.

• Tell students to use the menu items on page 170 to fill in the blanks in the conversation.
• Each group should choose a pair of students to act out the conversation between customer and waiter.

Culture Note

Ask students to compare the American amount of a tip with that of other cultures they know.

 What is the total for each bill? How much tip will you leave?

• Tell students that the easiest way to figure a tip in your head is as follows. Take 10% of the amount (if it's $4.50 then 10% is .45). Double that amount if you plan to tip 20%.
• Ask students to add the amounts in the two bills and then figure out the tip of either 15% or 20%.

More Action!

Have groups of students plan a menu of specialty items from several cultures for an international restaurant. Students can work in groups, each suggesting items for breakfast, lunch, and dinner. They should also work out reasonable prices. Once several menus are complete, ask pairs of students to role-play ordering food from the menus. What are their favorite dishes?

Jobs

Dictionary: Jobs and Occupations

  A Listen and repeat.

(CD3 • TR18)

- First, talk about the pictures. Ask:
Who is this person?
What's his/her job?
Where is he/she?
What's he/she doing?
- Students listen to the audio while looking at the pictures.
- Students listen again, this time pausing to repeat the words.
- Say the words out of order and ask students to point to the appropriate pictures.
- Call out picture numbers and ask students to tell you the job.

Dictionary   Jobs and Occupations

 A Listen and repeat.
CD3•TR18

1. a desk clerk   **2.** a babysitter   **3.** a busboy   **4.** a cashier

5. a cook   **6.** an electrician   **7.** a housekeeper   **8.** a landscaper

9. a laundry worker   **10.** a manager   **11.** a plumber   **12.** a security guard

13. a manicurist   **14.** a waiter /
a waitress   **15.** a van driver   **16.** a hair stylist

More Action!

Ask students to act out jobs that they've had while other students try to guess what they are. If this involves vocabulary not on this page, write some example words on the board. Each student who guesses correctly becomes the next one to mime.

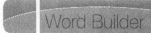

A **Write the jobs from the dictionary in the correct category.** You can write some jobs in more than one category. Add two more jobs to each category.

Works alone

a housekeeper   a cashier

a plumber   an electrician

Works outside

a landscaper   a security guard

_____   _____

Works in a restaurant

a busboy   a waiter

a cook   a waitress

Works in a salon

a hair stylist   a manicurist

_____   _____

Works with hotel guests

a desk clerk   a manager

a van driver   a babysitter

WORD PARTNERSHIPS	
get	hired
	fired
	laid off
look for	
find	a job
quit	

B **Match.**

g	**1.** a van driver	**a.**	serves food
d	**2.** a desk clerk	**b.**	washes and dries sheets and towels
h	**3.** a babysitter	**c.**	cleans and clears tables
a	**4.** a waitress	**d.**	takes reservations
i	**5.** a cook	**e.**	repairs bathrooms
b	**6.** a laundry worker	**f.**	supervises employees
j	**7.** a housekeeper	**g.**	drives guests to the airport
f	**8.** a manager	**h.**	watches and takes care of children
e	**9.** a plumber	**i.**	prepares food
c	**10.** a busboy	**j.**	cleans and vacuums rooms

Jobs • **173**

Teaching Tip

Ask students to brainstorm the best ways to find jobs. Make a list on the board and have students copy it in their notebooks.

Word Builder

A **Write the jobs from the dictionary in the correct category. You can write some jobs in more than one category. Add two more jobs to each category.**

• Do a warm-up exercise by calling out the numbers of pictures and asking questions that correspond to the categories. For example:
8. *Does she work outside?*
15. *Does he work with hotel guests?*
• Ask students to write in their answers.
• On the board, write the additional jobs that students added in each category. Correct any job terms or spelling, as necessary.

Word Partnerships

Ask students to work in pairs, making questions and statements from the phrases in the chart. For example:
S1: *Why are you quitting your job?*
S2: *I'm quitting because the pay is low.*

B **Match.**

• Go over the vocabulary in the phrases: *reservations, supervises, vacuums,* etc.
• Ask students to do the exercise and move among them, checking answers.
• Ask students to make complete sentences by combining the numbered and lettered items: *A van driver drives guests to the airport.*

Jobs • **173**

Active Grammar: Present Tense Statements Review

Ask students to look at the grammar chart. Explain that the simple present can be used to talk about general facts: *Waiters work in a restaurant. A landscaper works outside.*

A **Complete. Use the affirmative form of the correct verb.**

- Help students to work out the following vocabulary from context: *uniform, nails, styles, sinks.*
- Do the exercise orally as a class activity. Point out that while most of the verbs take *s* as an ending in third person singular, *fix* and *wash* take *es.*

B **Complete. Use the negative form of the correct verb.**

- Remind students that *does not = doesn't* and *do not = don't.*
- Do the exercise orally as a class activity. Point out that we do not need to change the base form of the verb in negative statements. It's correct to say: *A landscaper doesn't work in an office.* It is incorrect to say: *A landscaper doesn't works in an office.*

	Affirmative			Negative
Waiters	**work** in a restaurant.		Cooks	**don't serve** food.
A desk clerk	**works** at the front desk.		A waiter	**doesn't cook** food.

A **Complete.** Use the affirmative form of the correct verb.

		color	install
		cut	prepare
		drive	wash
		fix	wear

1. A van driver _____drives_____ guests to the airport.
2. A security guard _____wears_____ a uniform.
3. Cooks _____prepare_____ food for the guests.
4. A manicurist _____cuts_____ nails.
5. Electricians _____install/fix_____ lights.
6. A hair stylist _____cuts/colors_____ and styles hair.
7. Laundry workers _____wash_____ sheets and towels.
8. A plumber _____fixes/installs_____ sinks.

B **Complete.** Use the negative form of the correct verb.

drive	take
make	wash
need	wear
serve	work

1. Managers _____don't drive_____ guests to the airport.
2. Babysitters _____don't wear_____ uniforms.
3. A landscaper _____doesn't work_____ in an office.
4. A busboy _____doesn't take_____ orders from customers.
5. Laundry workers _____don't need_____ English for their job.
6. Security guards _____don't make_____ hotel reservations for guests.
7. A desk clerk _____doesn't serve_____ food.
8. A cashier _____doesn't wash_____ floors.

174 · Unit 13

More Action!

Ask students to work in pairs, asking each other what they **don't like** about their jobs. For example: *I don't like the low pay. I don't like my boss.* Then, each student reports to the class about his or her partner, switching to third person: *She doesn't like the low pay. He doesn't like his boss.*

A **Read the schedule.** Complete the information below.

	Sunday	Monday	Tuesday	Wednesday	Thursday	Friday	Saturday
Sam			3-11	3-11	3-11	3-11	3-11
Luis		12-5	12-5			12-5	12-5

1. Sam works ___8___ hours a day.

2. Sam works ___5___ days a week.

3. Sam works **full time** / part time.

4. Sam doesn't work on _Sun, Mon_

5. Sam starts work at ___3___.

6. Luis works ___5___ hours a day.

7. Luis doesn't work on _Sun, Wed, Thurs._

8. Luis works **full time** / **part time.**

9. Luis has ___3___ days off.

10. Luis goes home at ___5___.

> Full time: 35–40 hours a week
> Part time: under 35 hours a week

 Working Together **Work with a partner.** Complete your work or school schedule. Then, ask about your partner's schedule. (Answers will vary.)

	Sunday	Monday	Tuesday	Wednesday	Thursday	Friday	Saturday
You							
_____							

1. Where do you work?

2. What days do you work?

3. What time do you start work?

4. What time do you finish work?

 Join two other classmates and answer the questions. (Answers will vary.)

1. Who works on weekends?

2. Who works at night?

3. Who has a difficult schedule?

4. Who has an easy schedule?

Jobs · 175

More Action!

Internet Option: Ask students to think of their ideal job and have them search for it online. What training do they need? What experience is necessary? Do they need to live in a special place? Have them report back to the class.

Work Schedules

Read the schedule. Complete the information below.

- Ask students to look at the schedule. Who works longer hours, Sam or Luis? Who works full time and who works part time?
- Call on individuals to answer the questions with information from the schedule.

Working Together Work with a partner. Complete your work or school schedule. Then, ask about your partner's schedule.

- Tell students to fill in their schedules. In each box, they must put the times they start and finish work or school. If it's a free day, they should leave the box blank.
- Using the questions, students should find out the schedule information from their partners and then fill in the schedule in the same way that they did for themselves.

Join two other classmates and answer the questions.

Groups of three can ask and answer the questions. One person from each group should report the answers back to the class.

Active Grammar:
Present Tense:
Yes/No Questions

Ask students to look at the grammar chart. Have students work in pairs. Encourage them to make more job-related questions and answers:

S1: *Do you work at the mall?*

S2: *No, I don't.*

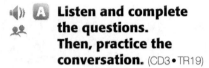 **Listen and complete the questions. Then, practice the conversation.** (CD3 • TR19)

• Have students listen to the audio while looking at the dialogue.

• Students listen again, this time pausing to fill in the questions.

• They listen a third time, checking what they have written. Ask a student to copy his or her questions on the board and check the spelling.

• Ask pairs of students to role-play the dialogue. They can substitute other kinds of work, if they like.

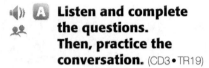 **Pronunciation: *Does he / Does she* Listen and repeat.**

(CD3 • TR20)

• Point out that it's important to listen for the *z* or *s* sound that connects the pairs of words. For example: *Does he* sounds like *duhzee? Does she* sounds like *duhshee?*

• Students listen to the audio while looking at the exercise. They listen again, repeating after the speaker.

176 • Unit 13

	Questions		Short Answers	
Do	you	work full time?	Yes, I **do.**	No, I **don't.**
	they	wear a uniform?	Yes, they **do.**	No, they **don't.**
Does	he	like the job?	Yes, he **does.**	No, he **doesn't.**
	she	use English at work?	Yes, she **does.**	No, she **doesn't.**

CD3•TR19 **A Listen and complete the questions.** Then, practice the conversation.

A: What do you do?

B: I'm a manicurist in a salon.

A: Do you <u>like your job?</u> ?

B: Yes, I do. I like it very much.

A: Do you <u>work in the day or in the evening</u> ?

B: I work in the day from 9:00 A.M. to 5:00 P.M.

A: Do you <u>need English for your job</u> ?

B: Yes, I do. Many of the hotel guests speak English, and I like to talk to them.

A: <u>Do you wear a uniform</u> ?

B: No, but I always wear an apron and gloves.

A: <u>Do you receive benefits</u> ?

B: Yes, I do. I work full time, so I get good benefits.

A: That's great. <u>Do you get tips</u> ?

B: Yes, I do. Sometimes I get big tips.

CD3•TR20 **B Pronunciation: *Does he / Does she* Listen and repeat.**

1. Does he work full time?   Does she work full time?

2. Does he wear a uniform?   Does she wear a uniform?

3. Does he get benefits?   Does she get benefits?

4. Does he like his job?   Does she like her job?

5. Does he work at night?   Does she work at night?

C Working Together **Look at the photos.** Work in a group and write four questions to ask each worker about his / her job. One student will be the waitress. The other students will ask their questions. Repeat for the barber and the desk clerk.

1. _Do you get good tips?_
2. _Do you work at night?_
3. _(Answers will vary.)_
4. _____

1. _____
2. _____
3. _____
4. _____

1. _____
2. _____
3. _____
4. _____

 D Working Together **Ask and answer the questions with a partner.**

> Does a cook wear a uniform?

> Yes, he does.

> Do waiters serve food?

> Yes, they do.

CULTURE NOTE

Many companies in the United States pay their employees **benefits** for full time work. Some employees receive benefits for part time work. Benefits include health and dental insurance, paid vacation, breaks, education, and retirement pension.

1. Does a waitress wear a uniform?
2. Do housekeepers make beds?
3. Does a manager get tips?
4. Do security guards wash towels?
5. Do cashiers give change?
6. Does a manager repair bathrooms?
7. Do plumbers prepare food?
8. Does a waiter serve food?
9. Do landscapers work outside?
10. Does a manicurist cut hair?

(Answers will vary.)

Jobs · **177**

C Working Together Look at the photos. Work in a group and write four questions to ask each worker about his / her job. One student will be the waitress. The other students will ask their questions. Repeat for the barber and the desk clerk.

Ask students to brainstorm questions before writing or asking them. Other question topics might include benefits, work hours, salary, and experience.

D Working Together Ask and answer the questions with a partner.

Students should role-play the dialogues. They can also act out the actions, such as *wash towels* or *serve food*.

Culture Note

Ask those students who are working what kind of benefits they receive. How are benefits paid in their native countries?

More Action!

Encourage students to learn more about health insurance and benefits. Ask working students to bring to class any literature they have concerning health care benefits. Display this on a table in front of the class and ask the class to look through it and find vocabulary or phrases they don't understand. Write these on the board and explain them: *inpatient, outpatient, quarterly deductible, preventive treatment, routine exams, diagnostic tests, physician visits, physical therapy.*

Teaching Tip

Make copies of student writing, omitting verbs in the present tense. Ask students to fill in the correct forms.

Active Grammar:
Present Tense:
Wh- Questions

Ask students to look at the grammar chart. Encourage them to ask other job-related *wh-* questions and to answer them.

Working Together Practice the conversation with a partner. Then, talk about your jobs. When you are finished, talk to three more students.

• Tell students to role-play the conversation and then to do it again using their real jobs or a job they would like to have.
• Students should move around the class, interviewing each other about their jobs.

Practice this conversation with a partner.

• Ask students to look at the picture. *Who is she? What's she doing?*
• Then, ask them to role-play the conversation. Have them repeat the conversation, substituting other jobs.

Working Together Talk about the jobs with a classmate.

For each of the three jobs, students should follow the process from Exercise B. They can work in pairs and they can substitute other jobs, if they wish.

Where		**do**	you	
When				**work**?
How many hours		**does**	she	

 Working Together Practice the conversation with a partner. Then, talk about your jobs. When you are finished, talk to three more students.

A: What do you do?

B: I'm a <u>cook</u>.

A: Where do you work?

B: I work at <u>an Italian restaurant</u>.

A: How many hours do you work?

B: I work <u>50 hours a week</u>.

B **Practice this conversation with a partner.**

A: Where does Marie work?

B: She works at a pharmacy.

A: What does she do?

B: She's a pharmacist.

A: When does she work?

B: She works Fridays, Saturdays, and Sundays.

Name: Marie
Place of Work: Pharmacy
Job: Pharmacist
Days: Friday, Saturday, and Sunday

C Working Together **Talk about the jobs with a classmate.**

1.

2.

3.

Name: Gina
Place of Work: Office Supply Store
Job: Manager

Name: Paul
Place of Work: Flower Shop
Job: Florist

Name: David
Place of Work: Hospital
Job: Custodian

A Working Together **Answer the questions about your daily schedule.** Then, sit with a partner and ask the same questions. *(Answers will vary.)*

Daily Schedule	You	Your Partner
1. What time do you get up?		
2. What time do you eat breakfast?		
3. What time do you leave the house?		
4. What hours do you work?		
5. What time do you study?		
6. What time do you go to bed?		

B **Look at the chart and write six sentences about your partner's schedule.**

My partner gets up at 7:00. (Answers will vary.)

C **Listen and answer the questions about Luis's job.**

1. What does Luis do?
   He's a valet.
2. How many hours does Luis work a night?
   4 hours
3. How many cars does he park a night?
   He parks 60 cars a night.
4. How many tips does he receive?
   He receives 50 tips.
5. How many breaks does he have?
   He gets one break (when it's quiet).

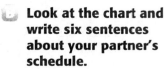

D **Listen and answer the questions about Jane's job.**

1. What does Jane do?
   She's a housekeeper.
2. How many hours does Jane work a day?
   She works 8.5 hours.
3. How many beds does she change?
   30 to 40
4. How many rooms does she clean?
   30 to 40
5. How many tips does she get per day?
   15 to 20

Jobs • **179**

Active Grammar: More *Wh*-Questions

 Working Together Answer the questions about your daily schedule. Then, sit with a partner and ask the same questions.

- Review telling time with the class. Make sure that when filling in the chart, they use *A.M.* and *P.M.* and not *o'clock*.
- After they've filled in the chart for themselves, they should ask a partner and fill in their partner's answers.

Look at the chart and write six sentences about your partner's schedule.

If students have problems thinking of sentences, they can write answers to the questions they asked their partners in Exercise A.

Listen and answer the questions about Luis's job. (CD3 • TR21)

- Tell students to look at the picture. *Who's he? What's he doing?*
- Students listen to the audio while looking at the picture. Ask them what they remember.
- Students listen again while looking at the questions about Luis. Ask students to write the answers to the questions.
- Students listen a third time, checking their answers

Listen and answer the questions about Jane's job. (CD3 • TR22)

Follow the same process as in Exercise C above.

Active Grammar: Present Tense: *Who* Questions

Ask students to look at the grammar chart. Encourage them to make more *Who* questions. For example: *Who has a job in a hotel?*

Ⓐ Working Together Work with a group of four or five students. Take turns asking the questions. If a student answers, "I do," write his or her name on the line.

Tell students that there may be more than one student who answers *I do* to any one question. They should write as many names as are applicable. Then, they should report to the class.

Ⓑ Read and write the question word. Some words will be used twice.

Do the exercise as an oral class activity. Ask one student to read the answer and another to call out the best question word.

	works	in a store?	I do.
Who	gets	benefits?	He does.
	has	a difficult job?	They do.

 Ⓐ Working Together Work with a group of four or five students. Take turns asking the questions. If a student answers, "I do," write his or her name on the line.

1. Who works in a store? _____
2. Who gets benefits? _____
3. Who works at night? _____ *(Answers will vary.)*
4. Who goes to work early in the morning? _____
5. Who has a difficult job? _____
6. Who has an interesting job? _____
7. Who has a boring job? _____

Ⓑ Read and write the question word. Some words will be used twice.

Do	Does	What	What time	Who	How many

1. __Does__ he get benefits?   Yes, he does.
2. __How many__ hours do you work?   I work 30 hours a week.
3. __What time__ do you begin work?   I begin work at 7:30 in the morning.
4. __Who__ works in a restaurant?   A waitress does.
5. __What time__ do you take a break?   I take a break at 10:30.
6. __Do__ waiters get tips?   Yes, they do.
7. __Who__ works outside?   Landscapers do.
8. __What__ does Jen do?   She's a hair stylist.

180 · Unit 13

More Action!

Using the information collected in Exercise A on page 180, ask students to make a bar chart about jobs on the board. Vertically down the left-hand side, write *fun job, difficult job, interesting job, boring job*. Fill in a one inch square horizontally for each student who has that kind of job. How many students have each kind of job?

Teaching Tip

Tell students they should check the employment ads regularly for new opportunities. Students should make use of ads both in English newspapers and newspapers in their own languages.

C **Put the words in the correct order to make questions.** Then, write the answers.

> No, she works part time.   She works four days a week.
> Yes, she does.   ~~She's a manicurist.~~
> She works from 10:00 to 6:00.   She works at the Sunrise Hotel.

1. does / do / Sheri / what ?
  What does Sheri do?   _She's a manicurist._

2. work / does / she / where ?
  Where does she work?   _She works at Sunrise Hotel._

3. does / work / how many days / she
  How many days does she work?   _She works four days a week._

4. full time / does / work / she
  Does she work full time?   _No, she works part time._

5. work / what hours / she / does
  What hours does she work?   _She works from 10:00 to 6:00._

6. like / she / does / her job
  Does she like her job?   _Yes, she does._

 D **Working Together** **Choose one of the jobs below.** Use your imagination. Write a conversation about the job. Act it out. (Answers will vary.)

1. What do you do?

2. Where do you work?

3. Do you work full time or part time?

4. What's your schedule?

5. Do you like your job?

6. Do you get benefits?

7. When do you have days off?

8. Do you use English at work?

Jobs • **181**

C **Put the words in the correct order to make questions. Then, write the answers.**

• Tell students that they should first look for the question word (*where*), then the auxiliary verb (*does*), then the subject (*Sheri*), and finally the main verb (*work*).

• Ask students to complete the exercise on their own and then call on different students to ask and answer each question.

D **Working Together Choose one of the jobs below. Use your imagination. Write a conversation about the job. Act it out.**

• You might want to introduce some vocabulary to go with each of the four jobs. Photographer: *shoot, develop, print, enlarge.* Florist: *bouquet, vase, arrangement, corsage.* Painter: *brush, roller, undercoat, prep work.* Cashier: *receipt, change, sales tax.*

• Ask students to role-play the conversation, choosing one or more of the listed jobs. They can answer other questions, using some of the vocabulary above. They can also choose other jobs to talk about.

More Action!

Ask students for ideas about what to ask an employer during a job interview. Write them on the board. For example: *What are the work hours? Is a uniform necessary? What qualifications are you looking for? Are there opportunities for promotion? What's the salary range?* Ask students to copy the list into their notebooks.

The Big Picture

The Big Picture: The Sunrise Hotel

 Look at the picture. Talk about the picture.

Ask students to talk about the picture, frame by frame. In the top left frame: *What's her job? Where is she? What's she doing right now? Describe the room.* In the top middle frame: *Who is he? What's he doing? What's on the cart?* In the top right frame: *Where is he? What's he doing? What's his job?* In the lower left frame: *Who are the people in the van? Who's the woman behind the desk?* In the lower right frame: *Where are they? What's the woman next to the piano doing?*

Listen and circle.

(CD3 • TR23)

• Have students listen to the audio while looking at the picture.
• Students listen again but to the first paragraph only. Ask them questions: *What's Ricardo's job? How many rooms does the hotel have?*
• Students listen to the next two paragraphs. *What employees does the hotel have? How many shifts? How much more do night employees make?*
• Students listen to the rest of the audio. *What kind of salaries does the hotel pay?*
• Ask students to answer the *true/false* statements. Call on individuals for the correct answers.

A **Look at the picture.** Talk about the picture.

1. Where are the employees working?   2. What are their jobs?

B **Listen and** circle.

(CD3 • TR23)

1.	Ricardo is the day manager of the Sunrise Hotel.	True	**(False)**
2.	The hotel has more than 200 rooms.	**(True)**	False
3.	The hotel has about 100 employees.	**(True)**	False
4.	The van driver parks cars.	True	**(False)**
5.	The hotel has three shifts.	**(True)**	False
6.	Night employees make more money than day employees.	**(True)**	False
7.	Everyone works full time.	True	**(False)**
8.	The salary is high.	True	**(False)**
9.	Some employees like the hours.	**(True)**	False
10.	The hotel has job openings.	**(True)**	False

182 • Unit 13

Teaching Tip

Explain that many companies ask for references before they hire a new employee. References are letters written about your character and experience from people you know well, such as former bosses or teachers.

Listen and write each question. Then, circle the answer.

1. What does Ricardo Lopez do?

   a. He's a tourist.   (**b.** He's the night manager.)   **c.** He's the desk clerk.

2. Does the hotel have a pool?

   (**a.** Yes, it does.)   **b.** No, it doesn't.

3. Where does the van driver go?

   a. To restaurants   (**b.** Downtown)   **c.** To other hotels

4. Who makes repairs?

   a. The plumber does.   **b.** The electrician does.   (**c.** Both a and b.)

5. Do all employees work full time?

   a. Yes, they do.   (**b.** No, they don't.)

6. How many employees does the hotel have?

   a. 200   (**b.** 100)   **c.** 20

Listen. Who is the manager speaking to? Complete.

1. He's speaking to the _____ housekeeper _____.

2. He's speaking to the _____ valet _____.

3. He's speaking to the _____ waiter/ waitress _____.

4. He's speaking to the _____ desk clerk _____.

5. He's speaking to the _____ laundry worker _____.

6. He's speaking to the _____ electrician _____.

7. He's speaking to the _____ van driver _____.

Answer the questions about the Sunrise Hotel.

1. What does Ricardo do? He's the evening manager.

2. Who drives guests to the airport? The van driver./ The van driver does.

3. Where does the singer work? She works in the club./ She works in the restaurant.

Jobs • **183**

Listen and write each question. Then, circle the answer. (CD3 • TR24)

• Students should listen to the audio while looking at the exercise.
• Students listen again, pausing to write in the questions they hear.
• Now they should go back and circle the correct answers to the questions.
• Call on individuals for the correct answers.

Listen. Who is the manager speaking to? Complete. (CD3 • TR25)

• Ask students to look back at the pictures of workers in this unit and review the vocabulary.
• Then, ask students to listen to the audio.
• Ask them to listen again, writing in the correct answers.

Answer the questions about the Sunrise Hotel.

After students have answered these questions, have them make more questions about the hotel. Have them work with a partner to and ask and answer the questions.

More Action!

Help students draft a letter of enquiry to a hotel about jobs. Have one student write the letter on the board: *I'm writing to ask if you have any job openings at present. I have experience as a _____ .* Be sure to use an appropriate opening and closing.

Reading: Working at the Hotel

A **Discuss these questions before you read.**

• Talk about hotels. Ask students if they've ever worked in a hotel. Ask about hotels they've stayed in.
• Ask students to scan the first reading for details. *How many hours does Richard work in a week? What are his busy days? Who are his customers? What does he do for them?*
• Have one student read the first few sentences and another finish reading the paragraph.
• Ask students to ask and answer questions about the paragraph in pairs.
• Follow the same process with the second paragraph, asking students to scan for details, read aloud, and ask and answer comprehension questions about the passage.

B **Complete each sentence using *Richard* or *Ana*.**

Tell students to look back at the two paragraphs and underline the information that will enable them to complete the sentences.

A **Discuss these questions before you read.**

1. Do you know anyone who works at a hotel? What do they do?

Richard is a hair stylist at a hotel. He works from Tuesday to Saturday. He works 40 hours a week, from 10:00 A.M. to 6:00 P.M. He is very busy on Fridays and Saturdays because everyone wants to look good for their special parties at the hotel. Most of Richard's customers are tourists or visitors to the city for a special occasion, such as a wedding, an anniversary, or a birthday. He washes, cuts, colors, curls, and blow-dries hair. He enjoys talking with his customers. He stands all day, and he's tired at the end of the day.

Ana is a cook at a hotel. She works from Friday to Sunday. She works 21 hours a week. She starts work at 2:00 P.M. and goes home at 9:00 P.M. She stands all day, so she is tired at 9:00 P.M. She is very busy on weekends because the kitchen has to prepare special meals for parties at the hotel. She cuts vegetables, makes soups, prepares all kinds of meats, and helps with desserts. During the week, Ana goes to cooking school because she wants to become a hotel chef. She wants to manage a hotel kitchen.

B **Complete each sentence using *Richard* or *Ana*.**

1. ___Richard___ works full time.   **5.** ___Ana___ works all weekend.

2. ___Ana___ works part time.   **6.** ___Richard/Ana___ stands all day.

3. ___Ana___ works in the evening.   **7.** ___Richard___ talks to customers.

4. ___Ana___ goes to school.

More Action!

Guide students in writing a resumé. Bring a sample resumé to class and hand it out. It should be for one of the jobs mentioned in this unit. Point out the placement of contact information and work objective. Then, show how to list experience in block form and in reverse chronological order. Now ask students to write their own resumés. Move among them, making suggestions.

A Read.

My Job

I am a security guard. I like my job.
I work at the Summit Mall in Westbrook.
I work full time. I work 40 hours a week,
from Wednesday to Sunday. My hours
are from 8:30 to 4:30, and I have a half hour for lunch. I
also have a fifteen-minute break. I receive benefits, too. I have
medical and dental insurance, vacation, and sick days.
    My job is easy, but sometimes it is difficult when the mall
is busy. I walk around the mall all day. I answer questions
and give directions. I carry a cell phone. In an emergency, I
call the police or an ambulance.

B Complete. (Answers will vary.)

1. I am a _____. **I like / don't like** my job.
   your job

2. I work at _____ in _____
   name of the company   location

3. I _____
   job responsibilities

C Write about your job. (Answers will vary.)

> **WRITING NOTE**
> The names of companies begin with capital letters:
> **C**lothes **C**loset

D Sharing Our Stories Read your partner's story.
Then, complete the sentences below about your partner's job.

1. My partner is a(n) _____

2. My partner works at _____

3. My partner **likes / doesn't like** _____

Jobs • **185**

Writing Our Stories: My Job

A Read.

• Ask students if they ever shop at malls. What kind of stores do they go to? Do they ever see security guards in the mall? Would they like to be a security guard? Why or why not?
• Ask students to read the passage to themselves. They may need help with some vocabulary: *insurance, emergency, ambulance.*
• Ask comprehension questions, such as: *Where does she work? What benefits does she have? What does she do all day?*

B Complete.

• Ask students to talk about their jobs, if they have one. Those who do not can talk about being students or other applicable experience.
• When students have completed the exercise, ask them to tell the class their answers.

C Write about your job.

Remind your students that they should choose a title for their paragraphs and write in complete sentences. They should use commas if they're including lists of job responsibilities.

D Sharing Our Stories Read your partner's story. Then, complete the sentences below about your partner's job.

Students should exchange papers, complete the sentences, and report to the class.

English in Action: Looking for Jobs

Ⓐ **Look at these job ads. Circle the names of the jobs.**

Make sure that students understand they only need to circle the job titles, nothing else in the ad.

Ⓑ **Work with a partner. Read these classified ads. Ask and answer the questions.**

• Ask students to scan the ads for details. They should look for experience, pay, benefits, phone number, etc.
• Ask them to write the answers to the questions and then read their answers to the class.

Ⓐ **Look at these job ads.** (Circle) the names of the jobs.

Help Wanted	Job Openings	Position Available
(Bellhop)	(Housekeepers)	(Cook)
(Desk Clerk)	(Laundry Workers)	Experience Required
Western Hotel	No Experience.	Paradise Hotel
137 Kennedy Street	Will train on job.	Call 644-8899
Apply in person.	Call the Carlton Hotel.	Ask for Mr. Thomas.
	555-6777	

Ⓑ **Work with a partner.** Read these classified ads. Ask and answer the questions.

COOK FT 2 years experience required. Excellent pay w/ benefits. Call Thurs. – Sat. 11:00 A.M. – 4:00 P.M. 555-2126

> FT = full time
> PT = part time

FRONT DESK CLERK for hotel PT Eve shift 3 P.M. – 11 P.M. Will train. Apply in person. Plaza Hotel. Seaside.

LANDSCAPER Immediate FT opening for landscape crew. Valid license required. $9.00/hour. Benefits, vacation. Call today. 555-9328

MAINTENANCE MECHANIC FT Must have painting, plumbing, and electrical skills. Salary based on experience. Good benefits. Sunrise Resort. 555-4334

1. Which jobs are full time?
cook, landscaper, maintenance mechanic

2. Which job pays $9 an hour?
landscaper

3. Which jobs have benefits?
cook, landscaper, maintenance mechanic

4. Which job requires a driver's license?
landscaper

5. Which jobs require experience?
cook, maintenance mechanic

6. Which job requires painting?
maintenance mechanic

7. Which job has excellent pay?
cook

8. Which jobs do you need to call?
cook, landscaper, maintenance mechanic

More Action!

Help students design ads for hotel jobs as if they were the manager. There are openings for desk clerks, bellhops, a van driver, and a maintenance man. Desk clerks and the maintenance man must have experience. The van driver must have a driver's license. Uniforms are provided for all staff. There are benefits for all positions and good salaries. Students can use the ads on this page as models. If they prefer, they can write ads for other kinds of jobs.

Teaching Tip

Tell students that during a job interview, it's a common practice for the interviewer to ask the applicant why he or she wants to leave his or her present position. A simple answer is to say *I want more opportunities*. It's not a good idea to say something negative like *I'm leaving because I hate my boss*.

Listen and read. Then, practice with a partner.

A: Hello. I'm calling about the job as a security guard.

B: Do you have any experience?

A: Yes. I was a security guard at a bank in Atlantic City for four years.

B: Can you come in for an interview?

A: Yes, I can.

B: We have appointments at 10:00 and at 12:00. What time is good for you?

A: 10:00 is good.

B: Okay. What is your name please?

A: My name is Brian García.

B: Okay, Mr. García. See you at 10:00, and please bring two references.

A: Thank you. See you at 10:00.

Complete the job application. (Answers will vary.)

				The Sunrise Hotel
Position _____				

Name _____
        Last   First   Middle

Address _____
        Number   Street   City   State

Social Security No. _____   Date of birth ____ / ____ / ____

Telephone _____

Work Experience			
From	To	Employer	Position

Signature of applicant _____

Jobs • **187**

Listen and read. Then, practice with a partner. (CD3 • TR26)

- Get students to discuss job interview habits, good and bad. What are some good things to do? What are some things you should never do?
- Students listen to the conversation and then tell you what they remember from it.
- Have students practice the conversation with a partner.

Complete the job application.

The application can be for any kind of job students choose. If they don't have work experience, they can use any other relevant skills. Tell students that they should not make up information on a real job application.

Teaching Tip

Some cultures emphasize modesty about accomplishments. Tell students not to be modest in job applications and interviews. Employers really want to know their strengths.

Unit 14

A Visit to the Doctor

Dictionary: Parts of the Body

  Listen and repeat.
(CD3 • TR27)

• Ask students to look at the pictures. They may already know some of the vocabulary. Ask: *Can anyone name the parts of the body without looking at the words?*
• Have students listen to the audio for parts of the body, repeating after the speaker.
• Say the numbers of the various parts of the body and ask students to call out the correct terms.
• Tell a student to point to parts of himself or herself while others say the words.

Parts of the Body

Dictionary

 Listen and repeat.
CD3·TR27

Parts of the body

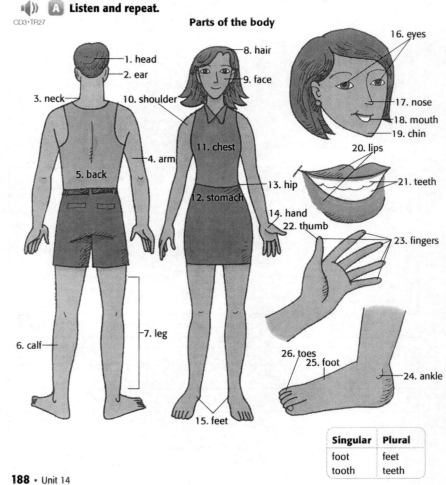

1. head
2. ear
3. neck
4. arm
5. back
6. calf
7. leg
8. hair
9. face
10. shoulder
11. chest
12. stomach
13. hip
14. hand
15. feet
16. eyes
17. nose
18. mouth
19. chin
20. lips
21. teeth
22. thumb
23. fingers
24. ankle
25. foot
26. toes

Singular	Plural
foot	feet
tooth	teeth

188 · Unit 14

More Action!

Ask students to take a poll, asking class members how often they go to the doctor each year. Make a pie chart on the board showing what percentages of students go once, twice, etc. Ask what kind of doctors they go to and write some of the terms on the board: *pediatrician, dentist, neurologist, ophthalmologist, dermatologist.*

Health Problems

1. an allergy

2. asthma

3. a burn

4. a cold

5. chicken pox

6. a cough
He's coughing.

7. a fever

8. a headache

9. a sore throat

10. a stomachache

11. a toothache

12. a sneeze
She's sneezing.

  C **Listen and repeat.**
CD3·TR29

Remedies

1. aspirin

2. ibuprofen

3. an ice pack

4. a heating pad

5. an inhaler

6. lotion

7. a dentist

8. a doctor

A Visit to the Doctor · **189**

B **Listen and repeat.**
(CD3 • TR28)

• Ask students to look at the pictures of common health problems. Have they ever had any of these problems? Which ones? What did they do about it/them?
• Students listen to the audio while looking at the pictures.
• Students listen again, repeating after the audio.
• Call out individual numbers and ask students to identify the health problems.
• Have students ask and answer questions about the health problems:
S1: *What's health problem number 4?*
S2: *A cold.*

C **Listen and repeat.**
(CD3 • TR29)

• Ask students if they've ever used any of these remedies. Which ones? Did they feel better?
• Students listen to the audio while looking at the pictures.
• They listen again, repeating the words.
• Call out individual numbers and ask students to tell you the remedy. Ask them not to look at the words.

More Action!

Mime one of the health problems and ask students to guess what it is. For example, put both hands to your head and look as if you're in pain to illustrate *a headache*. The first student who guesses correctly does the next mime.

A Visit to the Doctor · **189**

Word Builder

Word Builder

A Complete.

• Ask students to complete the labeling exercise using the words in the answer boxes. If they need to, they can look back to page 188.

• Call on individuals to tell you what they've written. Correct pronunciation.

Word Partnerships

Ask students to ask and answer questions using the phrases in the box and the present continuous:

S1: *Are you catching a cold?*
S2: *No, I'm not.*

S1: *Are you getting well?*
S2: *Yes, I am.*

The verb *get* can also be used with *sore throat, stomachache, cough,* and *fever*. The verb *catch* can also be used with *chicken pox*.

A Complete.

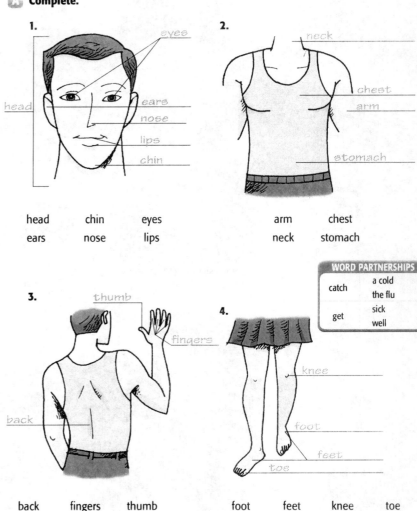

1.

head   chin   eyes
ears   nose   lips

2.

arm   chest
neck   stomach

3.

back   fingers   thumb

4.

foot   feet   knee   toe

WORD PARTNERSHIPS

catch	a cold
	the flu
get	sick
	well

More Action!

Play *Simon Says*. Ask students to stand beside their seats. Tell them that if you say the words *Simon says* before a command (*Simon says touch your nose*), they should act out the command (touch their noses). If you say the command *touch your noses* without saying *Simon says* before it, they should do nothing.

If student follows the command when you didn't say *Simon says* he or she is out of the game and must sit down. Use all the parts of the body mentioned in this unit. At the end, the students still standing are the winners.

Teaching Tip

In some cultures, it's not polite to mention parts of the body. If students find this embarrassing, don't force them, as long as they can write the words.

A Listen. Look at the pictures and complete.

My back **hurts**.
My feet **hurt**.

1. Her _head hurts_. 2. Her _back hurts_. 3. Her _stomach hurts_

4. His _ear hurts_. 5. His _feet hurt_. 6. His _tooth hurts_

B Listen again and repeat.

hurt = ache

C Pronunciation: *ache* Listen and repeat.

1. a backache 2. an earache 3. a headache 4. a stomachache 5. a toothache

D Listen and complete the sentences.

1. He has a _toothache_.
2. She has a _backache_.
3. I have a _headache_.
4. He has a _stomachache_.
5. I have an _earache_.

E Working Together **Act out a problem from page 189 or page 191.** The other students will guess the problem.

Active Grammar: Present Tense

A **Listen. Look at the pictures and complete.** (CD3 • TR30)

• Ask students to look at the pictures and guess what is wrong with the six people.
• Students listen to the audio while looking at the pictures.
• They listen again, pausing to fill in the blanks.
• Students listen a third time, checking their answers.

B **Listen again and repeat.** (CD3 • TR30)

C **Pronunciation: *ache* Listen and repeat.** (CD3 • TR31)

Write the words *stomach*, *back*, and *ache* on the board. Ask students what letters make the *k* sound in each word. Students listen to the audio, repeating the words.

D **Listen and complete the sentences.** (CD3 • TR32)

Students listen to the audio, repeating the sentences and filling in the blanks. Correct any problems with final *k*.

E **Working Together Act out a problem from page 189 or page 191. The other students will guess the problem.**

See **More Action!**, page 189, and the **Teaching Tip**, page 190.

Active Grammar: *Have/Has*

A Match.

- Introduce *has* and *have*. Ask students to look at the grammar chart. Using the health problems on page 189, ask them to make more *has/have* sentences. For example: *He has an allergy*.
- In the exercise, tell students to look for the health problem that the person or persons have and then to find the sentence that best describes it.
- Call on individuals to read their matches aloud and make any corrections necessary.

| I You | **have** | a sore throat. |
| He She | **has** | |

| We They | **have** | sore throats. |

A Match.

_____e_____ **1.** She has the chicken pox.   **a.**

_____h_____ **2.** She has a sore throat.   **b.**

_____g_____ **3.** They have allergies.   **c.**

_____d_____ **4.** They have colds.   **d.**

_____a_____ **5.** He has a headache.   **e.**

_____f_____ **6.** They have stomachaches.   **f.**

_____c_____ **7.** He has asthma.   **g.**

_____b_____ **8.** She has a fever.   **h.**

192 • Unit 14

More Action!

Explain that many different medical conditions have similar symptoms. Doctors often diagnose an illness by a process of elimination and by finding out what the patient *doesn't* have. Ask a student to choose an illness or symptom and write it on the board. The other students must say what the patient *doesn't* have. If a student writes *stomachache*, students should respond: *He/she doesn't have a sore throat. He/she doesn't have a headache.* Students should continue this until they have used all of the health problems.

Teaching Tip

On the board, write vocabulary for other common medical conditions and their symptoms. You might want to include *flu, rash, acne, sprained ankle,* and *athlete's foot.*

Listen and repeat.
CD3·TR33

1.
2.
3.
4.

5.
6.
7.
8.

B Read and number the remedies in Exercise A.

<u>5</u> Take some aspirin.   <u>8</u> Drink liquids.   <u>6</u> Stay in bed.

<u>2</u> Call the doctor.   <u>4</u> Put on lotion.   <u>7</u> Use a heating pad.

<u>1</u> Use an ice pack.   <u>3</u> Use an inhaler.

C Working Together Tell your partner about a health problem. Your partner will give you advice. Use the remedies below or give your own advice.

Health Problems	Advice
a cough	Call the doctor.
a headache	Call the dentist.
a backache	Drink some hot tea.
a toothache	Drink some soda.
a burn	Put ice on it.
a bad cold	Stay in bed.
a fever	Take aspirin.
a sore throat	Take ibuprofen.
	Take some medicine.
	Use a heating pad.

I have a sore throat.

Drink some hot tea.

A Visit to the Doctor · **193**

Household Remedies

A Listen and repeat.
(CD3 • TR33)

• Ask students to talk about the pictures. What is each person doing? What are the items in numbers 3 and 5 for?
• Students listen to the audio while looking at the pictures.
• Students listen again, repeating each command.
• Say numbers of the pictures out of order and ask students to give the command.

B Read and number the remedies in Exercise A.

Do this as a class activity. Have students tell you which picture goes with which remedy.

C Working Together Tell your partner about a health problem. Your partner will give you advice. Use the remedies below or give your own advice.

• Tell students to work in pairs. One student states a health problem and another student tells him or her what to do about it. They can use the dialogue in the speech balloons as a model.
• Have students reverse roles and repeat the process.
• Call on pairs of students to role-play the dialogues for the class.

More Action!

Most cultures have home remedies for common health problems. Ask students to be prepared to talk about remedies from their cultures. They can also ask older family members for some home remedies.

Active Grammar:
Must / Must Not

Ask students to look at the grammar chart. Can they think of other examples using *must* and *must not*? For example: *Drivers must stop at a red light.* Point out that *must not is* sometimes contracted to *mustn't.*

 Read the directions. Circle *must* or *must not.*

• Point out the directions on the medicine bottle. Explain *adult dose* and the abbreviations *tsp.* and *yrs.*
• Ask students to do exercise items 2 and 3.
• Point out the directions in the box. Explain *capsules* and *alcohol.*
• Tell students to complete the exercise and compare their answers with a partner.

A Read the directions. Circle *must* or *must not.*

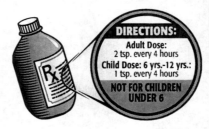

| You | **must** | take this medicine with food. |
| Children | **must not** | take this medicine. |

> must = It is necessary.
> must not = Don't do it.

1. Adults (must) / must not take two teaspoons every four hours.
2. Adults must / (must not) take four teaspoons every two hours.
3. Children under six must / (must not) take this medicine.

> **Directions:**
> Adults: Take 2 capsules every 4–6 hours.
>   Do not give to children.
>   Do not use with alcohol.

4. An adult (must) / must not take this medicine every four to six hours.
5. Parents must / (must not) give this medicine to children.
6. A patient must / (must not) drink alcohol and take this medicine.

> **Directions:**
>   Take 1 capsule once a day.
>   Take with food or milk.
>   Do not drive; may cause drowsiness.

> once a day = one time a day

7. A patient (must) / must not take one capsule a day.
8. Patients (must) / must not take this medicine with food or milk.
9. Patients must / (must not) drive if they take this medicine.

> **CULTURE NOTE**
> To get a prescription, you must see a doctor.

194 · Unit 14

More Action!

Print out copies of labels of non-prescription drugs commonly used. Write out phrases from the labels on the board and help students work out their meaning. For example: *Do not use if seal is missing or broken. Do not crush, chew, or break tablet.*

Teaching Tip

The word *once* means *eleven* in Spanish. Make sure Spanish speaking students understand that *once a day* means one time, not eleven times.

Teaching Tip

Review the process of getting prescribed medicine: a visit to the doctor, then to the pharmacist (where they give an insurance number).

B Read the label. Complete the directions. Use *must* or *must not*.

Greenway Pharmacy
Dr. Brown
Patient: John Smith
Penicillin 250 mg.
Qty: 30

Take 1 tablet in the morning and 1 tablet before bed. Take all tablets. Refrigerate.

1. The patient ___must take___ (take) two tablets a day.

2. He ___must eat___ (eat) food with this medicine.

3. He ___must not drink___ (drink) alcohol with this medicine.

4. He ___must take___ (take) all the tablets.

5. He ___must put___ (put) this medicine in the refrigerator.

C Pronunciation: Medical Specialists Listen and repeat.

1. a pediatrician   3. an obstetrician / a gynecologist   5. a psychologist

2. an allergist   4. an optometrist   6. a dermatologist

D Match.

___b___ 1. A pediatrician   a. checks your eyes.

___f___ 2. An allergist   b. takes care of children.

___e___ 3. An obstetrician / a gynecologist   c. talks to people about their personal problems.

___a___ 4. An optometrist   d. checks your skin.

___c___ 5. A psychologist   e. takes care of women's health.

___d___ 6. A dermatologist   f. helps people control their allergies.

E Working Together With a partner, write the names of three drugstores or pharmacies in your area. Which one do you use? (Answers will vary.)

1. _____

2. _____

3. _____

A Visit to the Doctor • 195

Teaching Tip

Tell students if they can't understand the doctor's English, they should ask for a translator or bring one with them.

More Action!

Hospitals can be confusing places. Teach students some useful questions and then ask them to make dialogues using them. For example: *Where is the emergency room? Is there a handicapped access ramp at that entrance? May I speak to the doctor? Are you the nurse in charge? What's his/her blood pressure / temperature? Can he/she have visitors?*

B Read the label. Complete the directions. Use *must* or *must not*.

• Ask students to look at the label. Talk about any new vocabulary words.
• Tell students to do the exercise and go over the answers orally.

C Pronunciation: Medical Specialists Listen and repeat.

(CD3 • TR34)

• Ask students if they know the terms for any other kinds of doctors, such as *pediatrician*.
• Students listen to the audio while looking at the words.
• They listen again, repeating the words.
• Explain what each kind of specialist does.

D Match.

Ask students to match definitions with specialists. Can they think of any other kinds of specialists?

E Working Together With a partner, write the names of three drugstores or pharmacies in your area. Which one do you use?

Point out that a drugstore and a pharmacy are really the same thing, depending on where you live.

The Big Picture: In the Waiting Room

🔊 A Listen and label the people in the waiting room. (CD3 • TR35)

- Ask students to talk about the picture. What is each person doing? Can they tell what's wrong with some of the patients? Which ones?
- Students listen to the audio while looking at the picture.
- Students listen again, pausing to label all the people in the picture.
- Students listen a third time, checking their labels.
- Ask questions about the picture: *What season is it? Who's Mrs. Jacob? What's wrong with Mrs. Lee? How old is Mr. Green?*

B Answer the questions.

Ask students to write answers about the people in the picture. They may need to hear the audio again at this point.

🔊 A Listen and label the people in the waiting room.
CD3·TR35

~~Dr. Johnson~~	Mrs. Lee	Julia	Mr. Henderson
Mrs. Jacob	Mr. Green	Mr. Patel	Andy
Mrs. Jackson	Mrs. Rios	Miss Gonzalez	

B Answer the questions.

1. Who is getting a checkup? Mr. Green
2. Who has an allergy? Miss Gonzalez
3. Who has a burn? Julia
4. Who has a bad cough? Mrs. Lee
5. Who is working in the office? Mrs. Jacob
6. Who is sick? Mrs. Lee
7. Who has a headache? Mr. Patel
8. Who is getting a tetanus shot? Andy
9. Who is a new patient? Mrs. Jackson

tetanus shot

196 • Unit 14

More Action!

Write the names of the patients in Dr. Johnson's waiting room on labels with adhesive backing. Put them on the backs of students but don't tell them who they are. Say that they all have a case of *amnesia* and have lost their memories. They must find out who they are by asking questions about their reasons for being in the waiting room in the picture.

For example:
S1: *Do I need a tetanus shot?*
S2: *No, you don't.*
S1: *Do I have a headache?*
S2: *No, you don't.*
S1: *Do I have a burn on my finger?*
S2: *Yes, you do.*
S1: *Am I Julia?*
S2: *Yes, you are.*

C **Listen again.** Read and (circle).

1. Mrs. Jacob is the doctor.   True   (False)
2. Mrs. Lee has a headache.   True   (False)
3. Mr. Green has a cold.   True   (False)
4. Mrs. Rios has allergies.   True   (False)
5. Julia's finger hurts.   (True)   False
6. Mr. Patel has a bad back.   True   (False)
7. Mrs. Jackson is a new patient.   (True)   False
8. Miss Gonzalez's throat hurts.   True   (False)
9. Andy has a stomachache.   True   (False)

D **Complete.**

allergies	bad-cough	prescription
checkup	head	tetanus shot

1. Mrs. Lee has a _____ *bad cough* _____.
2. Mr. Green needs a _____ *checkup* _____.
3. Mr. Patel's _____ *head* _____ hurts.
4. Miss Gonzalez has _____ *allergies* _____.
5. She needs a _____ *prescription* _____.
6. Andy needs a _____ *tetanus shot* _____.

E **(Circle).**

1. The waiting room is busy because . . .
   a. it's late.   **b.** the doctor is away.   (**c.** many people are sick.)
2. Mrs. Jackson is going to fill out . . .
   a. a prescription.   (**b.** a patient information form.)   **c.** an application.
3. Mrs. Lee . . .
   (**a.** is coughing.)   **b.** is talking to the nurse.   **c.** is sneezing.
4. Miss Gonzalez needs a prescription for . . .
   (**a.** allergies.)   **b.** asthma.   **c.** a cold.
5. Andy feels . . .
   a. sick.   **b.** happy.   (**c.** scared and nervous.)

A Visit to the Doctor • **197**

◀)) **C** **Listen again. Read and circle.** (CD3 • TR35)

- Students listen to the audio one more time, if necessary.
- Then, they answer the *true/false* questions as an in-class exercise.
- Call on individuals for the correct answers.

D **Complete.**

Ask students to fill in the blanks with what they remember from the story. They can exchange papers and compare answers.

E **Circle.**

Ask students to circle the best answers according to what they heard on the audio.

More Action!

Make sure students understand the difference between an illness and an immediate medical emergency. If they have a medical or other kind of emergency requiring immediate help, they should dial 911 and explain the emergency. Then, they will be asked to give their name, address, and phone number and may be given other instructions. It's important to understand what is and is not an emergency. Put a list of situations on the board and ask students to explain why or why they're not emergencies. You can include the following:

My husband/wife is having bad chest pains.
My cat is in a tree.
Our house is on fire.
My family doesn't have enough food.
I have a cold.
My baby is drinking some bathroom cleaning liquid.
My dog is acting really funny.
Someone I don't know is in my house.
I have a headache.

Reading: A Good Night's Sleep

A **Look at the chart. How many hours of sleep do you need?**

- Encourage the class to talk about their sleep habits. Does anyone have problems sleeping?
- Ask them to look at the chart. Where do they fit in the chart? Do they get fewer or more hours of sleep than their level in the chart?

B **Read.**

- Ask students to scan the reading quickly, trying to pick up some of the six suggestions.
- Ask: *What are the suggestions?* Get students to tell them to you in their own words.
- Ask individuals to read each of the six suggestions. Does anyone in the class have other ways of falling asleep?

C **Read each problem. Give some good advice.**

- Ask students to read about Joseph and then tell you what his problem is. One possible problem is that he may not be getting as many hours of sleep as he needs.
- What is Maribel's problem? Perhaps she needs to relax before closing her eyes.
- What about Mr. Andaba? Does he eat dinner too late at night?

A **Look at the chart.** How many hours of sleep do you need?

Age	Hours of sleep per night
Adults	7–8 hours
Teenagers	8–9 hours
Children	10–12 hours

B **Read.**

Tips for Getting a Good Night's Sleep

Is it difficult for you to fall asleep? Here are some ideas for a good night's sleep:

1. Try to go to bed and get up at the same time every day.
2. Take a warm shower or bath before you go to bed.
3. Relax before you close your eyes. Read a book or listen to soft music.
4. Don't eat late at night.
5. Make your room quiet and comfortable. Turn off the light.
6. Drink a cup of warm milk before you go to bed. Don't drink coffee or tea. Caffeine will keep you awake.

Everyone has trouble sleeping sometimes. If you have trouble sleeping for more than one month, see your doctor.

C **Read each problem.** Give some good advice. *(Answers will vary.)*

1. Joseph is 16 years old. He goes to school, plays soccer after school, works from 6:00 to 9:00, and then he does his homework until 12:00 A.M. He can't concentrate in school.
2. Maribel has many family problems. When she goes to bed, she thinks about her children, her husband, and her sisters. She can't sleep.
3. Mr. Andaba works from 3:00 to 11:00. When he gets home, he eats dinner. He goes to bed at 1:00, but he doesn't sleep well.

198 · Unit 14

More Action!

Ask students if their cultures have any special cures for insomnia. What are they? Do they work?

Teaching Tip

There may be more than one correct answer for each part of Exercise C. Accept any reasonable answers.

A. Read.

I am 70 years old. I am a senior citizen. I think I am healthy. I am very active. I am retired, but I volunteer three days a week at the elementary school. I help the children read. I go to the park with my wife, and we walk two miles every morning. I go to the doctor every year for a checkup, and I see my dentist twice a year. I am a healthy person.

B. Complete the sentences about your lifestyle. (Answers will vary.)

1. I **am / am not** healthy.

2. I **always / sometimes / never** exercise. I exercise _____ time (s) a week.

3. I **sleep** _____ hours a night.

4. I go to the doctor **every year / twice a year.** *OR* **I never get a checkup.**

5. I visit the dentist **once a year / twice a year.** *OR* **I never go to the dentist.**

6. I need to ❑ exercise more.

           ❑ sleep more.

           ❑ lose weight / gain weight.

           ❑ visit the doctor for a checkup.

> **WRITING NOTE**
> Check the plural nouns in your story. Most plural nouns end in *s*: *days, nights*. Some plural nouns are irregular: *children*.

C. Write a paragraph about your lifestyle. (Answers will vary.)

D. Sharing Our Stories Read your partner's story. Complete the sentences.

1. _____ **always / sometimes / never** exercises.

2. _____ sleeps _____ hours a day.

Writing Our Stories: My Lifestyle

A. Read.

- Encourage students to talk about the picture. Ask: *Who are these people and what are they doing? How old do you think they are?*
- Before the students read, explain what a *senior citizen* is. See if students can guess the meaning, from context, of the words *retire* and *volunteer.*
- Ask students to read silently. Have them tell you the main facts.

B. Complete the sentences about your lifestyle.

- Encourage students to talk about their health and lifestyle. What kind of exercise do they get? Do they take any medications?
- After students have answered the questions, tell them to compare their answers with those of a partner.

C. Write a paragraph about your lifestyle.

Suggest that students write a bit about what makes their lifestyle unique.

D. Sharing Our Stories Read your partner's story. Complete the sentences.

Ask students to write another paragraph, this time in third person singular, summarizing their partner's lifestyle.

English in Action: Making an Appointment

  A **Listen and practice with a partner.**

(CD3 • TR36)

• Ask students if they've ever made a medical appointment in English. Was it for themselves or for someone else?

• Have students listen to the conversation while looking at it in their books.

• Students listen again, repeating every line.

• Say only the receptionist's lines and call on individuals to provide the patient's lines. Then, do the opposite.

 **B** **Working Together Complete the conversation with a partner.**

Tell one student in a pair to complete the missing parts of the receptionist's lines and the other to do the same with the patient's lines.

C **Working Together Act out the conversation in Exercise B.**

Students can continue to substitute lines and make up different symptoms.

A **Listen and practice with a partner.**

CD3•TR36

Receptionist:	Hello, Dr. Walsh's office.
Patient:	Hello, this is Mrs. Moreno.
Receptionist:	Hello, Mrs. Moreno. How can I help you today?
Patient:	My daughter is sick, and I need an appointment.
Receptionist:	What's the problem?
Patient:	She has a high fever and a sore throat.
Receptionist:	Can you come in today at 2:00?
Patient:	Yes, I can.
Receptionist:	OK, Mrs. Moreno. See you at 2:00.

B **Working Together Complete the conversation with a partner.** (Answers will vary.)

Receptionist: Hello, Dr. _____'s office.

Patient: Hello, this is _____.

Receptionist: Hello, _____. How can I help you today?

Patient: I'm sick, and I need an appointment.

Receptionist: What's the problem?

Patient: _____.

Receptionist: Can you come in today at _____?

Patient: _____.

Receptionist: OK, _____. See you at _____.

C **Working Together Act out the conversation in Exercise B.**

Teaching Tip

Students may not feel comfortable talking about their real medical conditions or medications. If so, they can just make them up.

D **Complete.** Use your own information. *(Answers will vary.)*

1. Dr. _____ is a good doctor.
2. Dr. _____ is a good dentist.
3. _____ is a good hospital.
4. _____ is a good drugstore.

E **Complete the form.** *(Answers will vary.)*

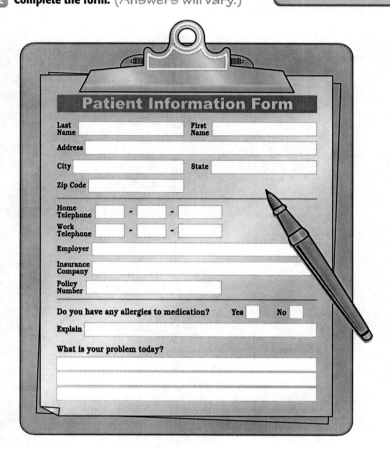

Patient Information Form

Last Name _____ First Name _____

Address _____

City _____ State _____

Zip Code _____

Home Telephone ____ - ____ - ____

Work Telephone ____ - ____ - ____

Employer _____

Insurance Company _____

Policy Number _____

Do you have any allergies to medication? Yes ☐ No ☐

Explain _____

What is your problem today?

_____

D **Complete. Use your own information.**

Tell students to write true information about doctors and medical services in their community.

E **Complete the form.**

Point out the **Culture Note** about filling out patient information forms. Then, ask students to fill out this form. Explain the terms *insurance company* and *policy number*. If students don't wish to fill in personal information, they can make up the information.

Teaching Tip

Bring a medical thermometer to class and talk about taking a temperature. Most students will be used to Centigrade, or Celsius, temperatures. Write these equivalents on the board:

$86\,°F = 30.0\,°C$
$100\,°F = 37.8\,°C$
$104\,°F = 40.0\,°C$

More Action!

Many people have difficulty understanding the health system and health insurance in the United States. If possible, ask an expert to come and speak to the class about it in very simple terms. If that's not possible, ask students what kind of health insurance they have here and what they had in their own countries.

Explain that most people get insurance and other benefits through their jobs (if they have a full-time job). Some states have *mandatory universal coverage*. As an Internet option, ask students to find out information about their own state and report back to the class. They can also research various local businesses and companies and find what kind of insurance coverage they offer.

Unit 15

Weekend Plans

Dictionary: Daily Routines and Activities

  Listen and repeat.

(CD3 • TR37)

- Ask students to look at the pictures on this page and talk about them. Ask: *Who are these people? What are they doing?*
- Students listen to the audio while looking at the pictures.
- They listen again, pausing to repeat the phrases.
- Ask students to work in pairs, one saying a picture number and the other making a sentence:

S1: *Number 3.*

S2: *They're going to the movies.*

Then, the students should reverse roles.

 Listen and repeat.

Daily Routines

1. get up early

2. do homework

3. go to the movies

4. go out to dinner

5. sleep late

6. rent a movie

7. visit friends

8. stay home

9. play soccer

10. watch TV

11. work

12. study

202 · Unit 15

More Action!

Ask students to mime activities from this page and the other students will guess what they are. Have them guess by saying the appropriate phrase and then using it in a complete sentence. For example: (*go out to dinner*). *Sophia is going out to dinner.* The student who guesses correctly becomes the next student to mime.

 **Listen and repeat.**

Celebrations

1. an anniversary   **2.** a birthday   **3.** a graduation   **4.** a wedding

  Listen and repeat.

Chores

1. iron clothes   **2.** do the laundry   **3.** do the shopping   **4.** vacuum the living room

  Listen and repeat.

Sports and Physical Activities

1. fish   **2.** dance   **3.** swim   **4.** camp

WORD PARTNERSHIPS	
play	soccer
	baseball
	volleyball
go	fishing
	dancing
	shopping

  Listen and repeat.
(CD3 • TR38)

- Ask students to look at the pictures and talk about them. Ask: *What are these people celebrating?*
- Students listen to the audio while looking at the pictures.
- They listen again, pausing to repeat the phrases.
- Ask students to work in pairs, one saying a picture number and the other making a sentence. Next, the students should reverse roles.

  Listen and repeat.
(CD3 • TR39)

- Encourage students to talk about chores they have to do regularly. What chores do they like and dislike?
- Students listen to the audio while looking at the pictures.
- They listen again, pausing to repeat the phrases.
- Ask students to work in pairs, one saying a picture number and the other making a sentence.

  Listen and repeat.
(CD3 • TR40)

Ask students what kinds of sports and activities they like to take part in or watch. Then, repeat the same process as in Exercises A, B, and C.

Word Partnerships

Ask students to add additional activities that can be used with the verbs *play* and *go*.

Word Builder

A. Match. What is each person going to do?

• Point out that the numbered statements are in the simple present but the lettered statements tell us about the future.

• Tell students to read the numbered statements first so that they understand that as a result of those facts, someone is *going to* do something. They must choose what that is. Call on individuals for the answers.

B. Complete with the correct celebration. You can use some words more than once.

Review with students the meaning of the celebratory occasions. Then, ask them to fill in the blanks.

A. Match. What is each person going to do?

___e___ **1.** Tom is driving to the river.

___h___ **2.** The students are walking to the library.

___g___ **3.** Mr. Lopez is at home. He's very tired.

___c___ **4.** Tonight is Nancy and George's anniversary.

___a___ **5.** We don't have any clean clothes.

___d___ **6.** Jimmy and Chen want to see a movie.

___b___ **7.** Ahmed needs a new suit for work.

___f___ **8.** Julia and her friends want to exercise.

a. We're going to do the laundry.

b. He's going to go shopping at the mall.

c. They're going to go out to dinner.

d. They're going to go to the movies.

e. He's going to go fishing.

f. They're going to go to the gym.

g. He's going to stay home tonight.

h. They're going to study for a test.

B. Complete with the correct celebration. You can use some words more than once.

anniversary	birthday	graduation	wedding

1. We're celebrating our twentieth ___anniversary___.

2. Tomorrow is my high school ___graduation___.

3. My niece's ___birthday___ is tomorrow. She's going to be 3 years old.

4. Our college ___graduation___ is going to be outside.

5. Jessica's husband gave her flowers and a necklace for their tenth ___anniversary___.

6. My best friend is going to get married next Saturday. The ___wedding___ is going to start at 2:00.

More Action!

Ask students to bring to class an item that is connected with a special festivity or celebration in their cultures. This item could be an article of clothing, a special food, or a photograph. Display these in front of the class and ask students to talk about the celebration. What is its meaning? What do people do, wear, eat, and drink? What is the history of the celebration?

Teaching Tip

If students have no experiences of celebrations in their own cultures, encourage them to research and talk about local celebrations in their community.

I	am			
You We	are	going to	study	at the library.
He	is			

A Complete with the future tense.

1. We __are going to celebrate__ (celebrate) our anniversary tonight.

2. The students __are going to take__ (take) a test next week.

3. My brother __is going to buy__ (buy) a smaller car.

4. There __is going to be__ (be) a sale tomorrow.

5. Sarah __is going to look for__ (look for) a new apartment.

6. It __is going to rain__ (rain) next weekend.

7. The children __are going to eat__ (eat) pizza for lunch.

8. I __am going to stay__ (stay) home tomorrow.

B Talk about your plans for the weekend. Use *be going to.*

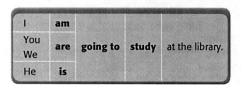

What are you going to do this Saturday?

I'm going to go to a birthday party.

C Read and circle.

1. The children are watching TV. — (Now) Future Every day

2. He works at an express delivery company. — Now Future (Every day)

3. They're going to move this year. — Now (Future) Every day

4. She is cleaning her apartment. — (Now) Future Every day

5. Belinda is going to make a salad for dinner. — Now (Future) Every day

6. I always eat cereal and fruit for breakfast. — Now Future (Every day)

Weekend Plans • **205**

Active Grammar: Future with *Be Going to*

Ask students to look at the grammar chart. Point out that *going to* tells us about an event that will take place in the future. The future with *be going to* is formed like the present continuous.

A Complete with the future tense.

Do the exercise orally, first showing students how to take the verb and convert it to the *going to* future.

B Talk about your plans for the weekend. Use *be going to.*

Tell students to work in pairs, using the dialogue in the speech balloons as a model.

C Read and circle.

• Ask students what time frame each of the tenses is used for. Write the time frames on the board and ask for example sentences for each one.
• Tell students to do the exercise and then read their answers aloud.

Active Grammar: Future with *Be Going to:* Negatives

Ask students to look at the grammar chart. Do a substitution exercise with students, calling out substitute pronouns and places so they can make new sentences. For example:

T: *They / at home.*
S: *They are not going to study at home.*

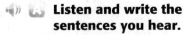 **Listen and write the sentences you hear.**

(CD3 • TR41)

• Students listen to all the sentences without writing.
• Remind them that it's sometimes helpful to repeat the dictated statements to themself before or while writing.
• Students listen again, writing the sentences.

Talk about the pictures.

• Ask students to look at the pictures and tell what is happening now.
• Ask them to predict what is *going to* happen, using the conversation in the speech balloons as a model.

S1: *What are they going to do? (#4)*
S2: *They're going to go on a vacation.*

I	am					
You	are	not	going to	study	at the library.	
They						
She	is					

 A Listen and write the sentences you hear.

CD3·TR41

1. I'm not going to watch TV tonight
2. She is not going to study this weekend
3. We aren't going to take a test tomorrow
4. They are not going to rent a movie tonight
5. He is going to go shopping on Saturday
6. It isn't going to rain tomorrow.

 B Talk about the pictures.

He's going to see the dentist. | The dentist is going to take out his tooth.

1. 2.  3. 4.

5.  6.  7.

206 · Unit 15

More Action!

Ask students to think of things they wouldn't enjoy doing and to make negative statements about them in the future (with *be going to*). For example: *I'm not going to clean my room tonight. I'm not going to go to the gym this weekend.*

C Pronunciation: *going to* versus /*gonna*/ **Listen and repeat**, *going to* and /*gonna*/.

1. Tom's going to sleep late tomorrow.
2. Mark and Ellen are going to celebrate their anniversary next week.
3. Are you going to do your homework tonight?
4. I'm going to do the laundry.
5. They aren't going to get up early on Sunday.
6. We're not going to watch TV.

> Do not write *gonna*. *Gonna* is only used in speaking.

 D Listen and complete.

1. I ___'m going to vacuum___ my living room tomorrow.
2. The students ___are going to go study___ after class.
3. Some students ___aren't going to do___ homework tonight.
4. My friend ___is going to visit___ this weekend.
5. My family and I ___are going to go to a wedding___ next month.
6. My brother ___isn't going to sleep___ late tomorrow morning.

E Practice saying the sentences in Exercise D. Use *going to* and /*gonna*/.

F Working Together **Plan your schedule for this week.** Complete the calendar with your activities for the next seven days. Share your schedule in a small group. (Answers will vary.)

Sun.	Mon.	Tues.	Wed.	Thur.	Fri.	Sat.

 Pronunciation: *going to* versus /*gonna*/ Listen and repeat, *going to* and /*gonna*/.
(CD3 • TR42)

- Students listen to the audio while looking at the statements in their books.
- Students listen again, repeating both long and reduced forms.
- They listen one more time, repeating only the reduced form.

Listen and complete.
(CD3 • TR43)

- Students listen while looking at the incomplete sentences in their books.
- They listen again while completing the sentences. Point out the note that reminds them /*gonna*/ is only used in speaking, not writing.

Practice saying the sentences in Exercise D. Use *going to* and /*gonna*/.

Point out that *gonna* shouldn't be pronounced too prominently. It's just an alternate way of saying *going to*.

Working Together Plan your schedule for this week. Complete the calendar with your activities for the next seven days. Share your schedule in a small group.

Tell students to fill in the calendar with work, school, and recreational activities.

Weekend Plans

A
Working Together Check your plans for this weekend. Then, read your sentences to your partner. Check your partner's plans.

Encourage students to talk about their weekend plans. Then, ask them to put checks in the chart where applicable and compare their plans with those of their partners.

B
Write sentences about your and your partner's plans for the weekend.

Using the chart, students should write two sentences for each of the five items. Then, ask them to tell the class about their weekend plans and those of their partners.

C
Working Together Find someone who... Ask students questions about their future plans. If a student answers "Yes," write that student's name. If the student answers "No," ask another student.

- Students can move around the room, interviewing each other until they've written a name for each future action, if possible.
- Then, they should compare notes. Which students are going to do each action?

D
Write four sentences about your classmates.

Ask students to pick any four of the classmates they interviewed and write statements about their weekend plans. Call on individuals to read the sentences to the rest of the class.

208 · Unit 15

A
Working Together Check (✓) your plans for this weekend. Then, read your sentences to your partner. Check (✓) your partner's plans. (Answers will vary.)

Weekend Plans	You		Your Partner	
	Yes	No	Yes	No
1. I'm going to get up early this weekend.				
2. I'm going to stay home this weekend.				
3. I'm going to work this weekend.				
4. I'm going to play a sport this weekend.				
5. I'm going to study English this weekend.				

B
Write sentences about your and your partner's plans for the weekend.

1. (Answers will vary.) _____
2. _____
3. _____
4. _____
5. _____

C
Working Together Find someone who . . . Ask students questions about their future plans. If a student answers "Yes," write that student's name. If the student answers "No," ask another student.

Yes, I am.
No, I'm not.

Questions	Classmate
	(Answers will vary.)
1. Are you going to go camping this year?	
2. Are you going to celebrate a birthday this month?	_____
3. Are you going to exercise tomorrow?	_____
4. Are you going to do the laundry this weekend?	_____
5. Are you going to go dancing this weekend?	_____
6. Are you going to eat at a restaurant this weekend?	_____
7. Are you going to study English this weekend?	_____
8. Are you going to speak English this weekend?	_____

D
Write four sentences about your classmates. (Answers will vary.)

208 · Unit 15

He's **going to** make a movie.
She's **going to** give a concert.

1. Marc Anthony,
Singer

2. Carolina Herrera,
Fashion Designer

3. Albert Pujols,
Baseball Player

4. Yao Ming,
Basketball Player

5. Barack and Michelle
Obama, President and
First Lady of the United
States

6. Beyoncé,
Singer/Actress

7. The Brazilian soccer team

8. Edwidge Danticat,
Author

Weekend Plans • **209**

 Working Together
Talk about these
famous people's
future plans.

• First, make sure that
students know who all
of the people are. Ask
individual students to
make statements about
the photographs.
• Then, go through
the photos one by one.
Get students to make
as many sentences as
possible about the
future plans of each
one. For example:
Edwidge Danticat is
going to write more
books.

Teaching Tip

Students may not know much
about Edwidge Danticat. She's
a Haitian-American writer who
has written novels, short stories,
and memoirs. Ask students if
any writers from their cultures
also write in English.

More Action!

Give each student a slip of paper with
the name of a famous personality. Select
people on this page or other figures of
your choice. Tell students not to show the
names to classmates. Each student says
several things that he or she is going to
do or is not going to do as that person.
For example:
S1: *I'm going to be the governor of*
California and I'm not going to be the
Terminator again.
S2: Are you Arnold Schwarzenegger?
S1: Yes, I am.

The Big Picture:
A Trip to the Beach

 Look at the picture and discuss the questions.

Ask students to talk about the individuals in the picture. Ask: *Where are they doing and what are they going to do? What are they going to take with them? What kind of car are they going to drive?*

 Listen and write each name on the correct person. (CD3 • TR44)

• Students listen to the audio while looking at the picture.
• Ask them what they remember from the audio. See if they can figure out the meaning of words and expressions: *come on, surfing, car seat, wallet.*
• Students listen again, pausing to write the names on the picture.

Look at the picture and discuss the questions.

1. Where is the family going?
2. What are they going to take with them?
3. Is the dog going to go on the trip?

Listen and write each name on the correct person.

Al   Emily   Rico   Linda   Paula   Pedro

More Action!

Ask students to imagine their ideal vacations without saying where they're going. Then, they should make sentences about what they're going to do in that place. For example:

S1: *I'm going to eat paella.*
S2: *Are you going to Mexico?*
S1: *No, I'm not. I'm also going to visit the Prado Museum.*
S2: *Are you going to Spain?*
S1: *Yes, I am.*

Teaching Tip

You might want to write all the place names students have chosen for ideal vacations on the board. Make sure they're all being pronounced correctly.

Listen again. Read and (circle.)

CD3·TR44

1. They're going to leave in an hour.   True   (False)
2. Linda is Emily's friend.   (True)   False
3. Paula is going to call the neighbors.   True   (False)
4. The neighbors are going to water the plants.   (True)   False
5. The dog is going to go with the family.   True   (False)
6. Al is going to use the surfboard.   True   (False)
7. Rico is going to take the surfboard with him.   (True)   False

Read and (circle) the correct answers.

1. Who is Emily waiting for?
   a. her cousin   **b.** her sister   (**c.** her friend)

2. Al is upset because they . . .
   (**a.** are going to be late.)   **b.** have too many bags.   **c.** are ready.

3. Who's going to walk the dog?
   a. Emily is.   (**b.** The neighbors are.)   **c.** Al is.

4. Where is Rico going to put the surfboard?
   a. In the house.   (**b.** On top of the car.)   **c.** Inside the car.

5. Why aren't they going to leave now? Because Dad needs to . . .
   a. get gas.   **b.** talk to the neighbor.   (**c.** find his wallet.)

Complete with the correct verb form. Some verbs are negative.

1. The surfboard ___*isn't going to fit*___ inside the car.
2. Rico ___*is going to put*___ the surfboard on top of the car.
3. The family ___*is going to take*___ a vacation.
4. The dog ___*is not going to come*___ on the trip.
5. The neighbors ___*are going to water*___ the plants.
6. Emily's friend ___*is going to go*___ with the family.
7. Pedro ___*is going to ride*___ in a car seat.

come
fit
go
put
ride
take
water

Weekend Plans · **211**

Listen again. Read and circle. (CD3•TR44)

Do the *true/false* exercise as a class activity. You can expand on this by making other statements about the picture. For example: *Rico has short hair. (F) The surfboard isn't going to fit in the car. (T)*

Read and circle the correct answers.

Ask students to compare their answers with a partner.

Complete with the correct verb form. Some verbs are negative.

Ask individuals to write the verb forms on the board.

More Action!

Play a memory game. Ask students to stand in line. The first student says, *On my vacation, I'm going to _____.* The next student says, *On his/her vacation, he/she is going to _____.* Then, the student adds, *And on my vacation, I'm going to _____.* Each student must remember and re-state everyone's sentence before before adding a statement about himself or herself. When someone makes a mistake, he or she sits down.

Teaching Tip

Tell students that *going on a vacation* means the same thing, more or less, as *going to go on a vacation.* They are often used interchangeably.

Reading: Planning a Trip to an Art Museum

A Circle your answers.

Encourage students to talk about visiting museums before they do the exercise. What kind of museums do they like to visit? Have they ever been to New York City?

B Read about the Metropolitan Museum of Art.

• Ask students to scan the brochure to find out specific things:
What time does the museum close on Friday? Can you go to the museum on New Year's Day? How much does it cost for children under 12? How old must you be to pay only $15?
• Now ask students to read the entire brochure. What can they tell you about it?

C Complete.

• Ask students to circle facts in the brochure which help them answer the questions.
• Have students write the answers to the questions on the board.

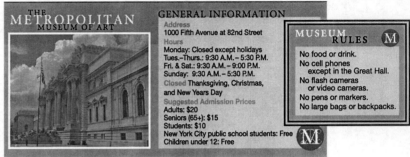

A Circle your answers. (Answers will vary.)

1. I want to visit New York City.   Yes No
2. I like to visit art museums.   Yes No
3. There are many interesting museums in New York City.   Yes No

B Read about the Metropolitan Museum of Art.

THE METROPOLITAN MUSEUM OF ART

GENERAL INFORMATION
Address
1000 Fifth Avenue at 82nd Street
Hours
Monday: Closed except holidays
Tues.–Thurs.: 9:30 A.M. – 5:30 P.M.
Fri. & Sat.: 9:30 A.M. – 9:00 P.M.
Sunday: 9:30 A.M. – 5:30 P.M.
Closed Thanksgiving, Christmas, and New Years Day
Suggested Admission Prices
Adults: $20
Seniors (65+): $15
Students: $10
New York City public school students: Free
Children under 12: Free

MUSEUM RULES Ⓜ
No food or drink.
No cell phones
    except in the Great Hall.
No flash cameras
    or video cameras.
No pens or markers.
No large bags or backpacks.

C Complete.

1. The museum's address is __1000 Fifth Avenue at 82nd Street__
2. The museum is open __Tuesday__ through Sunday.
3. The museum is open from __9:30__ A.M. to __9:00__ P.M. on Fridays and Saturdays.
4. Children under 12 are __free__.
5. Suggested admission for adults is __$20__.
6. Visitors cannot bring __food__, __cell phones__, or __flash or video cameras__.
(Additional answers for #6: drinks, pens or markers, large bags or backpacks)

More Action!

Internet Option: Ask students to search about a museum of their choice in any U.S. city. Some suggestions are Museum of Natural History in New York, De Young Museum in San Francisco, the Field Museum in Chicago, Smithsonian Institution in Washington, D.C., and the Museum of Fine Arts in Boston. Ask them to find information about museum hours, admission, and rules. They can report back to the class about their searches.

A Read.

> This weekend, I'm going to have a surprise party for my wife. We're going to have a cake, ice cream, and some punch. On Saturday morning, she's going to go to work. She doesn't know anything about the party. I'm going to clean our apartment. Then, I'm going to wrap her present in a special box. It's a pair of airline tickets to Brazil. Our children are going to decorate the apartment. They're going to give her presents, too. It's going to be a great party!

B Write some notes about your weekend plans. (Answers will vary.)

Friday	Saturday	Sunday
	do laundry	

C Write about your weekend plans.
(Answers will vary.)

> **WRITING NOTE**
> Use a comma after a time expression at the beginning of a sentence.
> **On Saturday evening,** we're going to go to a movie.

 ## D Sharing Our Stories **Read your partner's story.** Write two sentences about your partner's weekend plans.

Weekend Plans • **213**

More Action!

Play *Word Bingo.* Ask students to choose any ten words or phrases from pages 202 and 203 and write them on a sheet of paper. As you read the words or phrases from those pages, students cross off the ones they have written on their papers. The first student to cross off all of his or her words calls out *Bingo* and is the winner.

Writing Our Stories: My Weekend Plans

Ask students to look at and talk about the picture. Ask: *What are these people doing? What are they going to eat? What are they celebrating?*

A Read.

• Ask students to take turns reading sentences from the paragraph.
• Help students figure out new vocabulary from context clues: *surprise, punch, wrap, present, decorate,* etc.
• Tell students to ask each other questions about the reading and to answer them using the *going to* future.

B Write some notes about your weekend plans.

Ask students to fill in the chart with activities about work, school, and free time. Each note only needs to be a word or two.

C Write about your weekend plans.

Tell students to write this in paragraph form, indenting the first line and choosing a title. Ask them to read their compositions to the class.

D Sharing Our Stories Read your partner's story. Write two sentences about your partner's weekend plans.

Ask students to trade compositions and then write the two sentences.

English in Action: Reading a Community Calendar

English in Action

Reading a Community Calendar

Read the calendar of events from this community newsletter.

• First, ask students to look at the box below the calendar so they understand the abbreviations used in the calendar.
• Then, ask them to read the calendar to themselves, noting where and when events are going to take place.
• Have them ask each other questions: *What night is going to be movie night? What time are kids going to play soccer? Where is the rock concert going to be?* Continue around the class until everyone has had a chance to ask and answer questions about the calendar.

Read the calendar of events from this community newsletter.

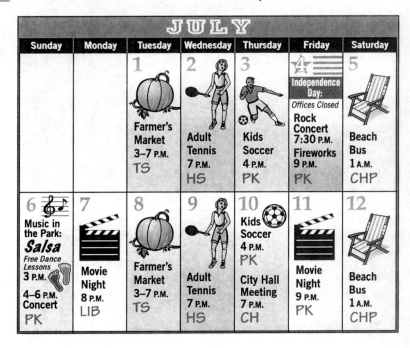

JULY						
Sunday	Monday	Tuesday	Wednesday	Thursday	Friday	Saturday
		1 Farmer's Market 3–7 P.M. TS	2 Adult Tennis 7 P.M. HS	3 Kids Soccer 4 P.M. PK	4 Independence Day: *Offices Closed* Rock Concert 7:30 P.M. Fireworks 9 P.M. PK	5 Beach Bus 1 A.M. CHP
6 Music in the Park: *Salsa* *Free Dance Lessons* 3 P.M. 4–6 P.M. Concert PK	7 Movie Night 8 P.M. LIB	8 Farmer's Market 3–7 P.M. TS	9 Adult Tennis 7 P.M. HS	10 Kids Soccer 4 P.M. PK City Hall Meeting 7 P.M. CH	11 Movie Night 9 P.M. PK	12 Beach Bus 1 A.M. CHP

LEGEND

LIB	- Public Library
CH	- City Hall
CHP	- City Hall Plaza
HS	- High School
PK	- Park
TS	- Train Station

A *legend* explains abbreviations in a map or chart.
Example: LIB - Library

More Action!

Ask students to find actual community calendars or event listings. They can usually find lists of events in their local newspapers and make calendars from them. Each student can present his or her calendar to the class, explaining the events and taking questions from the class about them. Which events is he or she going to attend and when are they going to take place? Take a class poll: How many students prefer music events, sports events, movie events, cultural events etc.?

Answer the questions about the calendar.

1. Where is the Farmer's Market? *At the Train Station.*

2. What day is the City Hall meeting? What time is the meeting? *Thurs. 7 P.M.*

3. When can you have free dance lessons? *Sun, July 6 at 3 P.M.*

4. What day is Kids Soccer? *Thursday*

5. Where can you see movies? *At the Park and the Library*

6. When can you listen to music in the park? *Sun, July 6 from 4-6 P.M.*

7. What time does the Beach Bus leave? *1 A.M.*

8. When are the fireworks? *Friday, July 4th at 9 P.M.*

 Working Together **Read and practice the telephone conversation.**

A: Hi, (B's name).

B: Hi, (A's name). What's up?

A: Nothing. Are you going to do anything on <u>Friday night</u>?

B: No. Why?

A: There's a <u>movie in the park</u> on <u>Friday night</u>.

B: That sounds like fun.

A: Good. Let's meet at <u>8:30</u>. <u>The movie starts at 9:00</u>.

B: Okay. See you then.

A: See you. Bye.

Working Together **Write a new conversation.** Look at the calendar and choose an activity. Then, act out your new conversation for the class.

Answer the questions about the calendar.

Use this as an extension of the previous exercise. Add more questions to the list.

Working Together Read and practice the telephone conversation.

• Assign roles to pairs of students. After they've read the conversation through once, they should exchange roles.

• Ask another pair to do the same but this time to substitute other events and times for the underlined words and phrases.

Working Together Write a new conversation. Look at the calendar and choose an activity. Then, act out your new conversation for the class.

The conversations can be about any kind of future event. One student can suggest an event and another can disagree. A third student can resolve the matter by suggesting a compromise.

Unit 1

Possessive Adjectives

Possessive Adjective	Noun	
My	name	is Adam.
Your	telephone number	is 555-1212.
His	teacher	is Miss Wilson.
Her	ID number	is 34345.
Our	classroom	is large.
Their	last name	is Brown.

Note:
A possessive adjective comes before a noun.

Present Tense of *Be*

FULL FORMS		
Subject	*Be*	
I	**am**	from Mexico.
You	**are**	a student.
He	**is**	a teacher.
She	**is**	from Haiti.
We	**are**	from Poland.
They	**are**	at school.
It	**is**	in Room 10.

CONTRACTIONS	
Subject + *Be*	
I**'m**	from Mexico.
You**'re**	a student.
He**'s**	a teacher.
She**'s**	from Haiti.
We**'re**	from Poland.
They**'re**	at school.
It**'s**	in Room 10.

Notes:
1. We often use contractions when we speak.
2. We usually use full forms in writing.

Wh- Questions with *Be*

What / Where	Be	
What	is	your name?
Where	are	you from?
Where	is	he from?

Notes:
1. Questions with *What* ask about things.
2. Questions with *Where* ask about places or locations.

Unit 2

Singular and Plural Nouns

REGULAR NOUNS	
Singular	Plural
a book	books
a pencil	pencils
a student	students
an eraser	erasers
an umbrella	umbrellas

IRREGULAR NOUNS	
Singular	Plural
a man	men
a woman	women
a child	children
a person	people

Notes:
1. Use an article with a singular noun.
2. Use *an* with nouns that begin with a vowel sound: *a, e, i, o*, and sometimes *u*.
3. Proper names do not take an article: *Tom, California, New York, Arizona.*

There is / There are

There	Be		
There	**is**	a book	on the desk.
There	**are**	books	on the desk.

Notes:
1. A sentence beginning with *There is* often tells about the location or existence of something.

   There is *a book on the desk.*
2. A sentence beginning with *There are* often tells how many.

   There are *twenty students in our class.*
3. We use *there* the first time we talk about a thing.

   There *is a book on the desk.* **It** *is a dictionary.*
   There *are many students in the classroom.* **They** *are from different countries.*

Yes / No Questions in the Present Tense with *Be*

QUESTIONS		
Be	Subject	
Is	this	your book?
Are	these	your books?

AFFIRMATIVE ANSWERS		
Yes	Subject	Be
Yes,	it	**is.**
Yes,	they	**are.**

NEGATIVE ANSWERS		
No	Subject	Be
No,	it	**isn't.**
No,	they	**aren't.**

Unit 3

Questions with *How old*

How old	Be	
How old	is	she?
How old	is	Tom?
How old	are	you?

Subject	Be	Number
She	is	27.
He	is	45.
I	am	14.

Adjectives

ADJECTIVES IN SENTENCES WITH *BE*

Subject	*Be*	Adjective
I	am	**heavy.**
She	is	**old.**
They	are	**tall.**

ADJECTIVES IN SENTENCES WITH *HAVE*

Subject	*Have / Has*	Adjective	Noun
I	have	**long**	hair.
She	has	**short**	hair.
They	have	**brown**	hair.

Notes:
1. Adjectives describe people, places, and things.
2. Adjectives are not plural, even if the noun is plural: ~~They are **talls**.~~   They are **tall**.

Yes / No Questions and Answers with *Be* and an Adjective in the Present

YES / NO QUESTIONS

Be	Subject	Adjective
Am	I	tall?
Are	you	short?
Are	we	old?
Are	they	married?
Is	he	young?
Is	she	thin?
Is	it	heavy?

AFFIRMATIVE ANSWERS

Yes	Subject	*Be*
Yes,	you	**are.**
Yes,	I	**am.**
Yes,	we	**are.**
Yes,	they	**are.**
Yes,	he	**is.**
Yes,	she	**is.**
Yes,	it	**is.**

Notes:
1. Do not contract affirmative short answers.   *Yes, he is.* NOT: ~~*Yes, he's.*~~

2. There is no contraction for *am not*, but the negative contraction for *I am not* is *I'm not*.

NEGATIVE ANSWERS

No	Subject	*Be*
No,	you	**aren't.**
No,	I	**am not.**
No,	we	**aren't.**
No,	they	**aren't.**
No,	he	**isn't.**
No,	she	**isn't.**
No,	it	**isn't.**

NEGATIVE ANSWERS

No	Subject + *Be*	*Not*
No,	you**'re**	**not.**
No,	I**'m**	**not.**
No,	we**'re**	**not.**
No,	they**'re**	**not.**
No,	he**'s**	**not.**
No,	she**'s**	**not.**
No,	it**'s**	**not.**

Unit 4

Where Questions with *Be*

Where	*Be*	
Where	is	the pillow?
Where	are	the pillows?

Subject	*Be*	Preposition
It	is	**on** the bed.
They	are	**on** the sofa.

PREPOSITIONS

Subject	Be	
The book	is	**on** the table.
		under the table.
		next to the chair.
The books	are	**between** the computer and the printer.
		in the desk.

Unit 5

Present Continuous Tense

AFFIRMATIVE STATEMENTS		
Subject	Be	-ing Form
I	**am**	study**ing**.
You	**are**	work**ing**.
We	**are**	sleep**ing**.
They	**are**	walk**ing**.
He	**is**	cook**ing**.
She	**is**	writ**ing**.
It	**is**	rain**ing**.

NEGATIVE STATEMENTS		
Subject	Be + not	-ing Form
I	**am not**	study**ing**.
You	**aren't**	work**ing**.
We	**aren't**	sleep**ing**.
They	**aren't**	walk**ing**.
He	**isn't**	cook**ing**.
She	**isn't**	writ**ing**.
It	**isn't**	rain**ing**.

Notes:

1. The present continuous tense tells about an action that is happening now.

2. Some common present continuous time expressions are: *now, right now, at this moment.*

3. The negative contraction of *I am not* is *I'm not.*

4. Some verbs are usually not used in the present continuous tense. These verbs include *have, like, want, need, see, know,* and *be.* We use the present tense with these verbs.

Yes / No Questions in the Present Continuous Tense

YES / NO QUESTIONS		
Be	Subject	-ing Form
Am	I	study**ing**?
Are	you	work**ing**?
Are	we	sleep**ing**?
Are	they	walk**ing**?
Is	he	cook**ing**?
Is	she	writ**ing**?
Is	it	rain**ing**?

SHORT ANSWERS	
Affirmative	Negative
Yes, you **are**.	No, you **aren't**.
Yes, I **am**.	No, I'm **not**.
Yes, we **are**.	No, we **aren't**.
Yes, they **are**.	No, they **aren't**.
Yes, he **is**.	No, he **isn't**.
Yes, she **is**.	No, she **isn't**.
Yes, it **is**.	No, it **isn't**.

Unit 6

Or Questions

Be	Subject	Adjective	Or	Adjective
Is	New York	small	**or**	large?
Are	the streets	clean	**or**	dirty?

Subject + *Be*	Adjective
It's	large.
They're	clean.

Adjective Word Order

Subject	Verb	Adjective	Noun
This	is	**a large**	city.
These	are	**large**	cities.

Notes:
1. Place the adjective before a noun.

2. Adjectives do not take the plural form.
   These are large cities. NOT: *These are larges cities.*

Unit 7

Prepositions

Subject		Be	Preposition
			on the corner of River Street and Pine Avenue.
			in front of the bank.
			in back of the drugstore.
The library		is	**next to** the park.
			between the hospital and the park.
			across from the police station.
			on River Street.

Giving Directions

Walk two blocks.
Turn right.
Turn left.

Note:
Use the base form of the verb to give directions.

Unit 8

Questions with *How much*

How much	Be	
How much	is	the printer?
How much	are	the batteries?

Subject + *Be*	Price
It's	$99.00.
They're	$7.95.

Notes:
1. *How much* questions ask about price.

2. For plural items, we often use *each* in the answer.
   How much are the donuts? They are $1.00. / They are $1.00 each.

Unit 9

Wh- Questions in the Present Continuous Tense

WH- QUESTIONS				ANSWERS			
Wh- word	*Be*	Subject	*-ing* Form	Subject	*Be*	*-ing* Form	
What	am	I	wearing?	You	are	wearing	a coat.
Where	are	you	driving?	I	am	driving	to the city.
What	are	we	doing?	We	are	studying	for a test.
Where	are	they	walking?	They	are	walking	in the park.
What	is	he	reading?	He	is	reading	the newspaper.
What	is	she	writing?	She	is	writing	a letter.

Who Questions in the Present Continuous Tense

WHO QUESTIONS			ANSWERS	
Who	*Be*	*-ing* Form	Subject	*Be*
Who	is	studying?	I	am.
Who	is	working?	You	are.
Who	is	sleeping?	He	is.
Who	is	walking?	She	is.
Who	is	cooking?	We	are.
Who	is	writing?	They	are.

Notes:
1. The word *Who* asks questions about people.
2. *Who* takes a singular verb. Who **is** sitting in the class? The students **are**.

Unit 10

How much Questions

How much	Be		Subject + Be	Price
How much	is	the shirt?	It's	$24.00.
How much	are	the jeans?	They're	$39.98.

Note:
How much questions ask about price.

WEATHER			Subject + Be	
Wh- word	*Be*		It's	sunny and hot.
What	is	the weather?	It's	windy.
How	is	the weather?		

Unit 11

Simple Present Tense

AFFIRMATIVE STATEMENTS		
Subject	Verb	
I	work	every day.
You	work	at night.
We	work	in the morning.
They	work	part time.
He	work**s**	full time.
She	work**s**	on the weekends.
It	work**s**	every day.

NEGATIVE STATEMENTS		
Subject	*do not / does not*	Verb
I	**don't**	work.
You	**don't**	work.
We	**don't**	work.
They	**don't**	work.
He	**doesn't**	work.
She	**doesn't**	work.
It	**doesn't**	work.

Notes:

1. The simple present tense tells about a repeated or routine action.

2. The present tense tells about facts that are true all the time.
   I live in the city. I like my class.

3. In affirmative statements, *he, she,* and *it* use *s* on the verb.

Common Time Expressions in the Present Tense

in	*on*	*every*	*at*	*from . . . to . . .*
in the morning	on Monday	every day	at 4:00	from Monday to Friday
in the afternoon	on Friday	every morning	at noon	from 1:00 to 3:00
in the evening	on the weekend	every evening	at midnight	
		every night	at night	

Unit 12

Adverbs of Frequency

I **always** drink water on hot days.
I **sometimes** drink coffee in the morning.
I **never** drink coffee at night.

Notes:
1. *Always* means 100% of the time.

2. *Sometimes* means about 50% of the time.

3. *Never* means 0%. You never do this action.

Yes / No Questions and Answers in the Simple Present Tense

YES / NO QUESTIONS		
Do / Does	Subject	Verb
Do	I	work?
Do	you	work?
Do	we	work?
Do	they	work?
Does	he	work?
Does	she	work?
Does	it	work?

SHORT ANSWERS	
Affirmative	Negative
Yes, you **do**.	No, you **don't**.
Yes, I **do**.	No, I **don't**.
Yes, we **do**.	No, we **don't**.
Yes, they **do**.	No, they **don't**.
Yes, he **does**.	No, he **doesn't**.
Yes, she **does**.	No, she **doesn't**.
Yes, it **does**.	No, it **doesn't**.

Wh- Questions in the Simple Present Tense

WH- QUESTIONS			
Wh- word	*Do / Does*	Subject	Verb
When	do	I	leave?
Where	do	you	work?
What	do	we	wear?
When	do	they	eat?
Where	does	he	work?
What time	does	she	get up?

ANSWERS		
Subject	Verb	
You	leave	at 2:00.
I	work	at the hotel.
We	wear	uniforms.
They	eat	at 7:00.
He	works	at the bank.
She	gets up	at 6:00.

Who Questions in the Simple Present Tense

WHO QUESTIONS		
Who	Verb + *s*	
Who	works	in a store?
Who	gets	benefits?
Who	wears	a uniform?
Who	has	a difficult job?
Who	works	at night?
Who	gets	tips?

ANSWERS	
Subject	*Do / Does*
I	**do.**
You	**do.**
We	**do.**
They	**do.**
He	**does.**
She	**does.**

Notes:
1. The word *Who* asks questions about people.

2. *Who* takes a singular verb.
   Who **works** full time?
   Nelson does.
   Who **works** full time?
   Nelson and Victor do.

Unit 14

Must / Must not

You	**must**	take this medicine with food.
Children	**must not**	take this medicine.

Note:
1. *Must* means that something is necessary.
2. *Must not* means that something is against the law. It is not permitted.

Unit 15

Future Tense Statements

AFFIRMATIVE STATEMENTS			
Subject	*Be*	*Going To*	Verb
I	**am**	**going to**	study.
You	**are**	**going to**	rent a movie.
We	**are**	**going to**	stay home.
They	**are**	**going to**	visit friends.
He	**is**	**going to**	play soccer.
She	**is**	**going to**	watch TV.
It	**is**	**going to**	rain.

NEGATIVE STATEMENTS			
Subject	*Be + Not*	*Going To*	Verb
I	**am not**	**going to**	study.
You	**aren't**	**going to**	rent a movie.
We	**aren't**	**going to**	stay home.
They	**aren't**	**going to**	visit friends.
He	**isn't**	**going to**	play soccer.
She	**isn't**	**going to**	watch TV.
It	**isn't**	**going to**	rain.

Note:
The future tense tells about actions that are going to happen tomorrow, next week, or sometime in the future.

Common Time Expressions in the Future Tense

in	*next*	*this*	Adverbs
in a minute	next Sunday	this morning	today
in a few minutes	next week	this afternoon	tomorrow
in an hour	next weekend	this evening	tomorrow morning
in two days	next month		tonight
in a week	next year		soon
in a month			later
in a year			
in 2020			

Plural Nouns

1. For most nouns, add an -*s*.
boy-boys　　*store-stores*　　*student-students*

2. If a noun ends with a consonant and a *y*, change the *y* to *i*, and add -*es*.
city-cities　　*dictionary-dictionaries*　　*baby-babies*

3. If a noun ends with *sh, ch, x,* or *z*, add -*es*.
box-boxes　　*dress-dresses*　　*watch-watches*

Present Continuous Verbs

1. For most verbs, add -*ing*.
walk-walking　　*play-playing*　　*eat-eating*

2. If a verb ends in *e*, drop the *e* and add -*ing*.
write-writing　　*come-coming*　　*drive-driving*

3. If a verb ends in a consonant + vowel + consonant, double the final consonant and add -*ing*.
sit-sitting　　*run-running*　　*put- putting*

Present Tense: Third Person

1. For most verbs, add -*s*.
make-makes　　*call-calls*　　*sleep-sleeps*

2. If a verb ends with a consonant and a *y*, change the *y* to *i*, and add -*es*.
try-tries　　*cry-cries*　　*apply-applies*

3. If a verb ends with *sh, ch, x,* or *z*, add -*es*.
wash-washes　　*watch-watches*　　*fix-fixes*

4. These verbs are irregular in the third person.
have-has　　*do-does*

For Page 76, Exercise C

Student 1: Read Questions 1-6 to your partner.

    1. Is this classroom large or small?

    2. Is the classroom clean or dirty?

    3. Is this school busy or quiet?

    4. Are the students friendly?

    5. Are the books boring?

    6. Is the classroom hot today?

Student 2: Listen and write your answers. Then, read Questions 7-12 to your partner.

    7. Is this city in the mountains?

    8. Is the traffic heavy now?

    9. Is the weather humid or dry today?

  10. Is this city noisy or quiet?

  11. Are the streets in this city clean or dirty?

  12. Are the parks beautiful?

Unit 1

CD1·TR4 (Page 4) **Listen and write the letter you hear.**
1. C   2. F   3. H   4. W   5. L   6. Z   7. S   8. G   9. J

CD1·TR8 (Page 8) **Listen and complete.**
1. I am from Mexico.   2. She's from Alaska.   3. They're from Chile.   4. We're from Cameroon.
5. He is from Ukraine.   6. I'm from Italy.   7. It is from Vietnam.   8. You're from Colombia.

CD1·TR9 (Page 11) **The Big Picture: My Classmates**
   Hi. My name is Tomás. I'm a student in English 1. I'm in class now. Here are four students in my class. This is Hiro. He's from Japan. This is Erica. She's from Mexico. This is Marie. She's from Haiti. This is Jenny. She's from Hong Kong. And this is me. I'm from Peru.

CD1·TR10 (Page 11) **Listen and write the answers.**
1. Who is from Peru?   2. Who is from Japan?   3. Who is from Mexico?   4. Where is Marie from?
5. Where is Jenny from?   6. Where are you from?

CD1·TR11 (Page 11) **Listen.** Write the number next to the correct answer.
1. What's your name?   2. Where are you from?   3. What's his name?   4. Where is he from?
5. What's her name?   6. Where is she from?

CD1·TR13 (Page 14) **Listen and write the numbers.**
a. six	b. eleven	c. zero	d. eighteen	e. two	f. fifteen
g. three	h. ten	i. seventeen	j. twenty	k. four	l. nine
m. thirteen	n. eight	o. twelve			

CD1·TR14 (Page 14) **Listen and write the words for the numbers.**
a. ten	b. six	c. eleven	d. three	e. twelve
f. eighteen	g. twenty	h. one	i. seventeen	

CD1·TR16 (Page 15) **Listen and write.**
a. 555-3231	b. 555-3080	c. 800-555-4242	d. 201-555-4413
e. 555-3692	f. 555-7548	g. 619-555-7042	h. 813-555-1624

Unit 2

CD1·TR19 (Page 18) **Listen and complete.**
1. Is this your dictionary? Yes, it is. Thank you.   4. Is this your notebook? Yes, it is. Thank you.
2. Is this your pen? Yes, it is. Thank you.   5. Is this your pencil sharpener? No, it isn't.
3. Is this your piece of paper? No, it isn't.

CD1·TR21 (Page 20) **Pronunciation: Plural nouns** Listen and circle.
1. a pencil	2. students	3. teachers	4. a man	5. a map
6. dictionaries	7. an eraser	8. a notebook	9. classrooms	10. women

CD1·TR22 (Page 23) **Listen and circle Desk 1 or Desk 2.**
1. There is a notebook on this desk.   3. There is a dictionary on this desk.
2. There are pencils on this desk.   4. There is a pencil sharpener on this desk.

5. There is a computer on this desk.
6. There are four textbooks on this desk.

7. There is a piece of paper on this desk.
8. There are two pens on this desk.

CD1·TR23 (Page 24)

The Big Picture: The Classroom

I am a student in English 1. My classroom is on the second floor in Room 204. There are ten students in my class. There are four men and six women. We are from different countries. There are five students from Mexico. There are two students from Vietnam. There is one student from El Salvador, one from India, and one from the Philippines.

Our room is small. There is a big table in the front for the teacher: There are twelve desks for the students. There is a chalkboard on the wall. There are two maps on the wall, one of the United States and one of the world.

Our teacher is Mr. Wilson. We like our teacher, and we like our class.

CD1·TR24 (Page 25)

Listen and circle.

1. The classroom is in Room 208.
2. There are twelve students in this class.
3. There are ten men in this class.
4. There are six women in this class.
5. There are four children in this class.

6. There are five students from India.
7. There is one student from El Salvador.
8. The room is small.
9. There are two maps on the wall.

CD1·TR25 (Page 25)

Listen. If the information is correct, write the sentence. If the information is wrong, put an X.

1. The teacher is a woman.
2. The classroom is in Room 204.
3. There are five students from Mexico.
4. There are ten women in this class.

5. There are ten students in this class.
6. There is a table for the teacher.
7. There is a computer in this class.
8. There is a board in the room.

Unit 3

CD1·TR30 (Page 31)

Listen and circle the correct name.

1. He is Sylvia's husband.
2. She is Sylvia's mother.
3. He is Sylvia's brother.
4. She is Eric's sister.
5. She is Annie's aunt.

6. He is Pedro's father.
7. He is Annie's uncle.
8. She is Annie and Eric's grandmother.
9. He is Elisa's nephew.

CD1·TR32 (Page 34)

Listen. Number the photographs. Then, listen again and write the relationships and ages.

Conversation 1

A: This is my daughter, Carmen, and her little boy. His name is Dennis, and he's two years old. He's our first grandchild.
B: How old is Carmen?
A: She's 35.

Conversation 2

A: This is my daughter, Gwen. She's 25. And this is her husband, Ellis. He's 28. They live in Florida.
B: Do they have any children?
A: No, they don't.

Conversation 3

A: This is my son, Brian. He's three. And this is our daughter, Erica.
B: How old is Erica?
A: She's six.
B: That's a cute picture.

B **Listen and write the questions.** Ask a partner the questions.

1. Are you at school?
2. Are you single?
3. Are you short?
4. Are you from China?
5. Are you young?

B **The Big Picture: A Family Photo**

A: I have the pictures from the party last week.
B: Oh, yes, your mom's birthday party. Let me see.
A: Here's a picture of everyone.
B: Oh, that's you and Steve. And your two little girls. Which one is Emily and which one is Kim?
A: Emily is five. She has long hair. And Kim is six. She has short hair.
B: Now, that's your mom and dad. Right? In the middle?
A: Yes. That's mom. It's her birthday. She's 55 years old. And that's dad, next to her.
B: Oh, your dad has a moustache?
A: Yes. He has a moustache. At one time, he had curly hair, but now he's bald.
B: Who's this?
A: These are my sisters. I have two sisters. This is my sister, Joanne. She's 21. And next to her, that's my sister, Mary. She's 23.
B: Joanne and Mary look a lot alike.
A: I know. They're tall and they both have dark, curly hair. But Joanne is a little heavy, and Mary is very thin.
B: Are your sisters married?
A: No, I'm the only one who is married.
B: And who's this?
A: That's my brother, Andy.
B: Oh, you have a brother?
A: Yes, I have a brother. Andy is the baby of the family. He's 18.
B: He looks like your dad.
A: Hmm. You're right.
B: That's a great picture.

G **Listen and complete.** Then, put a period (.) or a question mark (?) at the end of each sentence.

1. She is old.
2. Is he young?
3. Is it heavy?
4. It is tall.
5. She is thin.
6. Is he tall?
7. Is she short?
8. He is heavy.

C **Listen and write.**

1. January 4, 2005
2. February 11, 1992
3. April 17, 2010
4. July 25, 1990
5. August 18, 2015
6. September 7, 1964
7. November 30, 1999
8. December 25, 2000

Unit 4

A **Listen and write each question.** Then, look at the picture and write the answer.

1. Where is the end table?
2. Where are the books?
3. Where is the lamp?
4. Where is the rug?
5. Where are the pillows?
6. Where is the mirror?

C **Look at the picture on page 50 and listen to the conversation.** Write the missing questions.

Tom: Where is my cell phone?
Sara: Is it on the coffee table?
Tom: No, it isn't.
Sara: Is it on the desk?
Tom: No, it isn't.
Sara: Is it on the floor?
Tom: Yes, here it is!

Listen. Write the missing questions.

Tom:	Where are my keys?		**Tom**:	No, they aren't.
Sara:	Are they under the coffee table?		**Sara**:	Are they on the desk?
Tom:	No, they aren't.		**Tom**:	Yes, here they are!
Sara:	Are they on the sofa?			

  The Big Picture: A Messy Bedroom

Kathy: Hi, Mom.
Mom: Hi, Kathy. Doing your homework?
Kathy: Yes, I have a lot of homework.
Mom: How's your room?
Kathy: How's my room?
Mom: Yes, is it clean? Is it neat?
Kathy: Yes, Mom. My room is perfect.
Mom: Are your clothes on the floor?
Kathy: Are my clothes on the floor?
               Mom, my clothes are in the closet.
Mom: And your shoes and your boots?
Kathy: They're in the closet, too.
Mom: And your desk?
Kathy: My desk is perfect.
Mom: Are your books and papers on the floor?
Kathy: Mom, my books and papers are on the desk.
Mom: Good! Grandma is coming today.
               And you know Grandma!
Kathy: Oh, no! Grandma is coming?! When?
Mom: In about 10 minutes.
Kathy: Thanks, Mom.
Mom: Bye, Kathy. See you in a few minutes.

  Listen to the questions. Write the number of the question next to Kathy's answer.

1. Hi, Kathy. Doing your homework?
2. Is your room clean? Is it neat?
3. Are your clothes on the floor?
4. And your shoes and your boots?
5. Are your books and papers on the floor?

  Listen to each address and repeat.

a. 56 Main Street
b. 37 Maple Street
c. 244 Second Street
d. 872 Central Avenue
e. 1524 Park Avenue
f. 2159 North Avenue

  Listen. Complete the addresses. Then, repeat the addresses with a partner.

a. 73 North Avenue
b. 66 Maple Street
c. 143 Central Avenue
d. 861 Park Avenue
e. 9924 Second Street
f. 3285 Main Street

Unit 5

  Listen and circle the form you hear.

1. He is walking.
2. She's cleaning.
3. I'm making lunch.
4. You're driving.
5. They are watching TV.
6. We are studying.

  Listen and complete.

A: Hello.
A: I'm at home. I'm in the kitchen.
A: I'm cooking dinner.

B: Hi, Jenny. It's Sarah. Where are you?
B: What are you doing?
B: Okay. I'll call you later.

Listen and complete.

A: Hello.

B: Hi, Alex. It's Ben. Where are you?

A: I'm at work.

B: Are you busy

A: Yeah. I'm writing a report.

B: Okay. I'll call you later.

The Big Picture: Mom's on the phone!

Tommy: Hello.

Mom: Hi, Tommy. This is Mommy.

Tommy: Hi, Mommy. Are you at work?

Mom: Yes, I'm a little late. What are you doing? Are you doing your homework?

Tommy: No, I'm not. I'm watching TV.

Mom: Where's Brian? Is he doing his homework?

Tommy: Brian's in the living room. He's playing video games.

Mom: And Katie? Where's Katie?

Tommy: She's in her bedroom.

Mom: Good! Is she doing her homework?

Tommy: No, Mom. She's talking on the telephone to her boyfriend.

Mom: Where's Daddy? Is he cooking dinner?

Tommy: Daddy's in the living room. He's sleeping.

Mom: I'm coming home right now.

Listen and write short answers.

1. Is Mom at home?

2. Is she talking to Tommy?

3. Is Tommy doing his homework?

4. Is Brian doing his homework?

5. Is Brian playing video games?

6. Is Dad cooking dinner?

7. Is Katie doing her homework?

Listen and look at the message.

A: Hello.

B: Hello. Can I speak with Carlos?

A: I'm sorry. He's not here. Can I take a message?

B: This is Steve Carson.

A: Steve Carson?

B: Please ask him to call me. My number is 555-8341.

A: Please repeat that.

B: 555-8341.

A: Okay.

Listen to two phone calls. Take the messages.

CALL 1

A: Hello.

B: Hello. Can I speak with Maya?

A: I'm sorry. She's not here. Can I take a message?

B: This is Mary Lyons.

A: Mary Lyons?

B: Yes. Please ask her to call me. My number is 555-6672.

A: Please repeat that.

B: 555-6672.

A: Okay.

CALL 2

A: Hello.

B: May I speak with Mr. Pano?

A: I'm sorry. He's not here. Can I take a message?

B: This is Adam Madison.

A: Adam?

B: Adam Madison.

A: Please spell that.

B: M-A-D-I-S-O-N. Please ask him to call me. My number is 555-9143.

A: Please repeat that.

B: 555-9143.

A: Okay.

Unit 6

CD2·TR13
(Page 75) **Listen and point to each city on the map.** Listen again and repeat.

1. Seattle, Washington
2. San Francisco, California
3. Las Vegas, Nevada
4. Phoenix, Arizona
5. Detroit, Michigan
6. Chicago, Illinois
7. San Antonio, Texas
8. Boston, Massachusetts
9. New York, New York
10. Miami, Florida

CD2·TR14
(Page 77) **Listen and complete.**

Male: What city do you want to visit?
Female: I want to visit Miami.
Male: Why do you want to go there?
Female: I want to visit Miami because it's sunny and beautiful.
Male: Well, *I* want to visit New York City.
Female: Why do you want to go there?
Male: Because it's exciting. There are so many things to do!

CD2·TR15
(Page 80)   **The Big Picture: Chicago, Illinois**

Chicago, Illinois

Chicago, Illinois is one of the largest cities in the U.S. It's in the midwest of the country next to Lake Michigan. The summers are hot, and the winters are cold, so visit Chicago in the spring or in the fall.

There are many interesting places to visit. Many places are in busy downtown Chicago. If you like art, go to the Art Institute of Chicago. There are many famous paintings there. For children, the Brookfield Zoo is a fun place to visit. If you like something different, go to one of Chicago's blues clubs. You'll see great blues musicians. Maybe you'll want to dance.

If you like sports, Chicago is a great city. There are seven professional teams in Chicago. Wrigley Field, a baseball park, is the oldest baseball park in the United States. It's the home of the Chicago Cubs baseball team.

Do you watch TV talk shows? Then, you know Oprah Winfrey. Millions of people watch her TV show every afternoon. If you go to Chicago, maybe you can watch the Oprah show live! Finally, the 44th President of the United States—Barack Obama— worked in Chicago.

So, when do you want to visit Chicago? Chicago is waiting for you.

CD2·TR17
(Page 85)   **Listen and write the population.**

1. Seattle, Washington: 594,210
2. Phoenix, Arizona: 1,552,259
3. San Jose, California: 939,899
4. Boston, Massachusetts: 590,763
5. Chicago, Illinois: 2,836,658
6. Honolulu, Hawaii: 371,657
7. Dallas, Texas: 1,240,499
8. Greensboro, North Carolina: 258,671

Unit 7

CD2·TR20
(Page 88)   **Listen and complete the map.**

1. **A:** Where's the bakery?
   B: It's on Main Street, next to the park.
2. **A:** Where's the supermarket?
   B: It's across from the post office.
3. **A:** Where's the shoe store?
   B: It's on Main Street, across from the drugstore.
4. **A:** Where's the bookstore?
   B: It's next to the shoe store.
5. **A:** Where's the library?
   B: It's on Maple Avenue. It's behind the post office.
6. **A:** Where's the bank?
   B: It's on the corner of Main Street and First Street.
7. **A:** Where's the coffee shop?
   B: It's next to the post office.
8. **A:** Where's the laundromat?
   B: It's on the corner of Second Street and Maple Avenue.

CD2·TR22
(Page 91)

Listen and write the locations on the map on page 90.

1. **A:** Where's City Hall?
   B: Walk two blocks to Broad Street. Turn left. City Hall is on your right.
2. **A:** Where's the post office?
   B: Walk two blocks to Broad Street. Turn left. The post office is on your left.
3. **A:** Where's the hospital?
   B: Walk three blocks to the first traffic light. Turn right. The hospital is on your left.
4. **A:** Where's the aquarium?
   B: Walk four blocks to the second traffic light. That's Clark Street. Turn right. The aquarium is on your left.

CD2·TR23
(Page 94)

The Big Picture: Downtown

It's a busy afternoon downtown. People are busy, and the stores are busy, too. Oh, look! There's an accident at the intersection of Smith Street and North Main Street. Mr. Thomas works at the bakery, and he drives the delivery truck. He's talking to the other driver. Over in the park, Elena is watching the children. The children are playing on the swings. They're having a good time. There's a coffee shop on North Main Street. There are two tables in front of the coffee shop. Joseph is sitting at a table. He's reading the newspaper and drinking a cup of coffee. Jane is sitting at the other table. She's reading a good book. Mark is the waiter. He's bringing Jane some ice cream. Uh, oh. Mrs. Lee is running to her car. Officer Ortiz is standing next to her car. He's writing her a ticket. Oh, how wonderful! Michael and Luisa are in front of City Hall. I think they're getting married today.

CD2·TR24
(Page 94)

Listen and circle.

1. Who is watching the children?
2. Who is getting married?
3. Who is standing on the corner of Smith Street and North Main Street?
4. Who is running?
5. Who is working at the coffee shop?
6. Who is reading a book?
7. Who is drinking a cup of coffee?
8. Who is writing a ticket?

Unit 8

CD2·TR27
(Page 101)

Listen and write the amount.

a. two cents
b. ten cents
c. seventeen cents
d. twenty-five cents
e. thirty-eight cents
f. forty-nine cents
g. fifty cents
h. sixty-nine cents
i. ninety-eight cents

CD2·TR29
(Page 102)

Listen and write the amount.

a. a dollar
b. a dollar twenty-five
c. two dollars and fifty cents
d. three seventy-five
e. fifteen dollars and eight cents
f. seventy-nine twenty-five
g. one hundred fifty-seven dollars and sixty-two cents
h. two hundred thirty dollars and ninety-nine cents
i. four hundred fifty-seven dollars and twenty-four cents

CD2·TR31
(Page 102)

Circle the number you hear.

a. 13 b. 40 c. 15 d. 60 e. 70 f. $18 g. $19 h. $13
i. $15 j. $19 k. $14.14 l. $17.20 m. $16.16 n. $18.75 o. $10.50

CD2·TR32
(Page 108)

The Big Picture: I need a desk

Katrina: I can't study. It's too noisy.
Fabio: You can study in the bedroom. It's quiet in the bedroom.
Katrina: Yes, but I don't have a desk or a chair in the bedroom.
Fabio: Let's go to the office supply store tomorrow. You're right. You need a desk and a chair.
Katrina: And I need a light. It's too dark in the bedroom. I need a good light for reading.
Fabio: Anything else?
Katrina: I have my books and notebooks. But I need some folders.
Fabio: When we're there, I'm going to look at shredders.

Listen to the conversation. Then, write the items that Katrina and Fabio buy. Write the prices.

Katrina:	They have lots of desks.
Fabio:	This one is nice.
Katrina:	I think it's too big.
Fabio:	How about this one? It's a good price, $99.
Katrina:	But that one is too small. And it doesn't have a drawer.
Fabio:	This one is the right size, and it has a drawer.
Katrina:	I like that one. How much is it?
Fabio:	Not bad. It's $119.
Katrina:	Now, I need a chair.
Fabio:	Try out a lot of them. You want to find one that's comfortable. Do you want one with arms?
Katrina:	Well, I don't like this one. It's too big for me, and it isn't comfortable.
Fabio:	How about this one?
Katrina:	I like it. And it's a good price, $69. Okay, we have the desk, a chair, and now we need a lamp.
Fabio:	How much is this lamp?
Katrina:	It's on sale for $19.
Fabio:	Good! Let's buy it. We did well today. The shredder is on sale for $20, and your folders are $4. Let's go to the checkout counter.

  Listen and write the responses.

1. A: This desk is nice.	**B:** It's too big.
2. A: How about this desk?	**B:** It's too small.
3. A: This one is the right size.	**B:** Yes, I like that one.
4. A: Do you like this chair?	**B:** It's too big for me.
5. A: How about this one?	**B:** It isn't comfortable.
6. A: How about this one?	**B:** I like it. And it's a good price.
7. A: How much is this lamp?	**B:** It's on sale for $19.

Unit 9

  Listen to each question. Write the name of the correct person.

1. Who is looking at the bus schedule?
2. Who is listening to music?
3. Who is standing in back of Roberto?
4. Who is talking?
5. Who is running to the bus stop?
6. Who is reading a book?
7. Who is talking on a cell phone?
8. Who is playing a video game?
9. Who is carrying two large shopping bags?

  The Big Picture: The Train Station

1. Who is running for the train?
2. Who is carrying a briefcase?
3. Who is reading a newspaper?
4. Who is talking on a cell phone?
5. Who is looking at the clock?
6. Who is drinking a cup of coffee?
7. Who is buying a ticket?

  Listen to each sentence. Who is talking?

1. Hi! How are you? How's your new job?
2. I'd like a round-trip ticket to New York.
3. Good-bye! I'll miss you!
4. Is this the train to Washington?
5. I'm at the station now and my train is at 2:30. I'll call you again when I get to Trenton.

  Listen to the story and complete the questions.

Emily is standing next to the train and saying good-bye to her boyfriend. She's very sad, and she's crying. Emily is unhappy because her boyfriend is leaving for the army. He's standing on the train and waving good-bye. Emily is 18, and she's a senior in high school. Tom is 20, and he is going into the army. He is reporting for duty in New York. Tom is sad about Emily, but he's excited about his future. He's saying, "Don't cry, Emily. I'll call you when I get to camp. We can e-mail each other. I'll see you in eight weeks."

Unit 10

CD2·TR41
(Page 131) **Listen.** What is Amy wearing? Write the letter of the correct picture.

1. She's wearing a blue dress.
2. She's wearing beige shorts.
3. She's wearing black pants.
4. She's wearing a big white belt.
5. She's wearing a green shirt.

6. She's wearing a white blouse.
7. She's wearing sneakers.
8. She's wearing a green jacket.
9. She's wearing white sandals.
10. She's wearing a white sweater.

CD2·TR44
(Page 133) **Listen to the weather.** Find the city and write the temperature on the map.

1. Find Boston. It's cold in Boston today. It's snowing. The temperature is 20 degrees.
2. Find New York. It's cloudy and cold in New York today. The temperature is 35 degrees.
3. Find Miami. It's sunny and hot in Miami. The temperature is 90 degrees.
4. Find Houston. It's sunny and warm in Houston today. The temperature is 70 degrees.
5. Find San Diego. The weather is warm in San Diego all year. It's sunny and 75 degrees.
6. Find San Francisco. It's raining today in San Francisco. It's cool. The temperature is 55 degrees.
7. Find Seattle. It's raining in Seattle, too. It's 50 degrees in Seattle. You will need your umbrella and raincoat.
8. Find Denver. It's snowing in Denver today. It's 30 degrees.
9. Find Chicago. It's cloudy and cold in Chicago today. It's very windy. The temperature is 25 degrees.

CD2·TR45
(Page 135) **Josh needs a new pair of shoes.** Listen to the story and number the pictures from 1 to 8.

1. Josh needs a new pair of shoes for work. He's walking into a shoe store.
2. Josh is looking at all the shoes. He's picking up a nice pair of black shoes.
3. He's sitting down and putting on the shoes.
4. Josh is standing. He doesn't like the shoes. They're too tight.
5. Now, Josh is trying on another pair of shoes. The shoes are a larger size.
6. He is looking in the mirror. He likes the shoes. They're the right size.
7. Josh is standing at the counter and giving the box of shoes to the clerk.
8. Josh is paying for the shoes. The shoes are $49. He's giving his credit card to the clerk.

CD2·TR46
(Page 137) **Listen and complete the conversation.**

Clerk: Hello. Can I help you?
Customer: Yes. I'm looking for a shirt.
Clerk: What size?
Customer: Medium.
Clerk: The shirts are here.
Customer: I like this shirt. How much is it?
Clerk: It's $50. But today it's on sale for $25.
Customer: Great. I'll take it.

CD2·TR47
(Page 137) **Listen and complete the conversation.**

Clerk: Hello. Can I help you?
Customer: Yes. I'm looking for a pair of gloves.
Clerk: What size?
Customer: Extra large.
Clerk: Here they are.
Customer: I like these gloves. How much are they?
Clerk: They're usually $30. But today they're on sale for $19.
Customer: Great. I'll take them.

The Big Picture: The Clothing Store

Monica is from Cuba. Cuba is an island in the Caribbean. It's hot there all year. Now Monica is living in Boston. Monica came to the United States in May. She liked the weather in Boston in May, June, July, and August. It was sunny and hot. September was warm, and Monica was comfortable. But now it is December. Monica can't believe the weather! It's very cold. It's 30 degrees. Her friends tell her, "This isn't cold yet! In January, it's going to be colder. And it's going to snow soon." Monica is at the clothing store with her sister, Lydia. Monica needs warm clothes. She needs a coat. She needs a hat and gloves, too. She is also going to buy a sweater. Monica is standing in front of the mirror. She's trying on coats. She isn't comfortable. She's saying, "This coat feels so heavy."

Listen and complete the conversations.

1. **Monica:** I don't like this weather. It's too cold.
   Lydia: It's only December. It isn't cold yet. Wait until January!
2. **Lydia:** Here's a nice coat. Try it on.
   Monica: I don't like the color. Do they have a red or a blue coat?
3. **Monica:** Gloves? Why do I need gloves?
   Lydia: Try on these gloves. Believe me. You need gloves.
4. **Monica:** How do you like this coat?
   Lydia: It doesn't fit you. It's too big.
5. **Monica:** Do you like this sweater?
   Lydia: Yes, it looks good on you.

Unit 11

Listen and show the time on the clocks.

a. What time is it? It's four o'clock.
b. What time is it? It's six thirty.
c. What time is it? It's eight fifteen.
d. What time is it? It's ten fifty-five.
e. What time is it? It's one twenty.
f. What time is it? It's ten forty-five.
g. What time is it? It's five ten.
h. What time is it? It's seven thirty.

Listen to the conversation. Circle the correct answers about Pierre's day.

A: Where do you go to school, Pierre?
B: Bayside College.
A: How many days a week?
B: I go to school four days a week, Monday, Tuesday, Wednesday, and Thursday. I'm in an intensive program. School is in the morning, from 9:00 to 12:00.
A: Do you have a lot of homework?
B: Yes! About two hours a day. I eat lunch with my friends from school. And then, after lunch, I study with a friend. After that, I go to the library.
A: Do you work, too?
B: I don't work during the week. I work in a restaurant on Friday, Saturday, and Sunday.

Listen to the conversation. Talk about Maria's day. Some of the sentences are negative.

A: Where do you go to school, Maria?
B: South Street Adult School.
A: How many days a week?
B: Two days a week. I go to school on Tuesday and Thursday night, from 7:00 to 9:00.
A: Do you have a lot of homework?
B: Yes! About an hour a night. But, I don't have time to study. I have two children, and I work. I'm busy all day. And at night, I'm tired.

The Big Picture: Trouble with Math

Emily is sixteen years old and a sophomore in high school. Emily likes school, but she loves sports. She is busy from morning to night.

Emily has two alarm clocks. The first alarm clock rings at 6:00 A.M. Emily turns off the alarm clock, but she doesn't get up. The second alarm clock rings at 6:15. She gets up slowly. She gets dressed and

eats breakfast. Then, she takes the bus to school. Emily goes to school from 7:30 to 2:00. She likes all her classes except math. Math is difficult for her.

At 2:00, Emily goes to the gym and puts on her uniform. Emily plays baseball. She is on the school baseball team. Every day after school she practices or she plays a game. Sometimes her mother or father comes to her games.

Emily gets home at 5:30 and takes a long shower. Then, her family eats dinner at 6:00. Emily does her homework from 7:00 to 8:00. Then, she talks on the phone, plays video games, or watches TV. Emily sets her alarm clocks and goes to bed at 11:00.

CD3·TR9
(Page 153) **Listen and write each sentence you hear.**

1. Emily goes to high school.
2. She feels tired in the morning.
3. She doesn't like math.
4. Emily doesn't play tennis.
5. She doesn't have a lot of homework.
6. She goes to bed at 11:00.

CD3·TR10
(Page 153) **Listen to the conversation between Emily and her mother.** Complete the sentences.

Mom: Emily, your school grades are very good, except in math.

Emily: Mom, math is really hard.

Mom: Emily, you only study one hour a night. Then, you talk on the phone and watch TV. You need to spend more time on math.

Emily: Mom, I don't like math.

Mom: You usually do your homework from 7:00 to 8:00. You need to study one more hour. I want you to study math every night from 8:00 to 9:00. No TV, no computer, no cell phone from 7:00 to 9:00.

Emily: Mom!

Unit 12

CD3·TR12
(Page 160) **Listen and complete.**

BREAKFAST: Hi, my name is Mike. In the morning, I am always in a hurry, so I eat a small breakfast at 7:15. I eat cereal and toast. I always have a cup of coffee. Then, I go to work.

LUNCH: Hi, my name is Jenny. I have lunch from 1:00 to 2:00. I like to have a large salad with Italian dressing. I have cucumbers, tomatoes, carrots, and chicken or shrimp on my salad. To drink, I like iced tea. Sometimes, I have a piece of fruit for dessert.

DINNER: Hi, my name is Sara. My parents, my brother, and I always have dinner together. We eat at 7:00. Our favorite dinner is chicken or pasta. I like to have cookies for dessert. Oh, and my brother and I drink milk or water.

CD3·TR13
(Page 163) **Listen and complete.**

A: Hello?

B: Hi, honey. Guess who?

A: Hi, Mom! I'm so happy that you called.

B: Why Stacey? What's wrong?

A: Christopher is a fussy eater. He won't eat my food.

B: What? What do you mean?

A: Here's an example. I made spaghetti last night.

B: Good. All kids love spaghetti.

A: Well, I put vegetables in it: onions, broccoli, and spinach. He didn't eat it.

B: Why not?

A: He doesn't like vegetables.

B: All vegetables?

A: All vegetables.

B: How about pizza?

A: He doesn't like tomato sauce.

B: Okay, take off the tomato sauce.

A: He doesn't like cheese, either.

B: How about a hot dog?

A: He doesn't like hot dogs or hamburgers. Oh, and he doesn't like fruit.

B: What does he like?

A: He likes peanut butter, white bread, and milk.

B: Well, he's only six. You were a fussy eater, too. He will change.

A: I hope so. Thanks for listening, Mom.

B: You're very welcome, sweetheart.

The Big Picture: At Mario's Italian Restaurant

Faye:	Hi, how are you this evening?
Emma:	Hi, Faye! It's Friday, so here we are at your table again, right by the window.
Faye:	It's nice to see you every Friday.
Troy:	You're our favorite waitress.
Faye:	Thank you. And you're my favorite customers. What would you like to drink?
Emma:	I'll have iced tea.
Troy:	I'll have a soda.
Emma:	Here are the menus. I'll be back with your drinks.
Troy:	What are you going to have, Emma?
Emma:	I think I'll have a green salad and the pasta. How about you?
Troy:	I had pasta for lunch. I'll have a green salad and the chicken. Where's Faye?
Emma:	Here she comes.

Listen and look at the picture. Then, read and circle.

Bob:	How do you like the pizza, Ann?
Ann:	It's good, but I always like the pizza here.
Lori:	Me, too. I love cheese and pepperoni.
Matthew:	Dad, could I have another soda?
Bob:	Okay, I'll call the waitress.
Ann:	Bob, this was a great idea. We're all tired on Friday nights. I like to go out for dinner on Fridays.
Bob:	So do I.
Matthew:	Me, too. Let's have pizza every Friday!

Pronunciation: *I'll* Listen and write.

1. I'll have a hamburger.
2. He'll have the steak.
3. She'll have a salad.

4. I'll have the pasta.
5. She'll have a soda.
6. He'll have ice cream.

Unit 13

Listen and complete the questions. Then, practice the conversation.

A: What do you do?
B: I'm a manicurist in a salon.
A: Do you like your job?
B: Yes, I do. I like it very much.
A: Do you work in the day or in the evening?
B: I work in the day from 9:00 A.M. to 5:00 P.M.
A: Do you need English for your job?
B: Yes, I do. Many of the hotel guests speak English, and I like to talk to them.
A: Do you wear a uniform?
B: No, but I always wear an apron and gloves.
A: Do you receive benefits?
B: Yes, I do. I work full time, so I get good benefits.
A: That's great. Do you get tips?
B: Yes, I do. Sometimes I get big tips.

Listen and answer the questions about Luis's job.

I'm a valet at the hotel, so I park cars all day. I work part time, Tuesday to Sunday for four hours a night. When the hotel is busy, I park about sixty cars a night. I get a lot of tips. Maybe fifty people will give me a tip. Sometimes it's quiet, so I get a break.

Listen and answer the questions about Jane's job.

I'm a housekeeper at the hotel. I start work at about 9:00 A.M. and I work until 5:30 P.M. There are more than 200 rooms in the hotel, and I am in charge of the third floor. My co-worker and I work together, and we change thirty to forty beds a day. We clean thirty to forty rooms. We get fifteen to twenty tips per day.

The Big Picture: The Sunrise Hotel

My name is Ricardo Lopez. This is the Sunrise Hotel, and I'm the evening manager. The Sunrise Hotel is a big hotel with more than 200 rooms. There's a restaurant, a bar, two swimming pools—one indoor and one outdoor—and tennis courts. Many tourists stay here when they visit.

The Sunrise has about 100 employees. We have desk clerks, housekeepers, bellhops, landscapers, and restaurant employees. We also have a van driver. He drives guests to the airport and to downtown for shopping. And, we have an electrician and a plumber who make repairs.

We need people for all three shifts. People who work at night make one dollar more an hour than day employees. Some employees work full time, but we also have many part-time positions.

We are always looking for employees. The salary is low, but the employees work hard. Many employees leave us when they find a job with a better salary. But some people like the hours, and the workers like the tips. We have a friendly hotel here. Are you looking for a job? We have job openings now.

Listen and write each question. Then, circle the answer.

1. What does Ricardo Lopez do?
2. Does the hotel have a pool?
3. Where does the van driver go?
4. Who makes repairs?
5. Do all the employees work full time?
6. How many employees does the hotel have?

Listen. Who is the manager speaking to? Complete.

1. Please clean rooms 371 and 374.
2. Could you park the cars for these guests, please?
3. Table 4 needs more water and the dessert menu.
4. Do we have any empty rooms for Saturday?
5. Some of these towels are not clean. What kind of detergent are you using?
6. The air conditioner in Room 424 isn't working. Please check it.
7. Three guests need to get to the airport.

Unit 14

Listen and complete the sentences.

1. He has a toothache.
2. She has a backache.
3. I have a headache.
4. He has a stomachache.
5. I have an earache.

The Big Picture: In the Waiting Room

Dr. Johnson's waiting room is very busy. It's early spring, and many patients are sick. Mrs. Jacob is Dr. Johnson's nurse. She's talking to Mrs. Jackson. She's a new patient, so she's going to fill out a patient information form. Mrs. Lee is reading a magazine. She has a bad cough. The doctor is going to listen to her chest. Mr. Green is 75 years old, and he's in good health. He's in the office for his checkup. He has a checkup once a year. Mrs. Rios and her daughter, Julia, are in the office, too. Julia's crying because she has a bad burn on her finger. She burned her finger on the stove. Mr. Patel is holding his head. His head hurts. He has a bad headache. Miss Gonzalez is sneezing and coughing. She has allergies, and she needs a prescription from Dr. Johnson. Mr. Henderson is talking to his son, Andy. Andy cut his arm and he needs a tetanus shot. He's nervous and scared because he doesn't like shots.

Unit 15

CD3·TR41
(Page 206) **Listen and write the sentences you hear.**

1. I'm not going to watch TV tonight.
2. She is not going to study this weekend.
3. We aren't going to take a test tomorrow.
4. They are not going to rent a movie tonight.
5. He is going to go shopping on Saturday.
6. It isn't going to rain tomorrow.

CD3·TR43
(Page 207) **Listen and complete.**

1. I 'm going to vacuum my living room tomorrow.
2. The students are going to study after class.
3. Some students aren't going to do homework tonight.
4. My friend is going to visit this weekend.
5. My family and I are going to go to a wedding next month.
6. My brother isn't going to sleep late tomorrow morning.

CD3·TR44
(Page 210) **The Big Picture: A Trip to the Beach**

Al:	We're going to leave in a few minutes. Come on! Get in the car, Emily.
Emily:	But, Dad. My friend, Linda, is going to come with us, too.
Al:	Okay, where is she?
Emily:	Here she is!
Paula:	Al! I'm going to go talk to the neighbors.
Al:	Now? Paula, we're going to be late!
Paula:	They're going to water the plants and walk the dog, Al.
Al:	Oh, I forgot. Rico, what is that?
Rico:	I'm going to go surfing, Dad. I'm going to take my surfboard.
Al:	No, you're not. It's not going to fit in the car.
Rico:	No problem, Dad. I'm going to put it on top.
Al:	Hurry up, everybody. Come on, Pedro. Get in your car seat. Paula! Let's go!
Paula:	Okay, I'm ready. Let's go.
Al:	Great. Wait a minute. Where's my wallet?

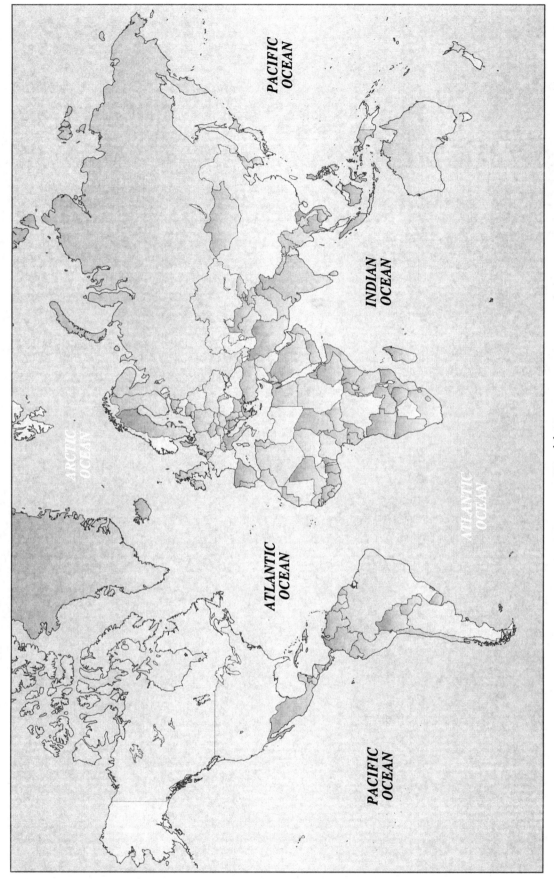

World Map

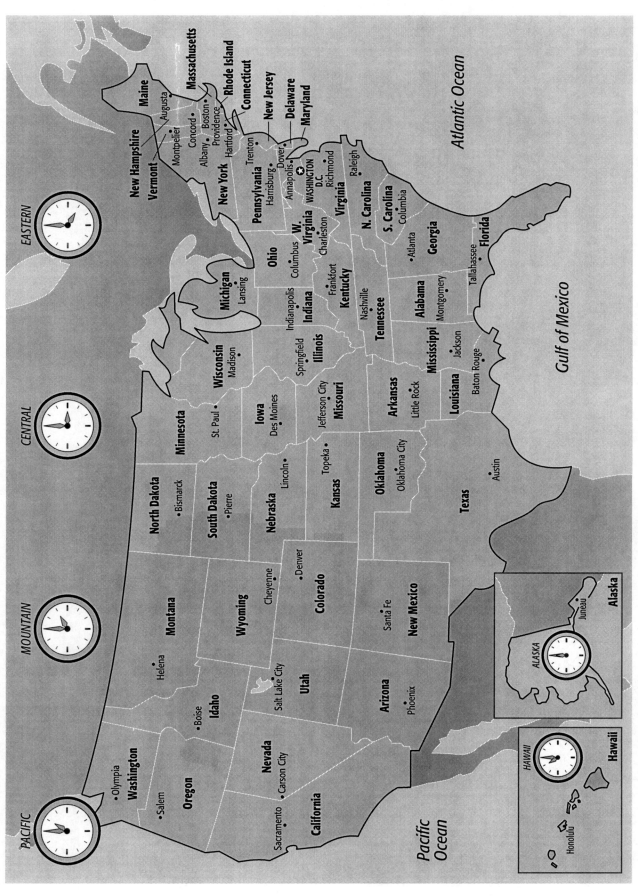

U.S. Map

Learner's dictionaries—essential tools for all stages
of English language learning!

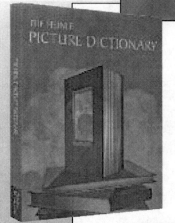

The Heinle Picture Dictionary

Low-beginning to low-intermediate

Unlike other dictionaries, *The Heinle Picture Dictionary* presents new vocabulary in contextualized, thematic readings and offers immediate practice and reinforcement to solidify the acquisition of new vocabulary.

Bilingual editions available

- Words in Context
- Word Partnerships
- Words in Action
- Workbooks, Audio, CD-ROM

Text   978-0-8384-4400-9

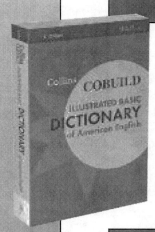

Collins COBUILD Illustrated Basic Dictionary of American English

Beginning to low-intermediate

The *Collins COBUILD Illustrated Basic Dictionary of American English* makes vocabulary acquisition efficient and effective by offering beginning-level students extra support through clear, level-appropriate definitions, unparalleled vocabulary support, and a controlled vocabulary list necessary for beginning-level learners.

- Word Worlds
- Spelling Partners
- Sound Partners
- Word Builders

Softcover
with CD-ROM   978-1-4240-0081-4

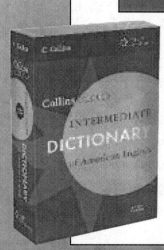

Collins COBUILD Intermediate Dictionary

Low- to high-intermediate

With full-sentence definitions and vocabulary builders, the *Collins COBUILD Intermediate Dictionary* transforms the learner's dictionary from an occasional reference to the ultimate resource for English language learners.

English/Spanish edition available

- Word Webs
- Word Links
- Word Partnerships
- Picture Dictionary boxes
- Thesaurus entries
- Interactive CD-ROM

Softcover
with CD-ROM   978-1-4240-0776-9

English in Action Series

Level 1

Student Book	978-1-4240-4990-5
Workbook with Audio CD	978-1-111-00565-8
Interactive CD-ROM	978-1-4266-3415-4
Teacher's Guide	978-1-4240-8497-5
Audio CD	978-1-4240-8501-9
Assessment CD-ROM with Exam*View*®	978-1-111-00164-3
Presentation Tool	978-1-111-00561-0

Level 2

Student Book	978-1-4240-4991-2
Workbook with Audio CD	978-1-111-00564-1
Interactive CD-ROM	978-1-4266-3416-1
Teacher's Guide	978-1-4240-8498-2
Audio CD	978-1-4240-8502-6
Assessment CD-ROM with Exam*View*®	978-1-111-00166-7
Presentation Tool	978-1-111-05779-4

Level 3

Student Book	978-1-4240-4992-9
Workbook with Audio CD	978-1-111-00563-4
Interactive CD-ROM	978-1-4266-3417-8
Teacher's Guide	978-1-4240-8499-9
Audio CD	978-1-4240-8503-3
Assessment CD-ROM with Exam*View*®	978-1-111-00167-4
Presentation Tool	978-1-111-00560-3

Level 4

Student Book	978-1-4240-4993-6
Workbook with Audio CD	978-1-111-00562-7
Interactive CD-ROM	978-1-4266-3418-5
Teacher's Guide	978-1-4240-8500-2
Audio CD	978-1-4240-8504-0
Assessment CD-ROM with Exam*View*®	978-1-111-00165-0
Presentation Tool	978-1-111-00559-7

CPSIA information can be obtained
at www.ICGtesting.com
Printed in the USA
FFOW02n1551100116
20213FF